moholy's edit

Chris Blencowe
Judith Levine

moholy's edit

the avant-garde at sea
august 1933

Lars Müller Publishers

‘The same object may appear entirely different depending on where you stand. Leonardo da Vinci once said to a pupil: “Listen to that bell ringing. There is only one bell, but it may be heard in an infinite number of ways”.’

Natsume Soseki, *The Three-Cornered World*

The film *Architect’s Congress* is available in full length online:
www.vimeo.com/larsmuellerpublishers/ciam1933
Time code along the text corresponds to this movie

I CIAM 4: a debacle avoided

1 reservations of 'the poet of architecture'

'Now, by what stroke of fortune was it decided that this most important subject should be discussed in our land by the most esteemed modern architects? What I want to say is obvious; it is difficult for anyone to imagine any modern city in such a state of deterioration as Athens.' The candid voice is that of Dimitris Pikionis, 46-year-old professor of architecture at the Athens Polytechnic University, and he has been provoked to go into print—in the journal *Τεχνικά Χρονικά* (Technica Chronica)—by the surprise announcement that the fourth CIAM congress 'will take place [...] during the course of a voyage from Marseille to Athens, and that two or three lectures will be given in our city'. What particularly disturbs him is the theme of the Conference: *'The Functional City'*—an oxymoron surely? Furthermore, the problems it raises 'are most complex, controversial and intractable; their implementation problematic to achieve'. His article finally appears on Tuesday, 1 August 1933, suggesting that it has been held over from a previous issue, since the event it announces is already underway.[1]

To a Greek intellectual like Pikionis, known to his students as 'the poet of architecture',[2] the premise of the congress appears scarcely relevant. Having recently celebrated the centenary of her independence, followed by the sudden influx of a million and a half refugees from Asia Minor in the aftermath of the *Katastrofí* of 1922, Greece in 1933 was experiencing profound political and cultural turmoil, to the point where even her traditional alignment with Western Europe was being debated.[3] Athens fell far short of other European capitals in terms of permanence and prestige; the city's neoclassical administrative core and low-rise inner suburbs were threatened with inundation by the refugees' chaotic bidonvilles. Clutching at straws, certain opportunistic politicians viewed the advent of CIAM as fortuitous, imagining that the new urban theories—largely based on Le Corbusier's radical 1922 proposal for rebuilding the centre of Paris—could be the panacea they sought.[4] Pikionis, though, rejected such generalised politically motivated solutions, believing rather in 'harmonisation of the proportions of spaces, volumes, shapes and textures [...] to the quality of light, rhythm of the landscape and climate'. Furthermore, he insisted that his fellow practitioners must take action 'to be in sympathy with the people if we want to be cultural workers rather than mere importers of culture'.

Invitations to membership of CIAM—Le Congrès international de l'architecture moderne—were issued exclusively to architects whose outlook matched that of the founders of the organisation: Le Corbusier, Dutch planner Cornelius van Eesteren, and the Swiss art historian Sigfried Giedion, who acted as its secretary. The founding principle, in Giedion's words, 'was to establish contemporary architecture's right to exist against the antagonistic forces of official architectural circles'. The rejection, on highly spurious grounds, of Le Corbusier's elegantly resolved entry to the competition for the League of Nations headquarters on the shores of Lake Geneva in 1927 exemplified these forces and provided the impetus for the first meeting of CIAM at the chateau of La Sarraz in June 1928. Subsequent congresses—in Frankfurt in 1929 and Brussels in 1930—focused on statistically based theories of mass housing; the short-hand terms *Existenzminimum* and Functionalism summarising the ethos of the movement. Thus, it had seemed entirely appropriate that an invitation should be received from the 15-year-old USSR to hold the fourth meeting in Moscow, since that nation was embarking on an ambitious programme of urban expansion.

This was how matters stood in April 1933 when, with a vast amount of research and planning work already completed on over thirty cities—including Athens, Amsterdam, London and Los Angeles, and all laboriously mapped to the same scale, a telegram arrived from Moscow postponing the meeting indefinitely. It could have been a devastating blow to the movement; instead, largely thanks to the resourcefulness of the Greek artistic community in Paris, not only was a debacle avoided but the fourth congress would become, by general agreement, the most successful in the history of CIAM. In Giedion's account of the crisis meeting in Le Corbusier's rue de Sèvres studio following the arrival of the telegram from Moscow, it was the Hungarian ex-Bauhaus teacher Marcel Breuer who promptly suggested that the congress should be held at sea, thus gaining a degree of detachment from a deeply troubled continent. 'Le Corbusier immediately telephoned Christian Zervos, editor of *Cahiers d'Art*.... Already the next day the confirmation of the Greek maritime company *"Neptos"* arrived, placing at our disposition the steamship *"Patris II"* under favourable conditions. The date was fixed for 29 July to 13 August 1933'.[5] A few days later an announcement was placed in Zervos's literary review *14 rue du Dragon* under the curiously provocative title 'Couteaux de jet' (Throwing knives): FIG. 1, 2

> The Congress of Modern Architects which should have been held in June in Moscow will not take place.
>
> The official pretext given is the need for savings to be realised. Well, we have experience of the cost of these CIAM congresses; they are practically non-existent. However pressing is the need in the USSR to make savings, we do not believe that is the real reason for this refusal to welcome the Congress of Modern Architects. It is, in truth [...] because in the USSR reactionary elements in architecture sweep it away a little more each day and are favouring outdated styles. In the end, the Soviets will respond to art in the same way as the Hitlerians. Except that with the Hitlerians, of whom we know several to be very sympathetic to modern art, it is only a provisional manoeuvre for opportunistic reasons, while with the Soviets there is the fear that

> the aversion to modern architecture becomes once more an instinct, and that Russia returns to her old habits of life burdened with outdated styles. That is the danger menacing the country that has given us the most hope of realising and perfecting modern architecture.

The hyperbolic style is Le Corbusier's. Whether it was written by him alone or jointly with Giedion is debatable, since both men had become deeply disillusioned with the USSR following the rejection of the architect's heroic 'constructivist' entry for the Palace of the Soviets competition. Worse, his elaborately detailed proposal had not even been shortlisted, while the project selected by Stalin in May 1933 was pure 'wedding cake'—risibly crowned by a monstrous statue of Lenin, arm upraised clasping a hammer and sickle. The equivocal attitude towards 'Hitlerians', disturbing in retrospect, testifies to a naïve opportunism within CIAM's inner circle convinced of the necessity of 'business as usual'. Thus, apparently unperturbed, the same issue of *14 rue du Dragon* carries an announcement of the cruise of *S/S Patris II* above the company name Neptos SA, complete with 'Conditions of Participation' and a price list.

The superior Paris-based travel agency had been set up by one Heracles Ioannides. In the words of his fellow ex-pat, the painter Ghika (Nikos Hadjikyriakos-Ghika, 1906–1994) FIG. 3, Ioannides was 'the indefatigable fellow countryman [...] full of enthusiasm, in the evenings he would leap onto benches along the boulevards, walking while balancing on their raised edges. He devoured books, tearing out pages with his fists as he read them'. More seriously, 'he had an idea that became an obsession. There was only one way to save the Greek economy: tourism, which he proposed to the Greek Government and Prime Minister of that time—but to no avail.'[6] Ioannides set about organising the passage to Piraeus and back on the *Patris II* and accommodation in Athens for around a hundred congressists, their partners and friends. He also

1 Zervos's monthly literary and philosophical review, *14 rue du Dragon:* front page of the May 1933 issue

2 'Couteaux de jet'—announcing the cancellation of the CIAM Congress in Moscow. The ambiguous and provocative title with its highly topical violent undertone was probably the work of the two young surrealist poet-editors of the journal, Pierre Guéguen and Gaston Bonheur. The latter also founded the short-lived surrealist review *Choc.*

3 Christian Zervos, Michael Tombros and Heracles Ioannides—virtually the ruling troika of the Greek avant-garde—photographed in Piraeus. From *20th Century.* Photographer unknown

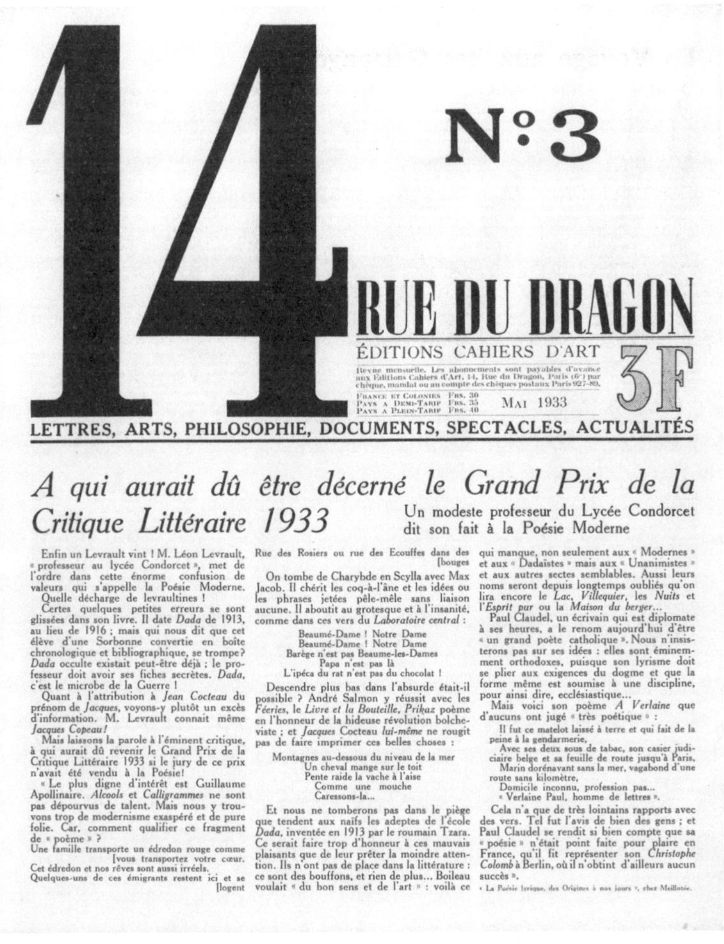

14 N° 3

RUE DU DRAGON

ÉDITIONS CAHIERS D'ART

Revue mensuelle. Les abonnements sont payables d'avance aux Éditions Cahiers d'Art, 14, Rue du Dragon, Paris (6e) par chèque, mandat ou au compte des chèques postaux Paris 927-89.

FRANCE ET COLONIES FRS. 30
PAYS A DEMI-TARIF FRS. 35
PAYS A PLEIN-TARIF FRS. 40

MAI 1933

3F

LETTRES, ARTS, PHILOSOPHIE, DOCUMENTS, SPECTACLES, ACTUALITÉS

A qui aurait dû être décerné le Grand Prix de la Critique Littéraire 1933

Un modeste professeur du Lycée Condorcet dit son fait à la Poésie Moderne

Enfin un Levrault vint ! M. Léon Levrault, « professeur au lycée Condorcet », met de l'ordre dans cette énorme confusion de valeurs qui s'appelle la Poésie Moderne.

Quelle décharge de levraultines !

Certes quelques petites erreurs se sont glissées dans son livre. Il date *Dada* de 1913, au lieu de 1916 ; mais qui nous dit que cet élève d'une Sorbonne convertie en boîte chronologique et bibliographique, se trompe? *Dada* occulte existait peut-être déjà ; le professeur doit avoir ses fiches secrètes. *Dada*, c'est le microbe de la Guerre !

Quant à l'attribution à *Jean Cocteau* du prénom de *Jacques*, voyons-y plutôt un excès d'information. M. Levrault connait même *Jacques Copeau!*

Mais laissons la parole à l'éminent critique, à qui aurait dû revenir le Grand Prix de la Critique Littéraire 1933 si le jury de ce prix n'avait été vendu à la Poésie!

« Le plus digne d'intérêt est Guillaume Apollinaire. *Alcools* et *Calligrammes* ne sont pas dépourvus de talent. Mais nous y trouvons trop de modernisme exaspéré et de pure folie. Car, comment qualifier ce fragment de « poème » ?

Une famille transporte un édredon rouge comme [vous transportez votre cœur.
Cet édredon et nos rêves sont aussi irréels.
Quelques-uns de ces émigrants restent ici et se [logent
Rue des Rosiers ou rue des Ecouffes dans des [bouges

On tombe de Charybde en Scylla avec Max Jacob. Il chérit les coq-à-l'âne et les idées ou les phrases jetées pêle-mêle sans liaison aucune. Il aboutit au grotesque et à l'insanité, comme dans ces vers du *Laboratoire central* :

Beaumé-Dame ! Notre Dame
Beaumé-Dame ! Notre Dame
Barège n'est pas Beaume-les-Dames
Papa n'est pas là
L'ipéca du rat n'est pas du chocolat !

Descendre plus bas dans l'absurde était-il possible ? André Salmon y réussit avec les *Féeries*, le *Livre et la Bouteille*, *Prikaz* poème en l'honneur de la hideuse révolution bolcheviste ; et *Jacques* Cocteau *lui-même* ne rougit pas de faire imprimer ces belles choses :

Montagnes au-dessous du niveau de la mer
Un cheval mange sur le toit
Pente raide la vache à l'aise
Comme une mouche
Caressons-la...

Et nous ne tomberons pas dans le piège que tendent aux naïfs les adeptes de l'école *Dada*, inventée en 1913 par le roumain Tzara. Ce serait faire trop d'honneur à ces mauvais plaisants que de leur prêter la moindre attention. Ils n'ont pas de place dans la littérature : ce sont des bouffons, et rien de plus... Boileau voulait « du bon sens et de l'art » : voilà ce qui manque, non seulement aux « Modernes » et aux « Dadaïstes » mais aux « Unanimistes » et aux autres sectes semblables. Aussi leurs noms seront depuis longtemps oubliés qu'on lira encore le *Lac*, *Villequier*, les *Nuits* et l'*Esprit pur* ou la *Maison du berger*...

Paul Claudel, un écrivain qui est diplomate à ses heures, a le renom aujourd'hui d'être « un grand poète catholique ». Nous n'insisterons pas sur ses idées : elles sont éminemment orthodoxes, puisque son lyrisme doit se plier aux exigences du dogme et que la forme même est soumise à une discipline, pour ainsi dire, ecclésiastique...

Mais voici son poème *A Verlaine* que d'aucuns ont jugé « très poétique » :

Il fut ce matelot laissé à terre et qui fait de la peine à la gendarmerie,
Avec ses deux sous de tabac, son casier judiciaire belge et sa feuille de route jusqu'à Paris,
Marin dorénavant sans la mer, vagabond d'une route sans kilomètre,
Domicile inconnu, profession pas...
« Verlaine Paul, homme de lettres ».

Cela n'a que de très lointains rapports avec des vers. Tel fut l'avis de bien des gens ; et Paul Claudel se rendit si bien compte que sa « poésie » n'était point faite pour plaire en France, qu'il fit représenter son *Christophe Colomb* à Berlin, où il n'obtint d'ailleurs aucun succès ».

« La Poésie lyrique, des Origines à nos jours », chez Meillotée.

Couteaux de jet

Le Congrès des Architectes modernes qui devait se tenir en juin, à Moscou, n'aura pas lieu.

Le prétexte donné officiellement est le besoin d'économies à réaliser. Or, nous avons l'expérience du coût de ces Congrsè des Architectes modernes. Ils sont presque inexistants. Si impérieux que soit en U.R.S.S. le besoin de réaliser des économies, nous ne croyons pas que ce soit là la raison vraie de ce refus d'accueillir le Congrès des Architectes Modernes. C'est, en vérité, comme nous le disions dans notre précédent numéro parce que en U.R.S.S. les éléments réactionnaires de l'architecture, l'emportent chaque jour un peu plus et cela en faveur des styles périmés. Au fond les Soviets finiront pas témoigner à l'égard de l'art la même réaction que les Hitlériens. Seulement chez les Hitlériens, dont nous connaissons plusieurs comme très sympathiques à l'art moderne, ce n'est qu'une manœuvre provisoire pour des raisons d'opportunité, tandis que chez les Soviets, il est à craindre que l'aversion envers l'architecture moderne devienne à nouveau un instinct et que la Russie revienne à ses vieilles habitudes de vivre aux dépens des styles périmés. Voilà le danger qui menace le pays qui nous adonné le plus d'espoirs pour réaliser et perfectionner l'architecture moderne.

★

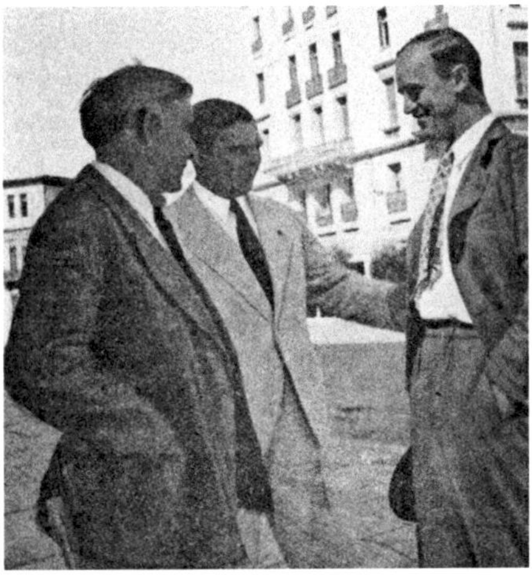

arranged the charter of a yacht on which invitees of CIAM's 'inner circle' could make a four-day excursion to the islands.

As for Pikionis's heroic intervention, if it was read at all during those heady August days, it must have been regarded as 'swimming against the tide'. Put off by their obsession with Functionalism, he had declined the invitation to join the select group of Greek architects who had affiliated with CIAM. As Ghika later recalled, 'Dimitris Pikionis wrote a classic article in sympathy with Greek perceptions in the *Technica Chronica* (without results, naturally)'.[7]

2 Piraeus

On that blazing Saturday afternoon, 5 August 1933, an observer on the dockside in the port of Piraeus casually watching the small white vessel as she steamed slowly towards the open sea might have instinctively felt that *something didn't quite add up* ... An antique hull, apparently, 'dolled up' to masquerade as a luxury yacht—the discordant impression reinforced by an unusually tall smokestack, most un-yacht-like winches and clumsy tackle dominating the foredeck. And, who were those men and women—self-consciously got up in evidently new 'yachting gear'—chattering in an assortment of languages as they settled into groups in the shade cast by the white awning?

3 Andreas Embirikos: a most untypical yacht-owner

Yacht owners typically enjoy impressing their guests with recitations of such matters as the luxurious accommodations, speed, safety, etc. of their vessels. But this was not a typical yacht, nor was Andreas Embirikos a typical yacht-owner. He would probably have preferred to be recognised by these celebrated members of the avant-garde as a philosopher and poet. Born in Romania in 1901 to a prominent Greek ship-owning family which—headed by his father Leonidas—also owned the *Patris II,* Andreas Embirikos had studied philosophy in Paris, where he had become acquainted with Leon Trotsky and André Breton among others; and it seems that the arch-surrealist had passed on to the young Greek a passion for 'automatic writing'.

While in Paris, he had also begun to study psychoanalysis with René Laforgue, to the point where it had become his dominant interest, and we may imagine that during the course of the four-day cruise he became increasingly fascinated by the idiosyncratic personalities of his fellow passengers.

For example, that shortish, bespectacled and somewhat obsessive fellow with dark wavy hair, wielding the very latest Zeiss movie camera: what drives him—and where does he fit in? An enthusiastic and original photographer himself, Embirikos would surely have been curious to learn how the unfamiliar machine worked. Before approaching László Moholy-Nagy, though, he checks on the logistics of the cruise with his partner in this enterprise, Heracles Ioannides.

4 Heracles Ioannides: 'traveller without baggage'

In contrast to the somewhat aloof 'aristocracy' of CIAM, Heracles Ioannides is the jovial and enterprising Greek who can 'fix it' with the impenetrable local bureaucracy—as you would expect from a competent travel agent. His friend, the art writer and publisher of Picasso, Tériade (Stratis Eleftheriades), also on board, recounts a saltier variation on Ghika's anecdote of the fluttering pages, in which Ioannides is 'an enigmatic figure stationed at the prow of the boat, book in hand, tearing out pages with the back of the hand and, as he read them, throwing them into the sea'.[8] Described as 'a traveller without baggage', the extravagant Dada-esque gestures concealed another, literary and philosophical, facet of this complex character who had already faced exile more than once in his life. Born in 1897 on the island of Marmara, in 1915 he escaped the clutches of the Turkish military authorities under a false identity; just three years later he was invited to be secretary to Leonidas Embirikos—at that time Minister of Food Supplies in the first liberal government of Eleftherios Venizelos.

After the fall of Venizelos's government in 1920, Leonidas Embirikos offered the 23-year-old Ioannides the direction of his Paris offices: Neptos SA. Here he represented the shipping line to New York, and it was in the thriving transatlantic emigrant traffic that the Embirikos line prospered until the US government placed an embargo on immigration following the Wall Street crash. Once again Ioannides demonstrated his initiative and instinct for survival, now launching a series of luxurious Mediterranean cruises on the *Patris II,* emphasising a historical and cultural dimension in his publicity material. Thus, his first brochure, published in 1930, contains an evocative essay by the theatre critic Gabriel Boissy: 'Vers la Grèce du passeé; Vers celle d'aujourd'hui' and dramatic photographs by Ioannides's friend Fred Boissonas, with whom he had climbed Mount Olympus. With the Neptos cruises the Greek tourist industry takes its first steps. FIG. 4

The intensity of the correspondence between Ioannides and Giedion in the few weeks leading up to the 1933 Congress gives a vivid impression of the cool professionalism of the experienced agent as he patiently accommodates the latter's exigent Swissness. Seeking to control matters from his Doldertal apartment in Zurich, Giedion writes to Ioannides on 27 June proposing that the entire complement of CIAM 4 should be conveyed to Crete for six days in the middle of their stay in Greece—there to visit Candia, Knossos and Phaistos, among other sites; he appears to be plotting a colonial expedition. If Ioannides had not succeeded in tactfully dissuading Giedion—quoting the 'excessive heat' of Crete in August, not to mention the length and discomfort of the ferry crossings and high cost of excursions on that island—the modest Aegean cruise, which was to have such far-reaching ramifications, would never have taken place.

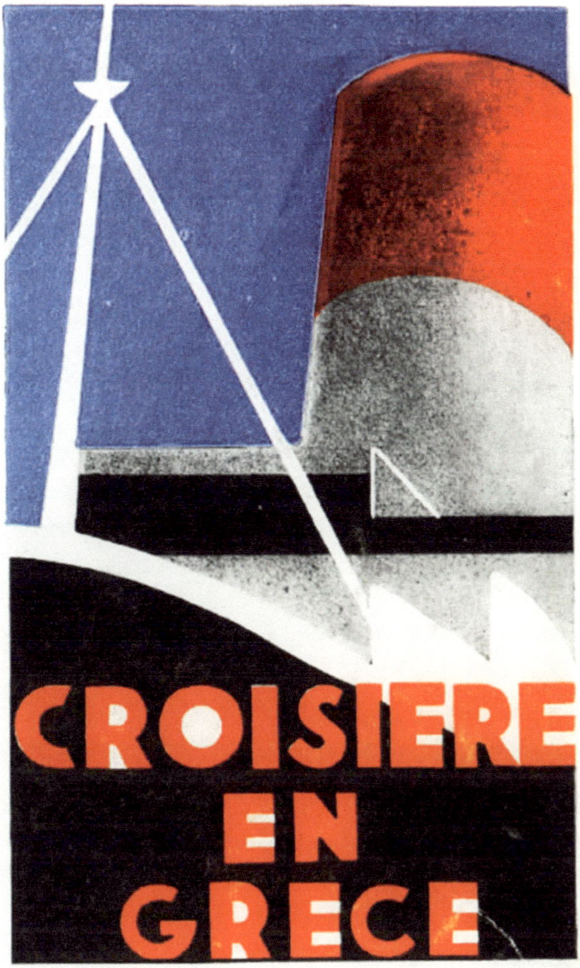

4 Cover of the first Neptos SA brochure in which Ioannides promoted cruises of the Aegean on the Embirikos liner *Patris II*, in the process launching the Greek tourist industry in 1930. A selection of essays by leading critics, with photographs by Fred Boissonnas, established the desired cultural cachet.

II Moholy—summoned to 'drop everything'—seizes a once-in-a-lifetime opportunity

1 the CIAM documentary and 'film within'

As Embirikos's yacht steamed towards the open sea, passing the variegated assortment of vessels that permanently line the quays of Piraeus, we can imagine the various *personae* looking around the deck to 'size up' the other invitees. Before them stretch four idyllic days of cruising to those legendary islands which, until this moment in time, had only existed in imaginations stimulated by rare travellers' accounts. Since the cruise had been conceived by Zervos and Giedion as a diversionary interlude, the *personae* could also look forward to convivial exchanges as welcome respite from the intense political manoeuvrings and interminable discussions of statistics that had filled the days since leaving Marseille.

Moholy, though, had a job to do. Giedion had abruptly summoned him to drop everything in Berlin and make a documentary film 'about the congress and about Greece'[9]; if sponsorship funding materialised, his expenses might even be paid. Sent by return, his creatively punctuated telegram of acceptance—'mitfahre mit freude = moholy +'—proves that he viewed the command from Giedion as felicitous. Following his resignation from the Bauhaus faculty in 1928, he had become disillusioned with painting—the medium that had brought him celebrity soon after his arrival in Berlin at the age of twenty-five in 1920. He was now determined to pursue photography and film-making and had already achieved a consistent portfolio of documentary films which would become recognised as classics in the genre. His first, *Berliner Stilleben,* a cinéma-vérité portrait of the city, had been shot in 1926 in the teeth of political harassment. This had been followed, in 1929, by *Marseilles, Vieux Port*—ten and a half minutes of evidently relished realism: street life (high and low), gypsy caravan with performing bear, the constructivist *Pont Transbordeur,* sublime abstractions of cable networks against the sky and reflections in water juxtaposed with piles of garbage, a child defaecating, cats and dogs foraging, and dilapidated buildings elaborately shored up against collapse. His last film had been *Gross-Stadt Zigeuner* (Urban Gypsies), made, in Sibyl Moholy-Nagy's words, 'in a spirit of defiance against the world without, and of confidence in the world which we had discovered within ourselves.... Gypsies had been the romantic element in his Hungarian childhood.... Europe's great vagabonds were disappearing fast, and Moholy decided on a last record.'[10] It was an attempt that almost cost the tenacious film-maker his life when one of the men, objecting to the alien presence in the encampment, shot at Moholy in earnest from the roof of his wagon. As Sibyl also recalled, 'The picture never passed the censor. The first objection was that it had been made by a foreigner who did not belong to the German Film Chamber ... it was rejected as showing German social conditions in an unfavourable light. Without complaint Moholy buried his last hope for creative work in Germany. His world became very abstract.'

Having, by the summer of 1933, scant means of support beyond selling prints of his photographs to American collectors, he had accepted Giedion's spur-of-the-moment commission with alacrity and was, as we know from eye-witness reports[11], totally focused on his task throughout the two weeks of CIAM 4. The 29-minute silent film that Moholy duly delivered to Giedion four months later was to become known as *Architect's Congress* and it's easy to imagine that the 16 mm original—filmed throughout on a hand-held Zeiss Kinamo—would have flickered ephemerally before the viewers' gaze, leaving them with little more than an impression of a convivial group of young men and women on shipboard and at large in the Greek landscape. With no more than a handful of prints in existence, the film acquired legendary

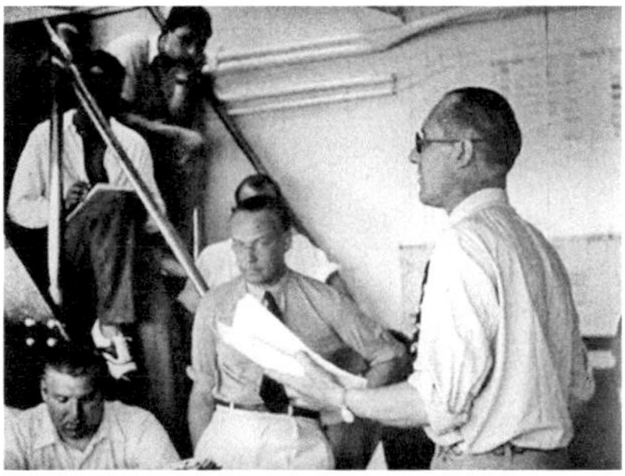

5 Le Corbusier addresses the assembled CIAM congressists on board *Patris II* on the outward voyage from Marseille to Piraeus. Standing centre is Sigfried Giedion, with Cornelis van Eesteren seated next to him. Still from *Architects' Congress* (**04'50"**)

status.[12] A typical recollection sets it in the context of the 4th CIAM congress, which took place at sea on the *Patris II* and in Athens:

> The laboratory scenes against the splendid background of the landscape have been preserved in some fascinating images by the camera of Moholy-Nagy. His film *Architects' Congress* gives us portraits of the congressists as slightly clumsy actors in an atmosphere of imperturbable sun. FIG. 5 Good humour was the order of the day—laughter, alcohol, games.... All of this spoke of the sociability of a large family. But at certain moments faces became more serious, as when the cases containing the city plans were unpacked, and later during the discussion sessions.[13]

Architects' Congress
A film by László Moholy-Nagy

Adopting an alternative viewpoint, there is another way of seeing Moholy's documentary in which a quite distinct 'film within' emerges into the foreground. This begins at a point 21 minutes and 12 seconds into the main 29-minute documentary, when, **21'12"** following a murky night shot of a ghostly Parthenon floodlit for the Congress, the title 'Cruise to the Greek Islands' appears and the screen suddenly fills with light. Moholy focuses on the vessel's wake streaming away from us: one of the longer shots in the mere 4 minutes and 28 seconds devoted to the cruise, the bleached screen clearly signalling a change of *mode.*

Thus, the departure from Piraeus marked the opening of a **21'19"** completely different phase of the filming. Perhaps feeling discharged from his documentary duties, he had begun to frame shots which were more 'Moholy', while simultaneously inspired to compose a vivid literary account to send to Sibyl—seven months pregnant and minding the studio back in Berlin, where she was obliged to work as a court reporter to make ends meet. He would not find time to commit these impressions to paper until near the end of the return voyage of the *Patris II* to Marseille;

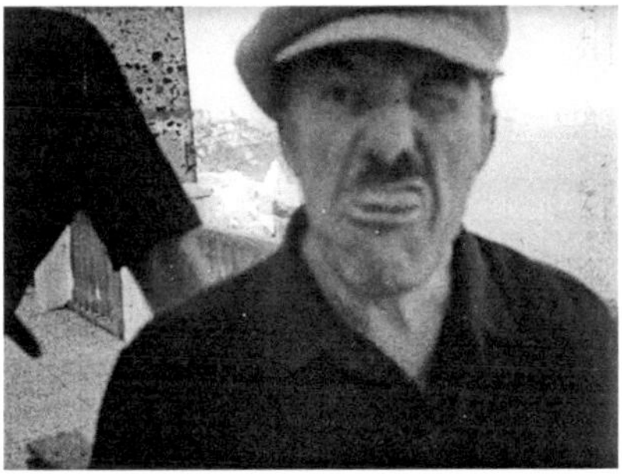

6 Léger cheekily pokes out his tongue at Moholy. The split-second shot coming soon after the opening of *Architects' Congress* was filmed on Santorini towards the *end* of the island cruise; thus the displaced shot becomes a striking demonstration of Moholy's signature montage technique. Still from *Architects' Congress* (**01'55"**)

then, in a colourful six-page letter—as ever, selecting his words carefully—he refers to his *compagnons de voyage* of the island cruise as a *gesellschaft.* A word that had definite sociological overtones in the Germany of that time and which would have resonated with Sibyl, since it implies a motley crew—especially now that its opposite, the cohesive *gemeinschaft*, had been conspicuously hijacked to bolster the *völkisch* national-socialist 'community'.

> *... it was an unusual experience. imagine a small nutshell on a rough sea, manned by a captain, helmsman and several sailors, and 25 chosen guests of the congress, mostly french, who like to keep to themselves, and several swiss, dutch and greeks + me.*[14]

While the French were cohesive in their isolation, we can't help noticing that there were no Germans—or Italians for that matter—on this trip.[15] As the sole Hungarian, Moholy wryly casts himself as the outsider.

But it wasn't mere nationality that prompted Moholy to regard events from a detached viewpoint peripheral to this company of earnest Westerners who preferred to talk among themselves. Having abandoned a promising career as innovative abstract painter to devote his creative energies to photography and film-making, his particular vision had surely been conditioned by the traumatic experience of fighting—and being wounded—in the trenches of the Great War.[16] There was one other artist on the vessel who had survived a similar ordeal: Fernand Léger. Soon after the opening of *Architects' Congress*, Moholy cuts to a split-second shot of Léger cheekily poking out his tongue at the cameraman, FIG. 6 in the process simultaneously hinting at a conspiratorial rapport between the two men, and establishing an irreverent tone for the documentary which follows. Filmed on Santorini towards the *end* of the island cruise, the displaced

7 *The City*—painted by Fernand Léger in 1919 as a mural-size celebration of modern urban technology—also evokes his youthful architectural studies and wartime experiences.

shot becomes a striking demonstration of Moholy's signature montage technique.

2 Léger's harsh critique

Now that's professionalism—reminding us that, from the viewpoint of the Parisian avant-garde, Léger was the artistic 'anchor' of this event. A deflationary heavyweight, though, whose tongue-poking is an indication of his affection for Moholy. Both men loved machinery, and the painter of *The City*—one of the greatest paintings of the twentieth century—must in turn have admired Moholy; FIG. 7 if nothing else, for his spectacular kinetic *Light-Space Modulator,* which he had probably seen at the Deutscher Werkbund exhibition in Paris in 1930. On his return to Paris after the congress, Léger would write an essay eulogising the Parthenon as a parallel proof of excellence to the Eiffel Tower and, ultimately, comparable in precision of concept and execution to the latest technological advance: the electron microscope.[17] Equally precise and impeccably constructed, Léger's painting style betrays the influence of his youthful architectural studies; thus it represents the opposite pole to the more Dionysian and prolific Picasso, whose provocative works fascinated the 1930s' public. As a determined part-time painter himself, the 'purist'

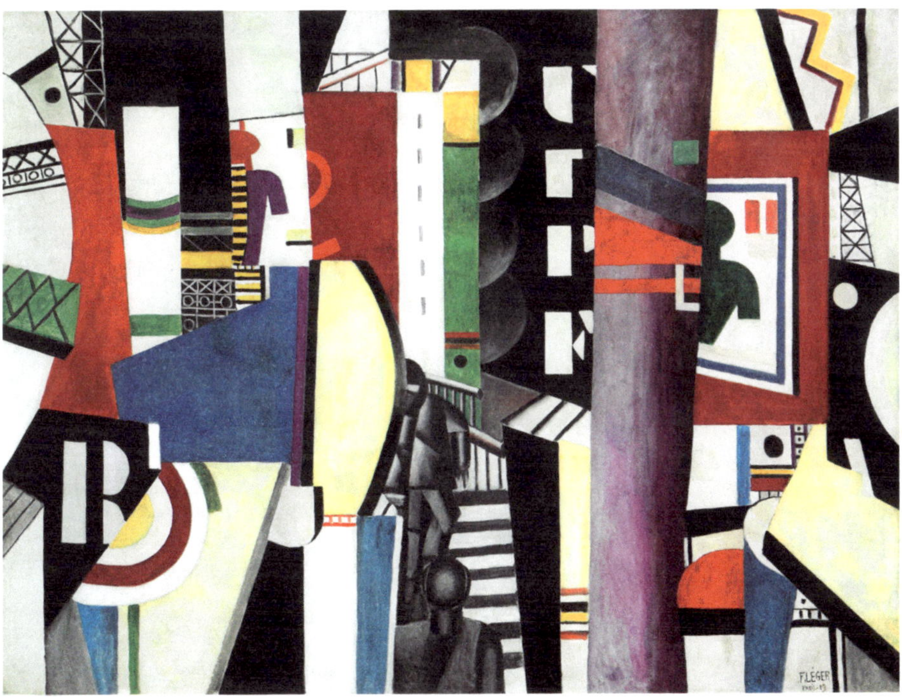

Le Corbusier clearly respected Léger's opinion; thus we may imagine that at some stage of this cruise he would have felt obliged to 'take on board' a harsh critique from his friend. The provocation for this was the iconoclastic lecture Le Corbusier had delivered to the assembled congress on the previous Thursday evening. Following a euphoric preamble invoking the spirit of the Acropolis, he had launched into a prepared text titled 'Air, Sound, Light'.[18] In essence this advocated the replacement of existing city quarters that he perceived to be obsolete with massive housing blocks 'equipped with tempered curtain walls'—incredibly, it now seems, as the environmental effect of large sheets of glass had been recognised in the forcing frames of Dutch and English gardens since at least the eighteenth century. The difference, in Le Corbusier's view, was that his curtain walls would be sealed so that 'the hermetic character of the glass facades will bring silence to the interior of the house, that's to say isolation from exterior noise'. That he had not reckoned on the 'greenhouse effect' must have left many of his audience bemused on a sweltering August evening.

Léger, the amiable countryman from Normandy, was less than enthusiastic about his friend's vision, arguing:

> You have discovered a new primary architectural material: 'air and light'. The materials and ornaments which suffocated the preceding architecture have disappeared; weights, volumes, thicknesses have vanished into thin air.... You have constructed houses for people who had become accustomed in advance to your radical formulae.... But your formula wants to extend itself. The word 'urbanism' wants, from now on, to dominate the aesthetic question. / Urbanism is social. You enter into a totally different *domaine,* a *domaine* where your pure and radical formulae are going to have to struggle. The drama begins precisely there for you; there will be a chilly reception. / You leave this elegant

> and established minority to attack the 'average' who, until now, have lived with furniture, reproductions and knick-knacks; who have always decorated their walls to the maximum and covered up the windows with curtains. These simple folk, slow and timid, you undress and stick completely stupefied in front of the 'curtain wall'. This wall, which you have brought back to life, their fathers and grandfathers spent their whole lives hiding. You impose it in a radical way. They find themselves suddenly enveloped in light in front of these glossy slick new surfaces where they cannot hide, where even the shadow no longer finds a place.[19]

As he had previously delivered the critique to a meeting of Zurich architects in April and it would also be published in the Italian journal *Quadrante* a month after CIAM 4, we can be sure that in the dazzling light and profound shadows of the islands Léger would, if anything, have become even more convinced of his reservations about the technological Corbusian vision.

Nevertheless, to a 20-year-old student of Pikionis at the National Technical University, Giorgios Kandilis—who as Georges Candilis would, some twenty years later, play a decisive role in the break-up of CIAM—Le Corbusier's visionary address came as a revelation:

> When he began to speak, the audience forgot his lateness, his tactlessness, and was transported, seduced by his impressive proclamation of the new reality, simple and true, which swept away [...] twenty centuries of architectural conformism. For us—young enthusiastic students—the columns of the temple came tumbling down. On the ruins, Le Corbusier made the new materials of architecture appear: they are not merely stone, cement, brick, wood or metal—but above all Space, Greenery, Sun![20]

3 the Corbusian view of Greece

Apart from a clutch of still photos and the 4 minutes and 28 seconds of Moholy's film footage that survived the editing process, the only documentation that was actually recorded during the island cruise to have come to light are six pages of Le Corbusier's pocket sketchbook 'carnet B5'. On two of these pages are sketches of the Temple of Aphaia on Aegina, while the remaining four are covered with a spidery and barely decipherable scrawl that Embirikos might have recognised as 'automatic writing'. The architect carried these 10.5 × 18.5 cm spiral-bound notebooks with him at all times, communing with them when an occasion arose, and relying on the notes he traced with soft pencil to preserve his impressions and insights for future reference. Inevitably, any attempt to interpret the ambiguous 'stream of consciousness' jottings must be conjectural. The pages frequently contain germs of ideas that only come to fruition months or years later; on the other hand, many notes and sketches would remain just that—hieroglyphics buried in a *carnet.* Thus, the battered notebook boards the boat in Piraeus in the architect's pocket. He's not alone but most probably accompanied by his closest friends: Fernand Léger, Christian and Yvonne Zervos, Jean Badovici and his loyal older brother, the composer Albert Jeanneret. We can be fairly sure about this because, immediately before he boards, he dashes off a postcard to his wife Yvonne in Paris—'We are leaving in a minute for the Islands in a small steamer (*petit vapeur*). Affectionately Dou'[21] (diminutive, apparently, of Edouard in the Le Corbusier household)—which he then got his 'gang' to sign: *Amicalement FLéger, Christian Zervos, Yvonne Zervos, A Jeanneret, Badovici.* The card, a reproduction of *Pericles' Funeral Oration* FIG. 8 painted in 1852 by the academic artist Philipp von Foltz, seems an odd choice to send to a stay-at-home wife who was not particularly renowned as a classical scholar; nor is it exactly a representative

8 *Pericles' Funeral Oration,* an 1852 painting by Philipp von Foltz, was the postcard Le Corbusier dashed off to his wife Yvonne in Paris immediately before departing from Piraeus.

image of Greece in 1933. It does, however, tell us something about the sender and his view of Greece at that moment in time, a viewpoint that Zervos will make a determined effort to reorientate during the coming days.

The architect had been top of the bill at the grand reception held for the entire CIAM complement and their friends in the courtyard of the neoclassical Athens Polytechnic on the previous Thursday evening. Crucially, government ministers had also been invited, and they had come expecting to be enlightened by the great man on how to solve Greece's severe urban crisis. At nine o'clock, the appointed time for his address, Le Corbusier was nowhere to be found; the organisers becoming increasingly embarrassed as the invited guests melted away and van Eesteren was obliged to apologise—aware that a valuable opportunity had been squandered. Finally, at a quarter to ten, a casually dressed Le Corbusier strolled up to the rostrum and proceeded to make light of his tardiness: 'Ladies and gentlemen, I've been told that I should have spoken at ten o'clock. It's now a quarter to ten. Please excuse me for starting a quarter of an hour too early'. Many years later he confessed to Georges Candilis that he had decided, after visiting the Acropolis one last time, 'to go for a wander, to look at the houses, the people, to gossip, go into the houses and drink some *retsina.* And time stood still in a bakery whose oven particularly impressed him. As he watched the baker kneed his dough he completely lost sight of the fact that he was expected at the conference.'[22] To regain the sympathy of the prestigious Greek audience, however, he spun a more flattering yarn:

> This morning at Piraeus we took a walk with some friends: Fernand Léger, the painter; Zervos, creator of Cahiers d'Art; Albert Jeanneret, the musician; Ghika from here—one of the painters who is making a name for himself. We stopped in front of the coastal boats, boats of today and through the ages, boats of your history. These boats are painted in very

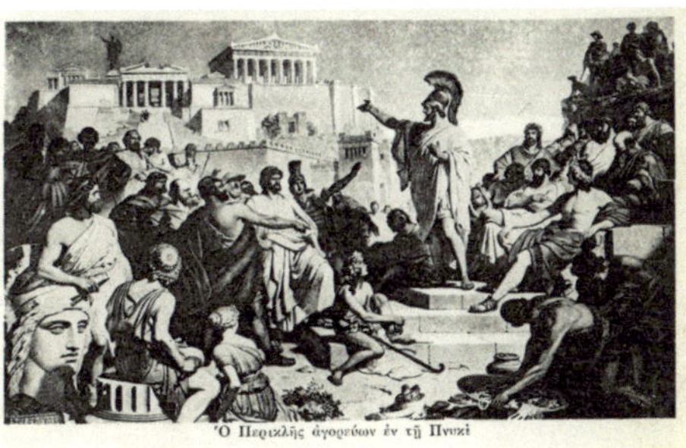

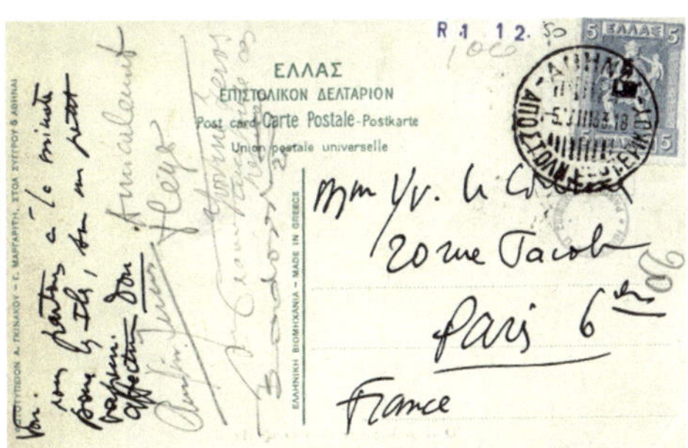

> strong colours. Colour, the very expression of life! In those boats of Piraeus which are painted like those of a thousand years ago, we found again the tradition of the Acropolis, which was not distinguished before Pericles. Which was strong, strict, exact and intense, sensual. The Greek spirit has remained the sign of mastery; mathematical rigour and law of numbers bringing in harmony.[23]

Pericles remains, two and a half millennia after his death, a controversial figure. Credited with getting the Parthenon built in record time, he was also accused of maladministration and certain perversions, while his friend Phidias—sculptor and architect of the building—was convicted of embezzlement and died in prison. In 1933 it was still taken for granted that the academically inclined would identify with the fifth-century statesman. The unequivocally anti-academic Zervos, on the other hand, had different ideas; he did *not* agree that the Greek tradition 'was not distinguished before Pericles' and thus, we imagine, set out to enlighten Le Corbusier.

4 Zervos's radical agenda

Christian Zervos (1889–1970)—as founder and editor of *Cahiers d'Art*, the luxurious quarterly review in which the leading European avant-garde artists aspired to appear—had been planning this cruise for years. Early in 1931 he had suggested to Giedion that they should together accompany the cinematographer Eli Lotar, poet Roger Vitrac and director Jacques Brunius on a journey through the islands which would result in the film *Le Voyage aux Cyclades*.[24] The film, which was subsequently lost, was premiered in March 1932, with music composed by Albert Jeanneret, in the cinema auditorium of the newspaper *L'Intransigeant* before an audience drawn from friends of *Cahiers d'Art*, the surreal ambience of the remote islands as portrayed in Lotar's images no doubt reinforcing the resolve of many in the audience to make the journey themselves.

If an encounter with unselfconscious proto-surrealism was one plank of Zervos's didactic mission, the other was his determination to reveal to his friends and readers the true essence of Greek art as he saw it, an essence that, in his view, had been eclipsed by the 'decadence' of the Periclean era. When they encountered the unforeseen beauty of the pre-classical temple of Aphaia on Aegina and, above all, the astonishingly 'modern' popular architecture of the islands, the eyes of the Westerners would, he firmly believed, be opened.

5 the incomparable light offers Moholy new creative possibilities

The most elusive of all the actors in this Greek drama had appeared to Giedion on board the *Patris II* a few days earlier. He describes the moment with characteristic accuracy:

> When the steamer hove-to outside Corinth to allow the Greek delegation to come on board, the quality of this light was suddenly made manifest to us by a detail, trivial enough in itself. There are many parts of the ocean where the water is transparent right down to the bottom. But here its limpidity was of a different order. The sun penetrated it with such power and brilliance that the bronze glint of the ship's screws was heightened to a positively unreal intensity. Light as a material and the consummate achievement of form, sought and striven for, was what Greece brought home to us.[25]

As his film eloquently demonstrates, Moholy seized with open arms the possibilities offered by this incomparable light and the way it played over the elemental island forms. He had considered experimental photography and film-making to be his métier since his resignation from the Bauhaus in 1928; Giedion's invitation to film the Greek adventure thus offered him an unrepeatable opportunity to pursue theories that he had first advanced in an article published in Hungary in 1930.[26] Here he reflected on the decline of traditional easel painting and the discovery, by his friend the suprematist Malevich, that 'his last picture—a white square on a square white canvas—is clearly symbolic of the film screen, symbolic of the transition from painting in terms of pigment to painting in terms of light'. Theorising that 'the essential medium of the film is *light* not pigment', Moholy rejected what he described as the 'misguided efforts of the present-day film-makers' to imitate studio painting or theatre—offering by contrast the montage technique of Dziga Vertov, best known for *Man with a Movie Camera:* 'The Russian director's sense of motion is impressionistic rather than constructive. Russian montage is particularly successful in the use of associative impressions.... Through rapid cutting often also of spatially and temporally distinct shots it created the necessary links between the individual situation and the whole'.

Moholy's frequently idiosyncratic choice of subject matter and camera angles were a source of fascination for the congressists. We may imagine also that his unconventional approach influenced their own attitudes to photography, which, as late as 1933, was not wholly accepted as an art form—Zervos, for one, having serious reservations. Giedion, on the other hand, was an accomplished photographer; he and Moholy had collaborated in curating one of the galleries at the celebrated *FIFO New Vision* exhibition of 1929 in Stuttgart.[27]

While Giedion and Moholy took a few photos on the cruise with a shared medium-format folding camera, the Zurich engineer-architect Carlo Hubacher came equipped with a 35 mm Leica—already at that date the preferred eye-level tool of the photo-journalist. He was thus able to present us with a coherent 'story' comprising over one hundred images, among which we find

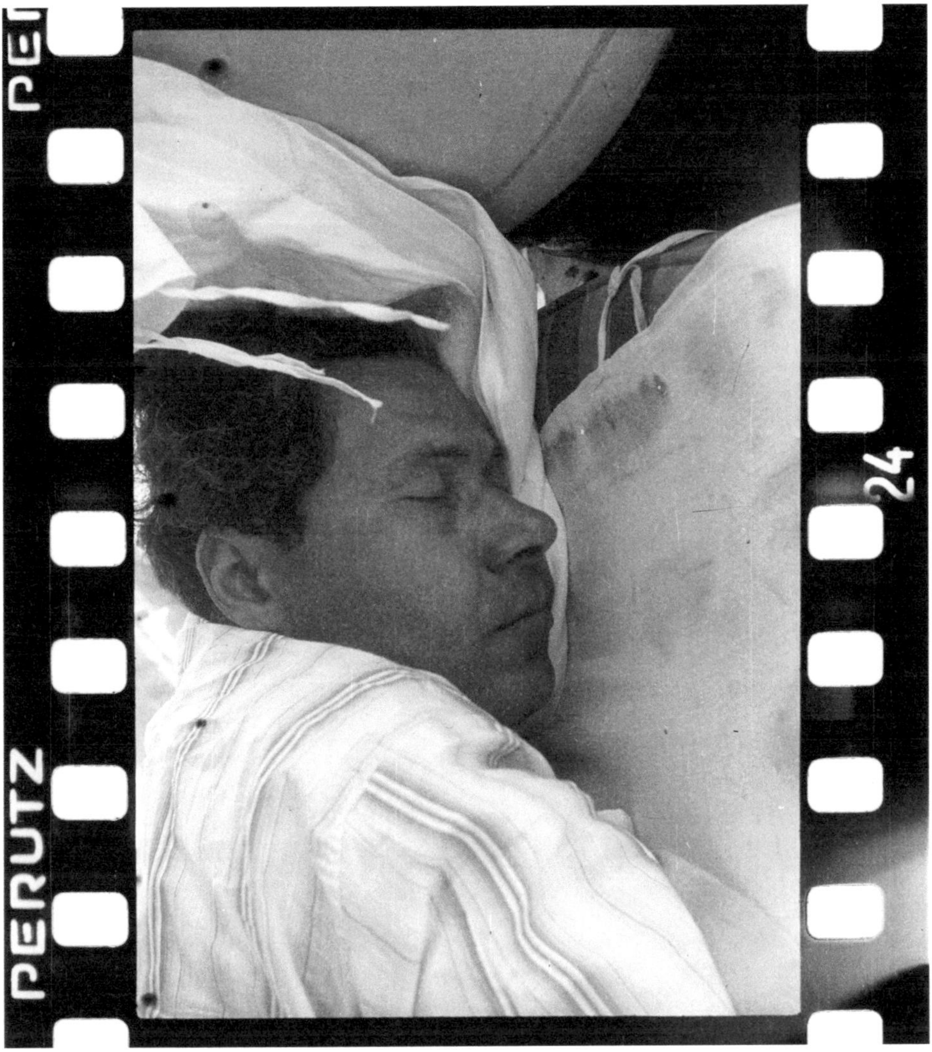

9 In his letter to Sibyl, Moholy claimed that he scarcely had time to rest; nevertheless, the alert Carlo Hubacher caught him deep in sleep on the deck of the *Afros*—an image he preferred to orientate vertically. Photo by Carlo Hubacher

shots of Moholy filming and, uncharacteristically, asleep on deck. FIG. 9 Hubacher's shots of the islanders and their houses reveal a perceptiveness and empathy, contrasting, for example, the vibrant plasticity of the white architecture in the astonishing light with the claustrophobic interiors, which were home to political exiles.

III from microcosm of the ancient Attic landscape to 'forest of symbols'

1 Aegina: a most impressive dialogue between architecture and landscape

Sometime in the late afternoon, the *petit vapeur* anchors in the bay below the village of Aghia Marina on the east coast of the island; there's no jetty, so the cruise party will have to be rowed ashore a few at a time. FIG. 10 Le Corbusier dives impulsively into the Aegean and swims with a strong crawl towards an islander's **21'26"** boat, a scene Moholy later described to Sibyl: *we swam in a charming small bay and were viewed and greeted as miraculous creatures by the nicest, most naive inhabitants of the island.*[28] He seems as fascinated by these islanders as he was by the gypsies of Berlin and Marseille, devoting a significant portion of his 4 minutes 28 seconds to a family group as they enjoy a convivial Saturday afternoon on the beach. One hirsute muleteer, distinguished by a tall straw hat with curious lampshade brim that **21'44"** casts a deep shadow over his eyes, particularly draws his attention. As Moholy raises his Kinamo to film a close-up, Hubacher snaps him with his Leica—so quickly, that he doesn't have time to level the camera. Thus, in an instant, are captured two of the most memorable images from the island cruise: Moholy totally focused on his task in front of a sloping horizon, FIG. 11 and the characteristic shot he has composed: muleteer's hat echoed by tall smokestack of the distant *vapeur.* FIG. 12

On landing from the rowing boats, the Western aesthetes are dismayed to learn that the Temple of Aphaia—today's goal according to Zervos's agenda—is 160 metres above sea level and reachable only by a steep and rocky *monopáti* through the pine forest. There's nothing for it but to mount the mules which just happen to be waiting silently on the beach; the ever-unfazed Moholy writes that he *rode up to the temple on a mule for the first*

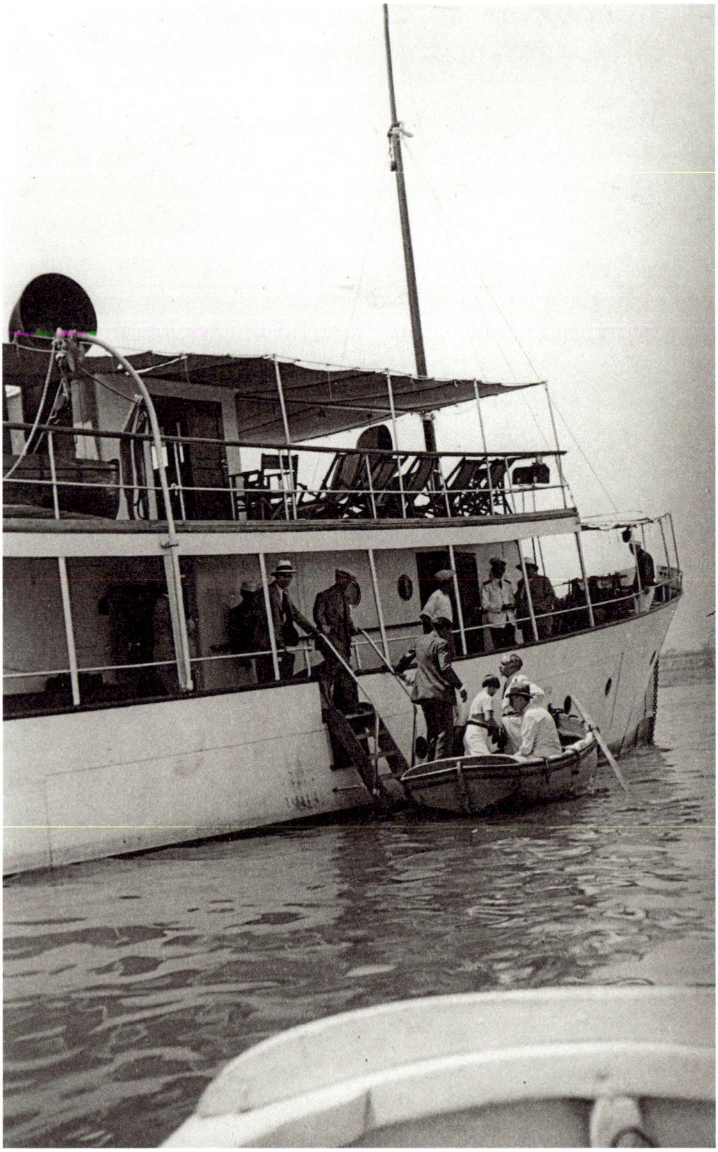

10 Members of the cruise party disembark from the *Afros.* As few of the island ports had jetties in 1933, passengers were rowed ashore in small boats. Photo by Ghika

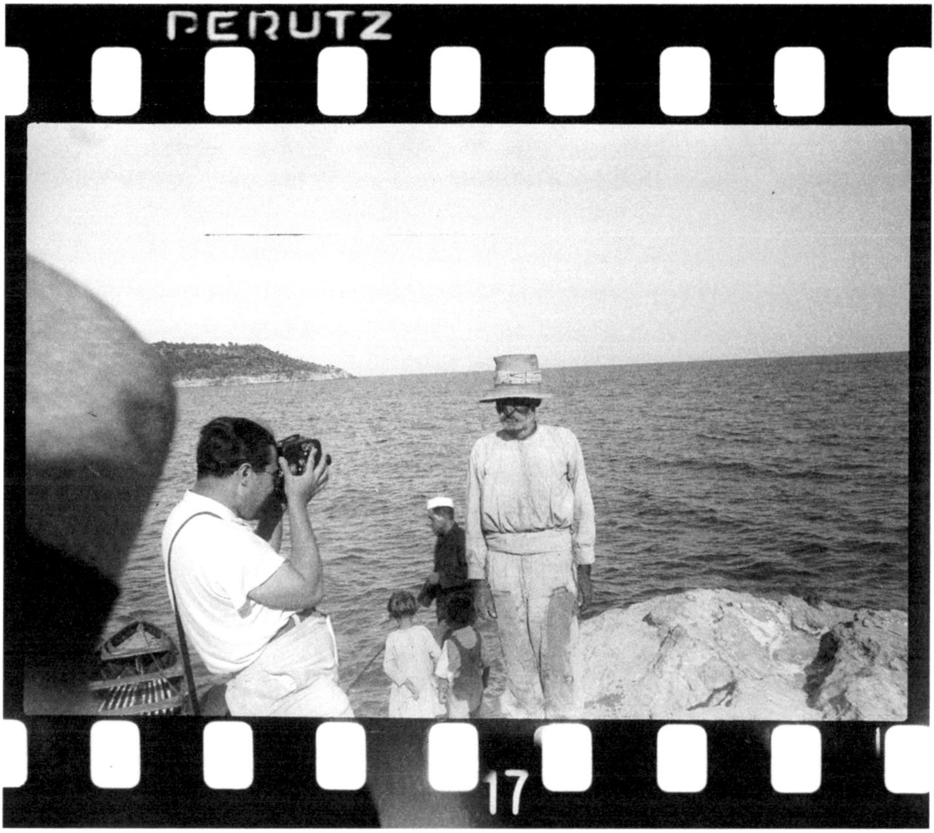

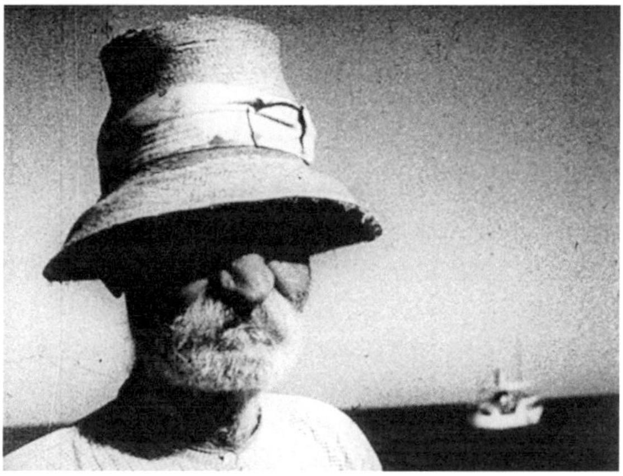

11 Hubacher's memorably spontaneous shot of Moholy filming the 'hirsute' muleteer on the beach at Agia Marina, Aegina. Photo by Carlo Hubacher

12 Moholy's close-up of the muleteer. Still from *Architects' Congress* (**21'43"**)

21'45" *time.* We catch a glimpse of a self-assured Giedion fully in control of his beast, while other members of the party appear less confident as they lurch unceremoniously up the track. The scene that greeted the riders as they gained the elevated temenos more than compensated for the sore posteriors acquired on the steep climb. The c.500 BCE Doric temple of Aphaia—raised on a precise platform with commanding views over the Saronic Gulf, island of Salamina and the Peloponnese to the north and west, and far over the Aegean to the south and east—survives to this day as one of the most impressive dialogues between architecture and landscape on earth. Aegina, a mere seventeen miles from Piraeus, also survives as a microcosm of the ancient Attic landscape; from fertile coastal plain of olive and pistachio groves, through protective valleys and small villages, to rugged mountain slopes clothed in aromatic pine forests, the island is the perfect introduction to the *poetic* reality of Greece.

However, it is the temple itself, standing on a site that has been occupied since Mycenaean times, that guarantees Aegina a unique status in the history of architecture. Since the excavations, led by the great Adolf Furtwängler in 1905, had been widely published, Zervos may have filled in the details of the mythological background for those, like Le Corbusier, who were interested in these matters. Aphaia was the ancient earth goddess related to Cretan Dictynna, protectress of both sailors and hunters. She was also associated with the virginal Artemis and had flung herself into the sea to avoid rape at the hands of Minos; thus Aphaia's name signified 'the vanishing one'. It seems probable that Zervos envisaged Aphaia's temple playing a vital didactic role at this critical juncture of the twentieth century and its architecture. Modestly scaled and unassuming in comparison with Pericles' muscular Parthenon, Aphaia appears to 'float' above the landscape; although built at the dawn of the classical era, in certain lights the ruin assumes an uncannily modern aura.

Moholy's camera pans for a few seconds over a cluster of surprisingly slender fluted columns poignantly lashed up with steel 'ligatures' and wooden wedges to prevent them from splitting apart, while the ground is littered with column fragments. He is filming from inside the *naós,* looking north towards the Saronic Gulf and mountains beyond. We catch a glimpse of Le Corbusier standing, sketchbook in hand, though—according to Giedion's later memoir—'Le Corbusier sat behind a column drawing in his blue sketch-book; van Eesteren had something to say about the lessons of this "cultural landscape". Otherwise—perhaps because what we saw in stones, or buildings, or the face of the ground stirred familiar chords in us—we mostly contemplated in silence'. Moholy, it seems, was content to observe and film, having, in Giedion's account, made his own peace with classicism the previous day: '"Never since my school days," Moholy said to me on the Acropolis, "have I been so conscious of how directly the Greek world speaks to us—though in a very different sense to what the nineteenth century understood by this".'[29]

22'00"

22'03"

Looking closely at Le Corbusier's sketches of Aphaia, we have the impression that they were rushed, and that he was unable to find the right frame of mind to do the temple justice; the others, perhaps, respectfully waiting in the failing light for him to finish so that they could set sail again. Then, another thought comes to mind. On his early backpacking travels through eastern Europe to the Balkans he had proved himself to be an enthusiastic and accomplished photographer; after 1911, however, he dropped it, Candilis claiming that it was because his countrymen had stolen the young traveller's camera.[30] Subsequently he seems to have taken a principled stand against photography, writing,

> I bought myself a little Kodak camera, which Kodak sold for six francs in order to sell film to those idiots who use it, and I was one of them, and I noticed that by entrusting my emotions to a lens I was forgetting to have them pass by

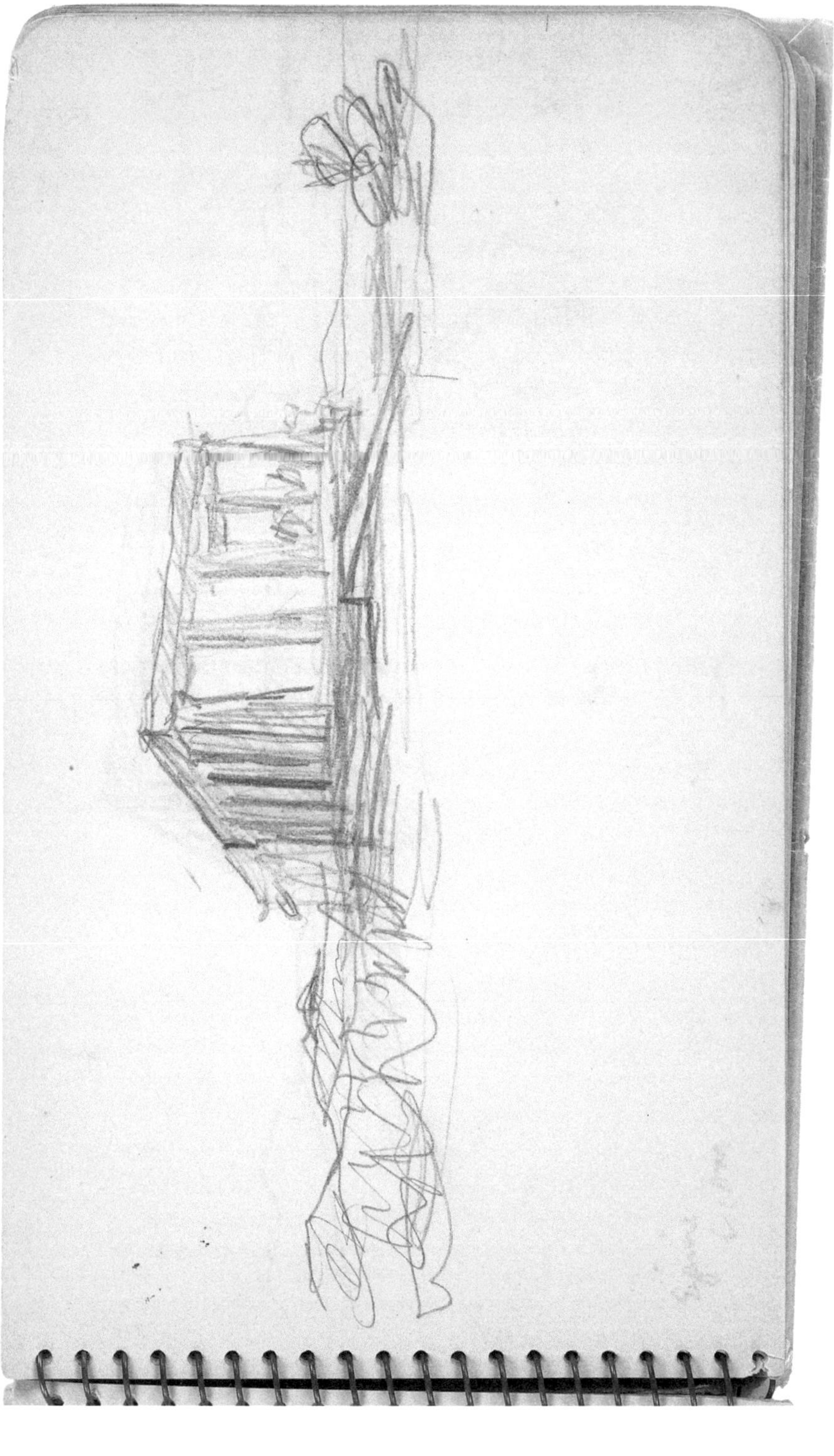

13 Pages from *Carnet B5.* Le Corbusier made two sketches of the temple of Aphaia on Aegina; in the first, which is carefully rendered, he emphasises the distinctive ramp up to the stylobate—he nevertheless shows only five columns on the east façade, simultaneously exaggerating their girth.

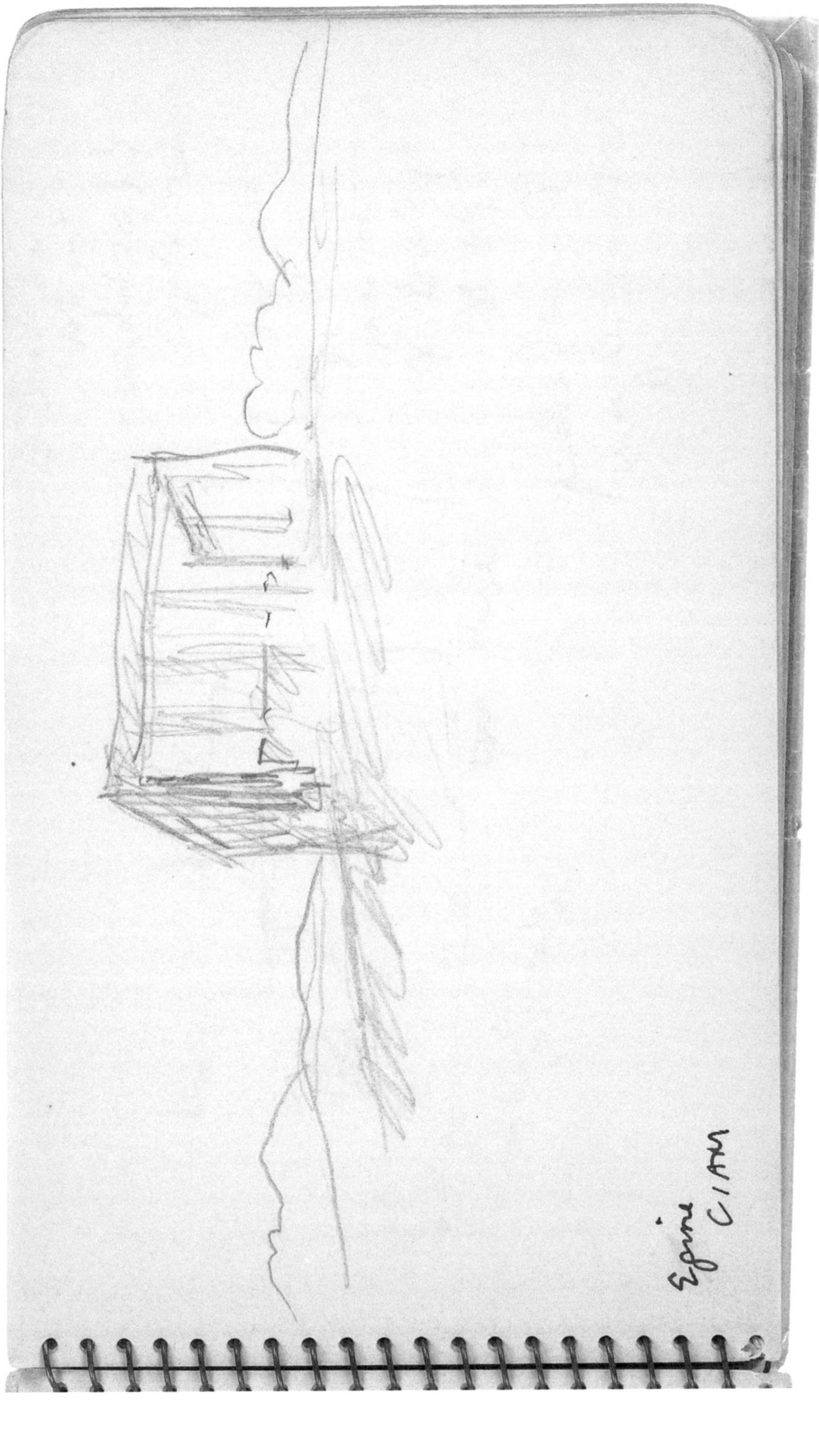

14 In the second, more rapidly executed sketch, he appears to rectify these faults. Apparently impressed by the dramatic siting of the temple, he sketches the profile of Mount Oros to the west.

> me—which was serious. So I abandoned the Kodak and picked up my pencil, and ever since then I have always drawn everything, wherever I am.[31]

The lone figure we see in Moholy's film feels compelled to sketch, but perhaps at this stage is merely *contemplating* how best to render these austere but slender columns. They have none of the bulging muscularity of the Parthenon's soaring trunks that he had drawn with such aplomb in 1911.[32] Doric temples are notoriously difficult to capture in this way; the columns—their proportion and spacing—defy the pencil. He is facing the north elevation, but the two sketches that survive in his *carnet* are of the *east* elevation with its distinctive ramp. Has his attitude to this architecture changed since his first overwhelming encounter with the Periclean monument which had been the goal of his epic 'Journey to the East'—the youthful epiphany he had recalled in his address to the congress two evenings earlier? Aphaia's façade is awkwardly sketched; FIG. 13 in his first attempt it has five columns—surely a mistake he would be anxious to correct in the second sketch. FIG. 14 What appears to have occurred then is that his attention was seized by the landscape beyond—his pencil rapidly rendering the profile of the surrounding mountains and islands. It seems that he has fallen under the spell of this landscape in a similar manner to Vincent Scully twenty years later:

> Aphaia's sanctuary is set upon an open saddle from which two seas are visible: the open Aegean to the south, the Saronic Gulf bounded by Salamis and Attica to the north. The easterly view is blocked near at hand by the greater height of the hills on that side. To the west are the deep gorges and peaks of the centre of the island.... The worshipper [...] went to the ramp, turned west upon it toward the temple and suddenly had before his eyes to the southwest the great mass of Mount Oros, symbol of Zeus Panhellenios and probably of the goddess before him.[33]

The presence of this peak—a volcano in antediluvian times and, at 532 metres, the highest on Aegina—is inescapable on the island.

As epigraph to his *Technica Chronica* article,[34] Pikionis had selected a couplet by the nineteenth century Cuban-born French poet José-Maria de Hérédia; intending no doubt to balance the journal's technical bias with the sensibility of one who also wrote: 'True poetry dwells in nature and in humanity, which are eternal, and not in the heart of the creature of a day, however great.'

Dans ce fauve terrain	*in this wild landscape*
la terre vainement éloquent	*the earth vainly eloquent*

He is concerned to impress on his pragmatic fellow-professionals the necessity for 'insight' to 'achieve [...] an effective creativity and the will to combat the powers of evil'. However, he acknowledges what he identifies as 'the greatest tragedy. This land, with its spirit still alive (despite its decayed form) and still with the supreme example of the most perfect "culture" ever developed, stood "vainly eloquent" for its progeny.' On the other hand, the Le Corbusier of *Vers une Architecture,* as Pikionis knew well, was acutely attuned to the mysterious lines of force and axes of the Greek landscape; thus we must assume that his fleeting encounter with 'the vanishing one'—recorded by his pencil—also entered deep into his subconscious.

2 Tombros's monument to Rupert Brooke prompts a Corbusian response

As the visitors wended their way back down the rutted *monopáti* to the beach, thence to be rowed out to the waiting *vapeur,* they must have been turning the encounter with Aphaia over in their minds. For Michael Tombros (he anglicised his given name from Michalis)—born in Athens in 1889 and, in 1933, Greece's most prominent sculptor—this landscape was anything but 'vainly eloquent'. The contrast between the masterful siting of the pre-classical temple and tragic missed opportunity of his monument to Rupert Brooke on the island of Skyros must have been painful. FIG. 15

The monument had been the idea of the Belgian poet Paul Vanderborght (1899–1971), who raised the necessary funds from the international artistic community by subscription. In 1921 Vanderborght had founded the artistic and literary movement La Lanterne sourde,[35] which published a review and organised exhibitions and conferences. The roll of contributors reads like a 'who's who' of the European avant-garde of the time: Blaise Cendrars, Paul Valéry, Darius Milhaud, Eric Satie, the proto-fascist Marinetti and, inevitably, Le Corbusier. Tombros had come into contact with the European avant-garde during a sojourn in Paris between 1925 and 1928 and had repeatedly attempted to break free from academicism, venturing into cubist and surrealist territory. For the Brooke commission, however, he adopted a quasi-academic style, producing a standing nude—believed to have been modelled on the young dancer Alexander Iolas, who, many years later, would become a flamboyant international gallery owner.

Tombros's monument was unveiled at a ceremony on 5 April 1931 by Prime Minister Eleftherios Venizelos—the event being filmed by the cinematographer Eli Lotar as the climax of *Le Voyage aux Cyclades.* To the viewer acquainted with Brooke's work, however distantly, the brazen male nude appears incongruous, its connection to the tragic poet obscure. Years later Lawrence Durrell would concede it a brief mention, reporting, 'I was [...] told that the nude youth in the sculpture caused a certain amount of middle-class distaste among the nicer sort of people in the capital. Well, it is epicene, but to feel shocked by a nude is surely simply out of date.'[36] From an architectural viewpoint, the overtly masculine statue is insensitively sited: isolated at the edge of an exposed open space high above the town, and lost against the broad horizon. Le Corbusier had been actively involved in promoting the Lotar-Vitrac-Brunius film; thus, it must also have been his introduction to the monument.

Having experienced the miracle of Aphaia and observed Le Corbusier's attempt to capture it with his pencil, Tombros may have mentioned his disappointment over the Brooke memorial to the architect as the two men returned to the *vapeur.* They find common ground in reminiscing about their mutual friend Vanderborght. Notwithstanding certain innuendos, Tombros is not embarrassed by his sculpture; what pains him is the perfunctory installation. Le Corbusier agrees and—sensing the pretext for an intervention—takes out his *carnet* and begins sketching and scribbling notes: *statue Tombros* in the top right-hand corner is the clue. FIG. 16 The page leaps out of the battered *carnet* as a map of the man's mind at that moment in time: top left, two minuscule sketches suggest islands glimpsed from far out to sea; below the lower sketch an arrow pointing right and, below that, the word *coupe* (section). Immediately to the right, a lightly sketched diagonal—the word *rampe* above it—then a hatched horizontal line and vertical line terminating in a black squiggle that resembles someone sitting up in bed. Above this squiggle the words *joues laterale* which suggest 'side walls', and a diagonal line linking them to the hatched lines. But 'side walls' of what? A possible answer can be seen to the right and below—again with a pointing diagonal line—*piscine salée* (saltwater swimming pool). Immediately below, and written with a flourish, the wonderful Greek sea word, *Thalassa,* underlined by a sweeping horizon that crosses the page rightwards from a third tiny 'island profile' sketch.

If we divide the page into three horizontal layers, we now come to the 'filling in the sandwich'. From left to right: *pas d'eau courant sur le terrain* (no running water on the site); immediately to the right of this note, the tantalisingly tiny but emphatically drawn plan of what appears to be a square building with

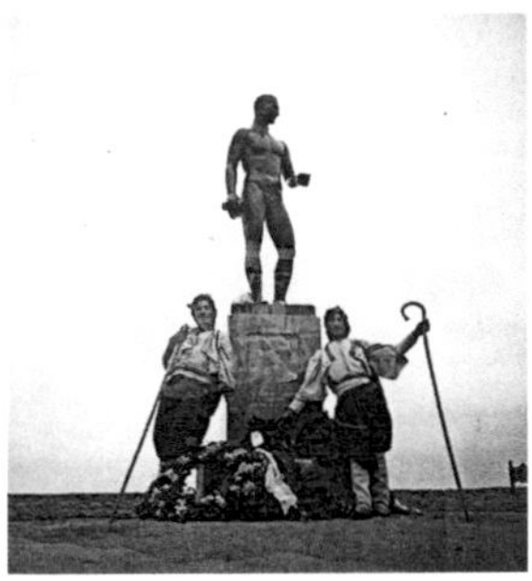

15 Dedication of the Rupert Brooke memorial by Michael Tombros on the island of Skyros, 5 April 1931. This event was filmed by the cinematographer Eli Lotar as the climax of the film *Le Voyage aux Cyclades*, which was premiered in Paris in 1932 and subsequently lost. Photo by Eli Lotar

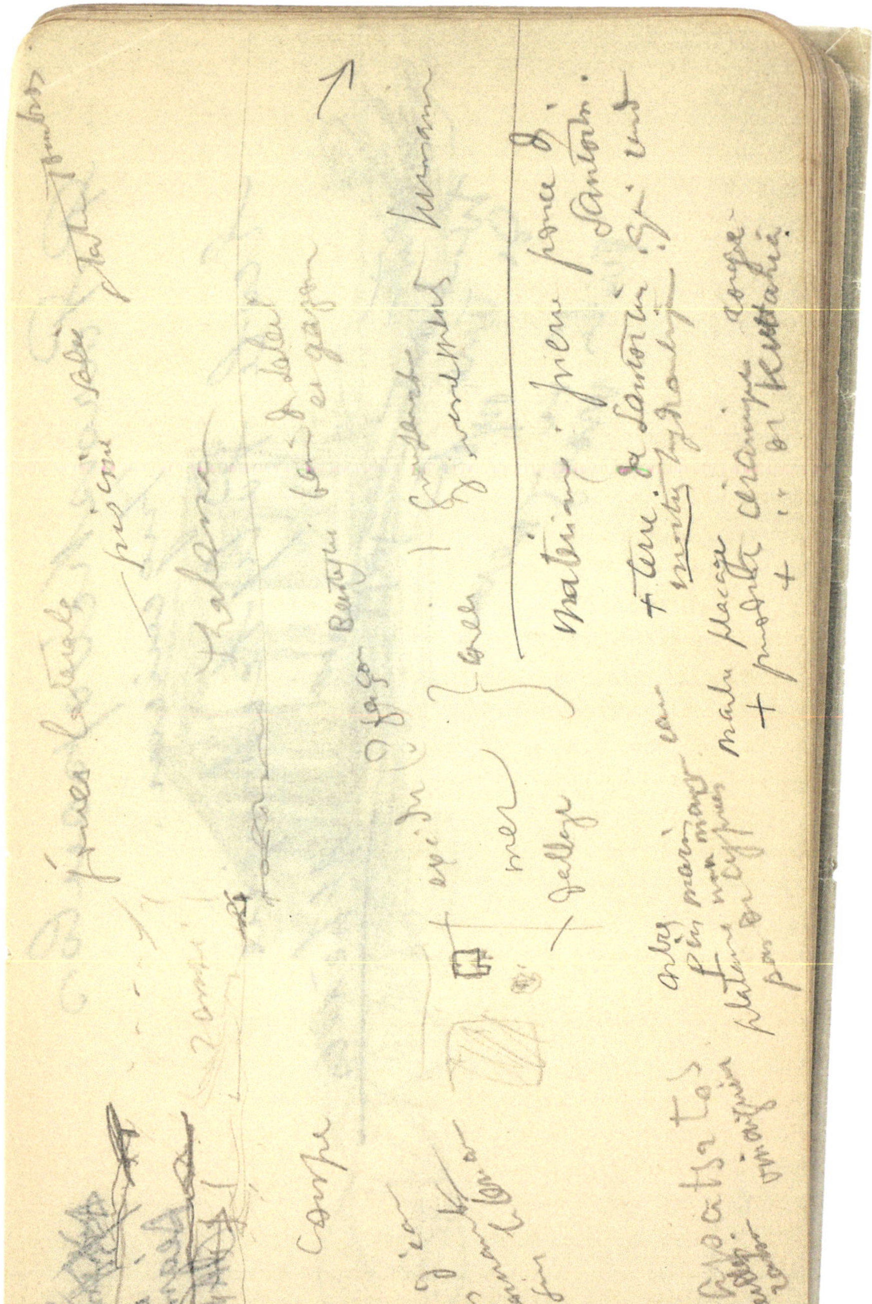

16 Page from *Carnet B5* with notes by Le Corbusier made on the *Afros: statue Tombros*, top right, and the fictitious *Papatsatos*, bottom left

projection lower left. To its left a shaded area and, beneath that, a squiggle—possibly a tree; surrounding this ensemble, a line apparently marking the site boundary. To the right, the words *mer* above *dallage* (paving): these two words bracketed with *créer – groupements d'evenements humains.* We understand that the square 'building', the sea and paving are there to create 'groupings of human events': celebrations of some kind. Now to the note that extends to the right of the emphatic tiny plan: *exèdre (? façon Beistegui bain de soleil en gazon.* What Le Corbusier appears to have in mind is a grass-carpeted 'room' surrounded by a high wall blocking horizontal views while framing the sky—like the unequivocally surrealist roof garden he had created above the Champs Elysées in 1929–31 for the legendary Mexican party-giver Carlos de Beistegui e Yturbe.[37] There should, first of all, be a wall: the beginning of architecture. The wall must be high enough to baffle the horizon-view, directing the viewer's attention to the sky—just as the Beistegui wall allows only the tops of familiar Parisian monuments to be glimpsed. The marble-faced wall encloses a sort of grass-carpeted open-air 'gallery' with Tombros's brazen nude (epicene indeed!) installed in the curved exedra. Perhaps Mies van der Rohe's installation of the Kolbe nude in his celebrated 1929 Barcelona pavilion was a subliminal reference, prompted by the quasi-academic character of both sculptures. From the paved area beyond the wall, a ramp descends to a saltwater pool, where visitors can athletically disport themselves safely separated from the rocks. Le Corbusier perhaps imagines a contemplative and memorable architectural space that somehow celebrates the physicality of youth, while evoking the idealistic sensibility of the young poet whose life was so tragically cut short.

3 moonlight

Our interpretation of the *Carnet B5* page takes its cue from the chaotic distribution of barely intelligible words and minuscule sketches.[38] Of course, it is not impossible that this was Le Corbusier's hand attempting to keep up with the pace of his thoughts in broad daylight; on the other hand, these scrawls could be the record of a discussion that took place at twilight.

22'13" The *vapeur* has now left the bay of Aghia Marina and set course for the island of Poros about two hour's voyage to the south, where, the illustrious Ioannides assures them, they will dine well: he 'knows a good place'. A few minutes before half past eight, the sun dips behind the mountains of the Peloponnese, throwing them quite suddenly into silhouette. Twilight falls over the silvery waters of the gulf: if anyone has been paying attention to the eastern horizon they might have noticed a red glow in the sky—a distant wildfire perhaps ... *Are* there any forests in that direction? The mystery is solved a minute or two later as a red-orange disc floats like a Japanese paper lantern clear of the Aegean horizon. Few amongst the group could have been impervious to the spell cast by the largest full moon of the year as it illuminated their first night at sea. An event pregnant with mythological and psychological significance; to those aware of these matters—Embirikos, Moholy and, almost certainly, Giedion—moonrise symbolised the threshold between conscious and unconscious states, a midsummer moonrise having particular resonance. Years later, perhaps, they would associate this unforgettable moment with limpidity, lightness and *colour*—the essence of *méditerranéité.* In Giedion's words, 'In those days we were still fired by the faith of the Nineteen-Twenties, a time when the colours of painters were more luminous and optimistic than they had ever been before or have ever been since. We were confident that our generation was destined to bridge at last the gulf between inward and outward reality.'[39]

4 Poros: introduction to a 'determinedly anti-metaphysical' philosopher contrasted with Moholy's view of Greek island reality

As the disc climbed into the heavens and assumed its characteristic luminosity, the *vapeur* rounded the southerly cape of the island and entered the strait, or *poros*—barely two hundred metres wide—that separates it from the mainland to the west and gives the island its name. In an atmosphere heady with the aroma of lemon groves, the white houses close in cinematically on the approaching vessel, giving the impression that she is sailing through the streets.[40] Pulling in to the quay on that warm Saturday night in August some eight or nine hours after they had lunched together in Piraeus, the disparate group—now feeling, after their shared experiences, more like a real 'party'—would have been as one in their desire for sustenance. The *tavernas* lining the *paralía* are bursting with Saturday-night crowds; though times are generally hard, somehow the Athenian elite who gravitate here on their luxurious yachts still manage to party extravagantly. Now Embirikos, who knows the place well, comes into his own; the *vapeur* moors opposite his favourite taverna—above it are the ascending terraces of neat white red-roofed houses crowned by the tall domed *orológio* standing on its rocky crag. The waiters set up a long, long table; there are around fifteen each side. At its head and foot will be the Greek hosts and 'fixers': Embirikos and Ioannides. Le Corbusier will not, on this occasion, be able to monopolise the conversation ... The rest, of course, must be conjecture; Moholy the cameraman, denied the use of his Kinamo, perhaps falls into conversation with another self-styled 'outsider' with an all-consuming interest in graphic communication.

Otto Neurath (1882–1945), FIG. 17 Austrian philosopher of science, sociologist, political economist, and formidable member of the logical-positivist and determinedly anti-metaphysical

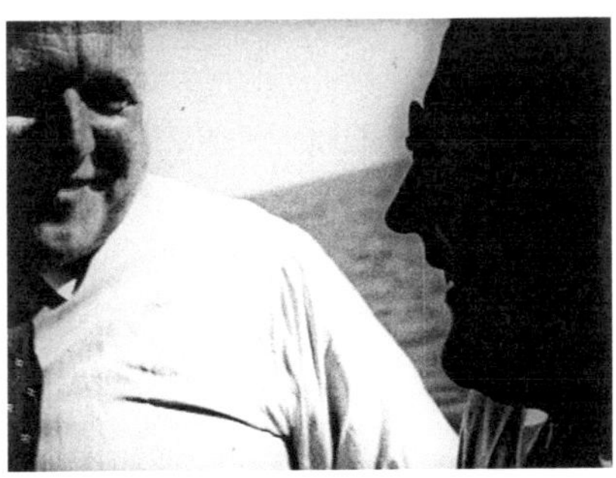

17 Close-up of Otto Neurath on *Patris II*. Still from *Architects' Congress* (**8'28"**)

Vienna Circle—had been admitted to the inner circle of CIAM as inventor of the universal 'Isotype' graphic language which CIAM had adopted, at van Eesteren's urging, to standardise the presentation of urban analyses. As advisor to the Soviet government, it was believed that his influence might also help to advance the CIAM cause in that vast territory. Beyond these already momentous attributes, he has been described as a 'great big elephant of a man',[41] who signed his letters with the symbol of an elephant and was also renowned for 'elephantine resources of energy and capacity for enjoying life'. As his beaming rotund visage pops up frequently in Moholy's film and the two men signed the congress register together, FIG. 18, 19 it is evident that they enjoyed each other's company, perhaps having Vienna in common—nevertheless agreeing to disagree about most things.

Taking a stroll through the narrow streets that lead up from the *paralía* to the *orológio* seemed the obvious way to pass the brief interval between after-dinner coffee and raki and re-embarking on *Afros.* Moholy would be moved by what he saw to write to Sibyl:

> *from aegina we went to poros, where we experienced the wonderful, simple, white architecture of the island by brilliant moonlight. the people whitewash their villages once a week; if emigrants from america, canada, etc. return on a wednesday, the playful young women, who are open to marriage, do not shy away from wielding the brush in the middle of the week. everything blazes with cleanliness. even the treads of the stairs are white, and on every tread there are only two specific places to step, hence permitted to become grey. the steps and large terraces are without railings, the houses are cubic, clear, sharp-edged, the numerous orthodox churches, like small baking ovens, according to old byzantine heritage in between. this white sharpness of the island architecture set with wonderful*

18 Cover of CIAM 4 register signed by the congressists, their partners and friends, as they arrived at the Athens Polytechnic on 3 August 1933

19 Page of CIAM 4 register with the distinctive signatures of *Otto Neurath* and *Moholy = Nagy*

clarity on the hills, which we later encountered everywhere, was the greatest experience for me. also the vivid blue sea and the mostly red-brown, yellow-brown rocks.[42]

The keen perceptiveness of Greek island reality and aptness of understated description is worthy of the great Alexandros Papadiamantis himself; he would have understood precisely the significance of the emigrant returning after years of back-breaking work in the New World to his impoverished island in search of a capable wife, and the anxiety of a young woman, no longer a girl, who had no better dowry to offer than a family home 'blazing with cleanliness'.

Such are the thoughts going through the mind of an artist and 'outsider', entirely free of preconceptions as he encounters this reality for the first time. By contrast, the didactic historian Giedion finds confirmation of his assumptions, recalling years later:

> At nightfall we anchored in the harbour of Poros, the last of the fertile islands. Those we were to see later, which were clothed in forests in Homer's days, are now bare and the standard of life on them is shockingly low. At midnight we sailed again, but found little sleep under the electric brilliance of a full southern moon.[43]

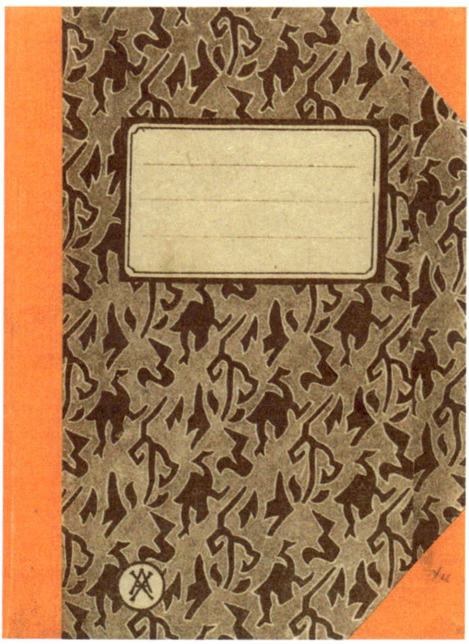

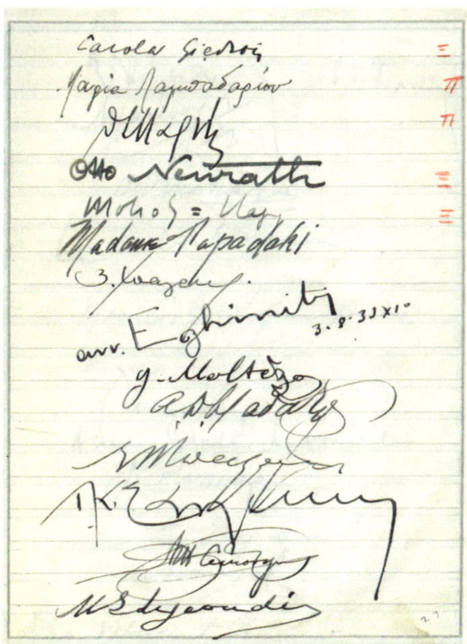

5 symposium: Moholy integrates the 'psychological and human' into the discussion

Giedion had asked Moholy to sit on the committee 'which was to deal with the findings of this Congress',[44] and the serious discussions may have begun during that sleepless night as the *vapeur* steamed eastwards across the open Aegean towards Serifos. In addition to Neurath, Moholy's fellow committee members were the Romanian architect and editor of *L'Architecture vivante,* Jean Badovici, and Swiss architect Rudolph Steiger. Badovici and Zervos had studied philosophy together in Paris; both subsequently publishing luxurious and complementary reviews. Steiger, with his partner Hubacher, had been responsible for the revolutionary Zett-Haus in the centre of Zurich—a multifunctional building notable for its rooftop 'ROXY' cinema, the roof of which could be slid open on fine evenings. Thus Giedion's *de facto* four-man committee could be said to present a representative sample of the various factions within CIAM at that point in time. FIG. 20 Perhaps he and van Eesteren were also trying to restore some cool objectivity after the heady plenary sessions both on *Patris II* and in Athens, in which Le Corbusier had persistently tried to pre-empt committee discussions.[45] Steiger represented the stolidly professional Swiss faction—all recruited by Giedion—and the largest national group in CIAM. Badovici, for his part, was a gifted publicist, his quarterly review an impeccably designed and printed record of the best European modern buildings from 1923 until unfavourable economic circumstances had put paid to it in 1932. It is true to say that both men represented the view, prevalent in CIAM at the time, of architectural production as primarily a technical matter and thus would have been less interested in any nebulous philosophical or political influences that might be said to shape it.

Neurath, on the other hand, insisted that 'the general rationalisation of the shaping of built form can only be possible within

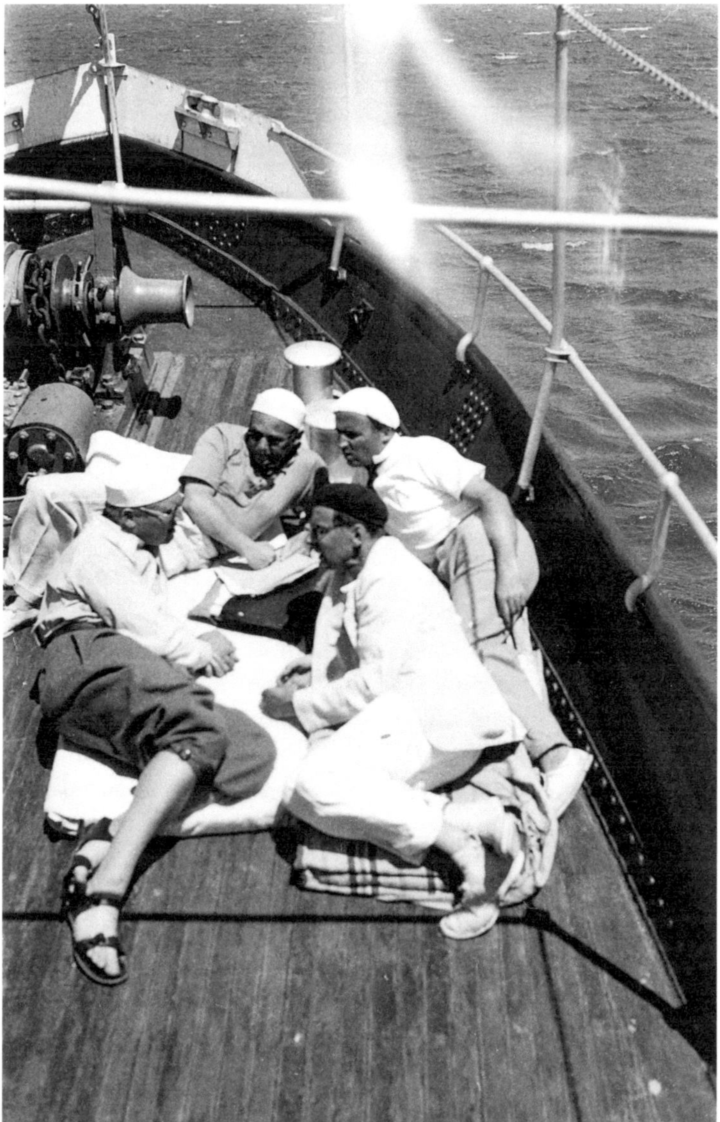

20 Working 'symposium' on the foredeck of *Afros*. Conjectural identification of the *personae* clockwise from top left: Sigfried Giedion, Rudolf Steiger, Alfred Roth and Cornelis van Eesteren.
Photo by László Moholy-Nagy

the context of the rationalisation of life itself.'[46] A tall order, but then as a Marxist sociologist who had founded the Museum of Society and Economy in Vienna in 1925, he believed it was his mission to bring 'social and economic facts to the masses, raise the self-awareness of the working class, and break down modern capitalism's fetishisation of the "object"'. Fundamental to this, in his terms, was the 'scientific world conception'—an empirical philosophy committed to removing metaphysics from everyday communication. These efforts led to the development of Isotype—International System of Typographic Education—designed to communicate social and scientific facts by means of standardised pictorial graphics. It was this system that van Eesteren imposed on the various national teams of CIAM, insisting that their urban analyses be presented using Isotype graphic symbols.

From Giedion's point of view, the use of standardised graphic symbols was a means towards re-establishing that 'common language which bound the leading spirits of all branches of art and science so closely together in previous ages'.[47] The loss of this common language was 'one of the great defects of our contemporary civilisation'; thus, Giedion was convinced that CIAM's embrace of 'the most diverse talents and personalities and considerable disparity in point of age' and 'the fact that [it] represents a balance between individual and collective thought [give] it a particular value at the present time. In the interests of the eventual emergence of a genuinely contemporary culture it is to be hoped that other fields of art and science will be able to recover their "common language" on similar lines.' Looking at these plans today,[48] however, it is difficult to relate them to the phenomena they were intended to describe, and we sense that Moholy experienced the same difficulty—as van Eesteren later acknowledged: 'I am truly happy that you participated [...] so actively in the Congress events.... In particular, what has stayed

21 Diagrammatic map of Barcelona prepared by the Spanish group of CIAM using standardised symbols from 'Isotype'—International System of Typographic Education developed by Otto Neurath. Van Eesteren had insisted that all national teams should present their urban analyses employing this common graphic language. All cities were also to be presented at the same 1:10,000 scale, leading to extreme differences in the size of display panels representing Los Angeles, for example, and those for smaller cites like Athens.
From *La Cité: Revue d'Architecture et d'Urbanisme* 8 (1934)

in my mind is how intensely you debated Neurath—in which you, very correctly, always integrated the psychological and the human into the discussion; had you not, we would have definitely fallen victim to Neurath's rather limited system.'[49]

The limitations become clear when we contemplate a city celebrated for its unique character—Barcelona, for example—as rendered in Isotype. FIG. 21 Less a topographical map, and more a chart composed of abstract symbols—each designed, according to an abstruse logic, to represent a specific function: industry, public services, recreation, habitation and, within the latter, 'working', 'middle' and 'upper' class areas. The city disguised as a 'forest of symbols'—apparently a chaotic jumble. And this, of course, is the point van Eesteren is trying to make with Neurath's 'system': re-planned on a rational basis, 'functional City' methodology will sort this mess out, neatly separating the four supposedly

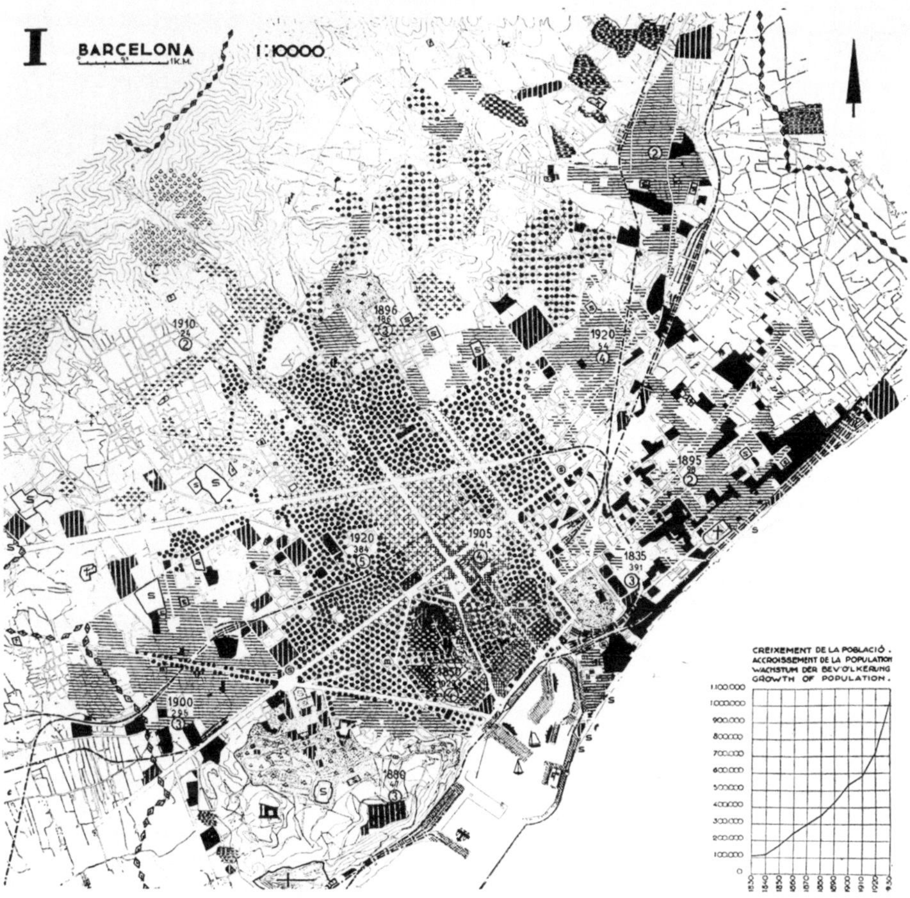

incompatible functional zones and, in the process, producing a clean diagram. It must have struck Moholy, who relished, and was adept at capturing, the minutiae of quotidian life in his writing and filming—as demonstrated by his classic *Marseilles Vieux Port,* for example—that the so-called 'anti-metaphysical' stance was incompatible with a sense of the everyday *quality* of a living city. Alongside the incomparable report to Sibyl, a document coded in Isotype resembles a dead letter.

Moholy's distinctive style of discourse had been formed in early experiences that set him apart from the rest of the group. He had been associated with the movement known as Hungarian Activism, the distinguishing ethos of which 'was that it regarded artistic revolution as inseparably linked with the idea of [. . .] social revolution'.[50] This interconnected social and artistic activity aimed at nothing less than 'the external and internal liberation of Man, his self-realisation'. Moholy had offered his services to the Hungarian Soviet led by Béla Kun following the defeat of Austria-Hungary in the Great War; the communists, however, rejected 'his newly-won assurance of nonrepresentational art as an essential revolutionary weapon'.[51] Following the fall of the Soviet, Moholy was forced into exile—briefly to the revolutionary hotbed of Vienna and, a few months later, to Berlin. Through it all, he held to the belief that *modern art is a way of life,* a notion that Neurath would have dismissed as inconsequentially 'metaphysical'. Thus, Moholy felt obliged to oppose the sectarian sociological bias of Neurath—no doubt associating it with the 'scientific empiricism' of the doctrinaire Marxist Hannes Meyer, whose appointment as head of the Bauhaus in 1928 had provoked Moholy's resignation from the school along with Walter Gropius. In an atmosphere of deepening crisis, the Weimar authorities had insisted on the school's syllabus being reorganised along specialist and vocational lines—a policy that was anathema to Moholy. As he wrote in 1932, 'We cannot establish a universal intellectual attitude or cultural standard from one vantage point only, such as cognition by means of logic, or the sciences; nor indeed from the arts exclusively. In order to form a comprehensive attitude to existence, we must start simultaneously from emotion and cognition'.[52]

In subsequent years Moholy pursued a more ambiguous line of thought that seems to owe much to his early education in rural Hungary, where he was taught by the aesthetician Iván Hevesy and two prominent poets, Gyula Juhász and Mihály Babits.[53] In addition to his experimental photograms and politically satirical *fotoplastik* collages, he would devote much of his time to pure engineering work on the celebrated *Light-Space Modulator*,[54] which was exhibited at the Deutscher Werkbund exhibition in Paris in 1930 and was itself the subject of an experimental film *Lichtspiel Schwarz-Weiß-Grau* (Light Play Black-White-Grey). Perhaps Moholy's consuming interest really was literature as, in a sense, his entire oeuvre betrays this sensibility, frequently expressed in densely argued theoretical writings. For example, in *Kestészet és fényképészet* (Painting and Photography), published in 1932, he writes,

> Optical works are one of the unconscious, unintentional educational tools with which we are trying to prepare a form of consciousness appropriate for the society of the future. But we are not thinking primarily of so-called propaganda art, which active politicians think exclusively important and are always urging. What we are thinking of, first of all, is the activation of the energies of the subconscious through the optical organ of the eye.[55]

Relying on the unconscious to bring about change seems to place Moholy in the surrealist camp, and much of his work of this period—in particular the *fotoplastik* collages and photograms—demonstrates an anarchic surrealist sensibility. From this standpoint he must have viewed the Greek island adventure as a once-in-a-lifetime opportunity to immerse himself in the distinctive ambience and fabled light quality of the archipelago, thus further extending his artistic explorations.

In the end, Giedion's ad hoc committee submitted no report; its 'findings'—if such there were—dispersed into thin air. As Walter Gropius, who claimed to have had no regrets about *not* attending CIAM 4, would later comment, 'CIAM was Le Corbusier's world'[56]—and indeed it was Le Corbusier's view that would prevail. That he regarded Neurath's 'system' as a strait-jacket inhibiting creativity seems clear from his reaction on first seeing the plans—all uniformly presented in Isotype[57]—on the *Patris II:* 'How are we to make use of this prodigious material? How are we to extract the pure metal from this mineral?' For him, as for Moholy, the suppression of metaphysics was unthinkable: poetic imagery being the beginning and end of all creative activity, the city plans should be read 'in the prism of the modern era' in which human beings formed 'the measure' at the heart of the struggle between the individual and the collective. Ultimately, he would edit the proceedings of the congress virtually single-handed during his wartime exile from Paris, producing in the process the 'Athens Charter', which was to have a dominant influence on post-war reconstruction worldwide.

Of course, it is not that straightforward; the complexity of the man—and indirectly the significance of the island cruise—is demonstrated by another 'mental map' in his *carnet.*[58] **FIG. 22** What appears to be the hastily drawn sketch-plan of a house in which *plan libre* partitions spider out from a diagonally crossed *circulation verticale* towards a surrounding glass membrane—*tout verre*—is accompanied by a loose weave of text: *on board / 'Agros' / August 1933 / Cyclades / the idea returns / of the / house / in Brittany / of 1924 / proceeding from 1 / central core.* The vessel's name, mistranscribed thus in the first 1984 edition of the *carnets*, was quoted down the years; even appearing in a

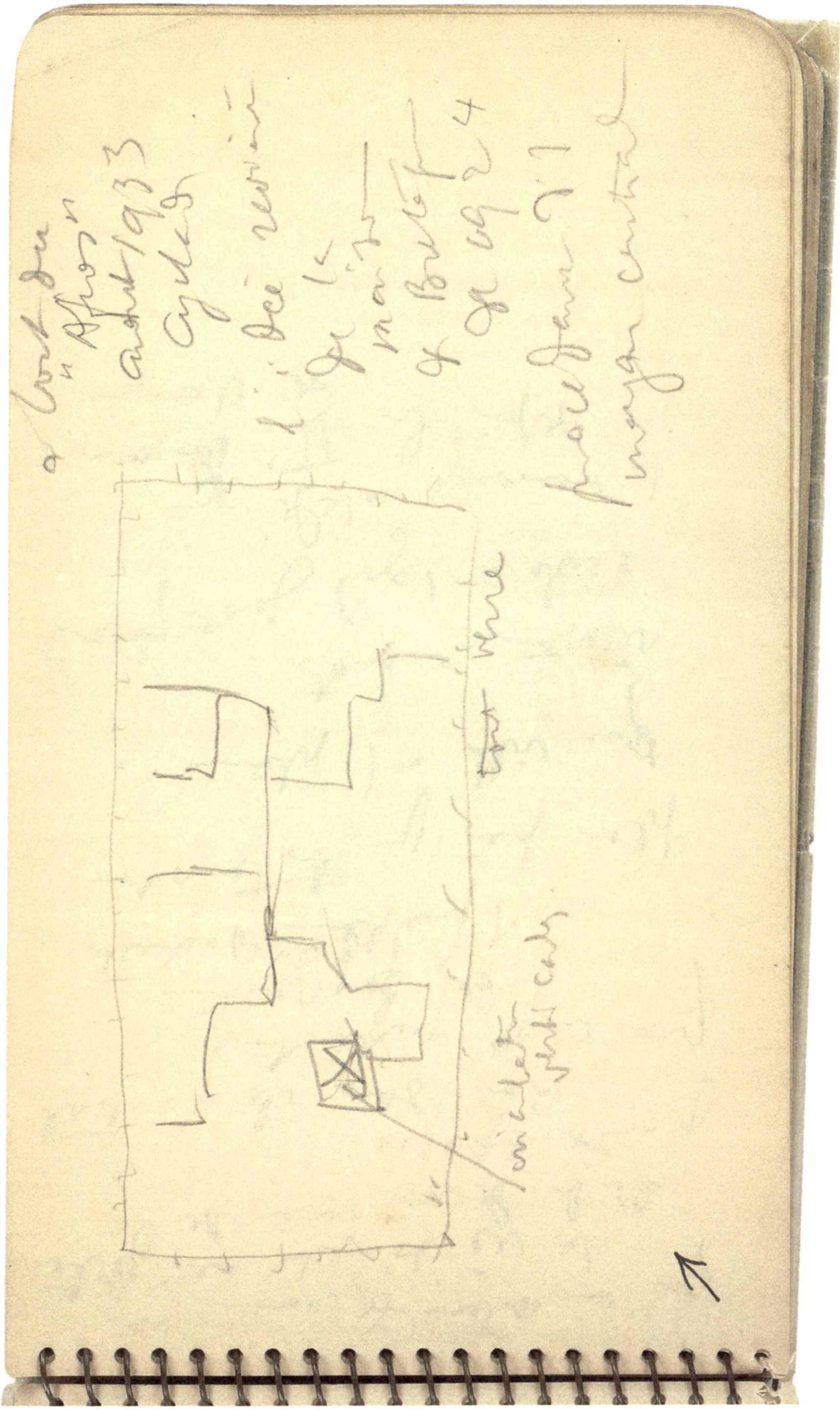

22 Page from *Carnet B5:* Could this be Le Corbusier's concept sketch for a waterfront villa in Piraeus that the cigarette manufacturer Sotiris Papastratos had commissioned from him two days previously?

The note translates: *on board / 'Afros' / August 1933 / Cyclades / the idea returns / of the / house / in Brittany / of 1924 / proceeding from 1 / central core*; and, on the plan: *vertical circulation / all glass.*

1987 essay 'The Last Trip to Greece' by Georgios Simeoforidis and Georgios Tzirtzilakis.[59] As the 'official' history of CIAM 4 began to be recorded in a series of weighty publications, the carefree island cruise was downgraded to 'peripheral', its significance lost; thus, a typical summing-up reads, 'the participants in the congress swarmed over the Greek mainland and the Cyclades. Giedion, van Eesteren, Le Corbusier, Léger, Moholy, Zervos, Badovici, Winter and several of the Swiss set out on a converted English collier for the island of Aegina.'[60]

IV the 'film within'

The film *Architect's Congress* is available in full length online:
www.vimeo.com/larsmuellerpublishers/ciam1933
Time code along the text corresponds to this movie

21'14"

wake of *Afros:*
opening shot of 'film within'

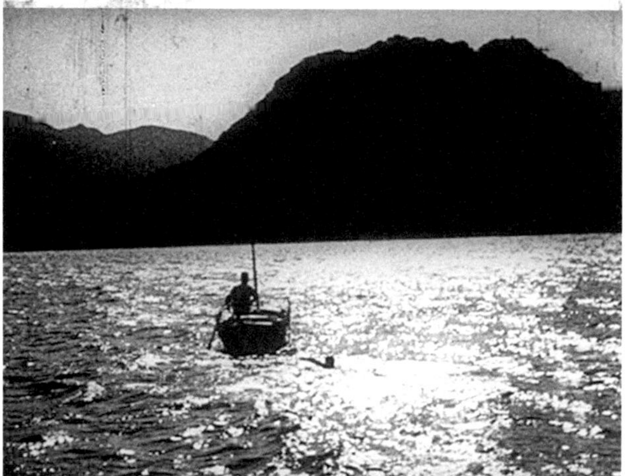

21'26"

Aegina:
Le Corbusier strikes out for
islander's boat

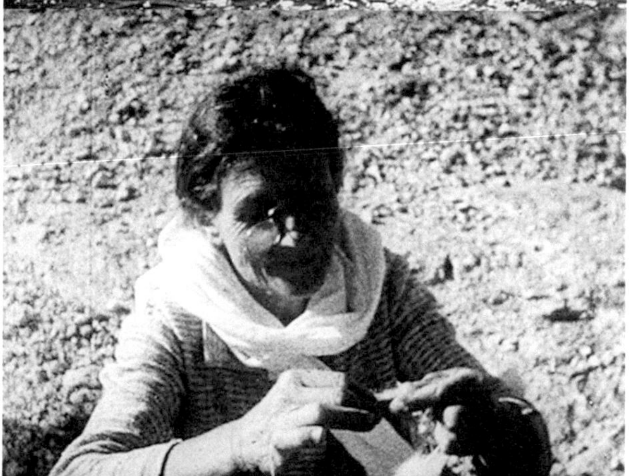

21'57"

island woman spinning wool
with a spindle

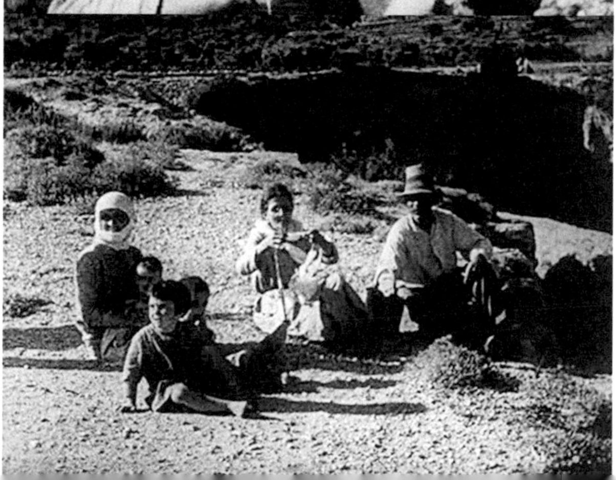

21'58"

island family enjoying Saturday
evening on the beach

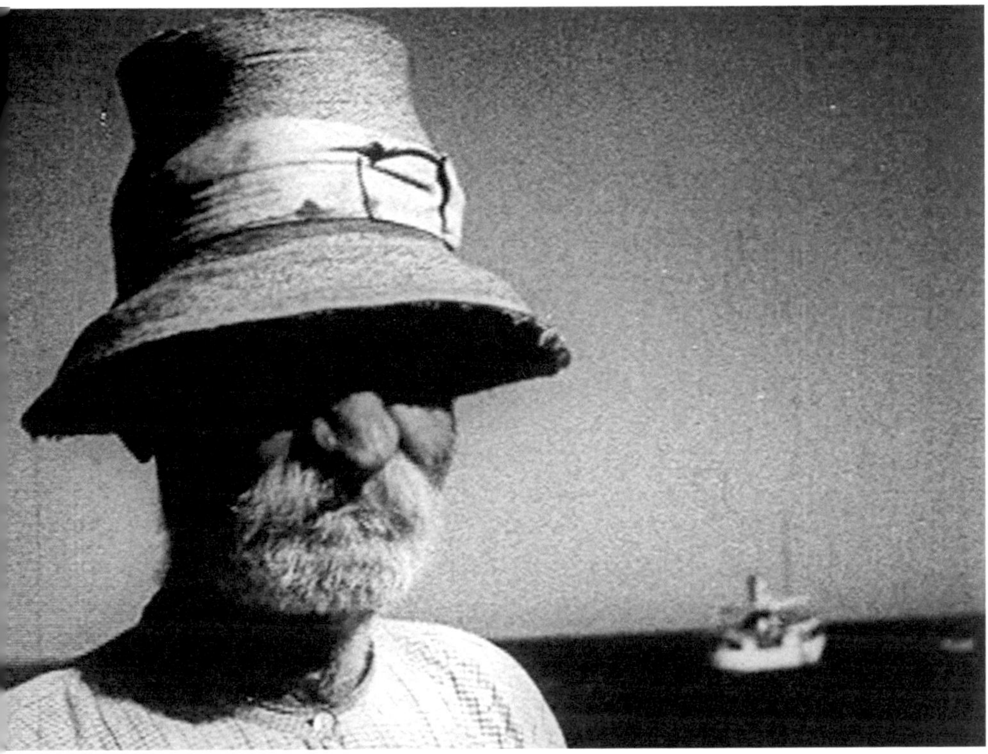

21’43”

the muleteer—*Afros* at anchor

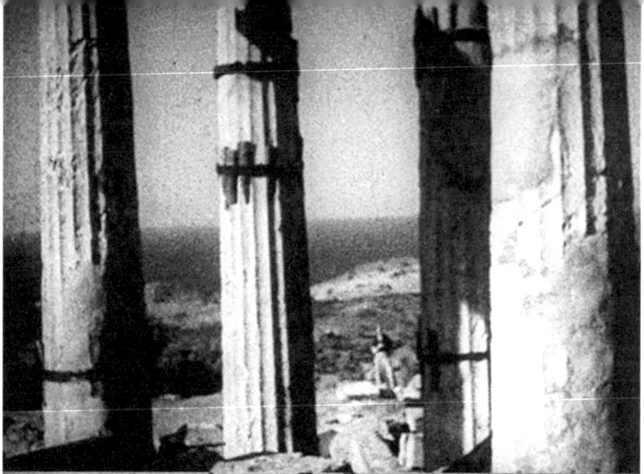

22’04”

temple of Aphaia: Le Corbusier sketching the north elevation

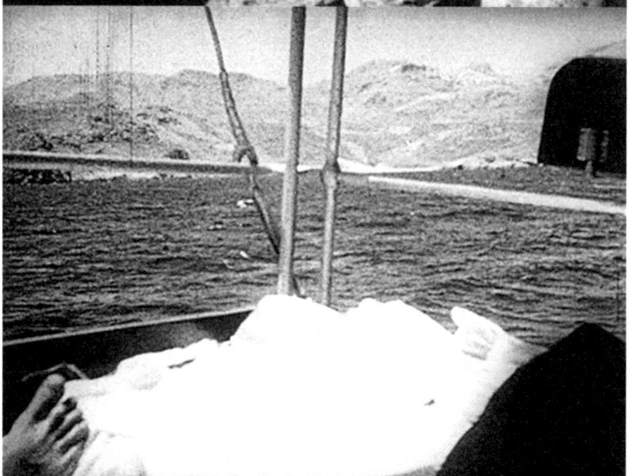

22’30”

Serifos:
approaching the village of Livadi

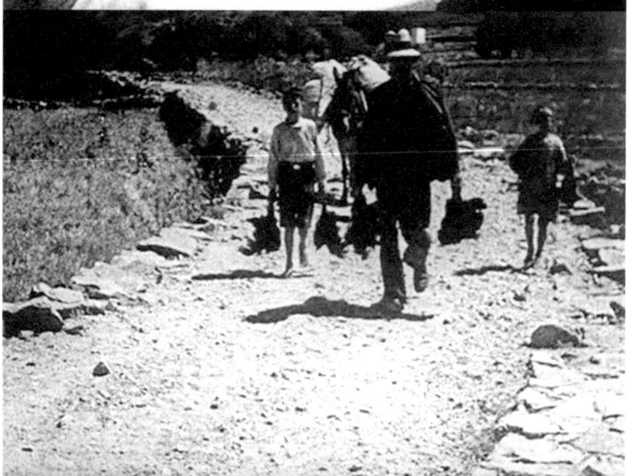

23’36”

islanders bring sustenance for the cruise party

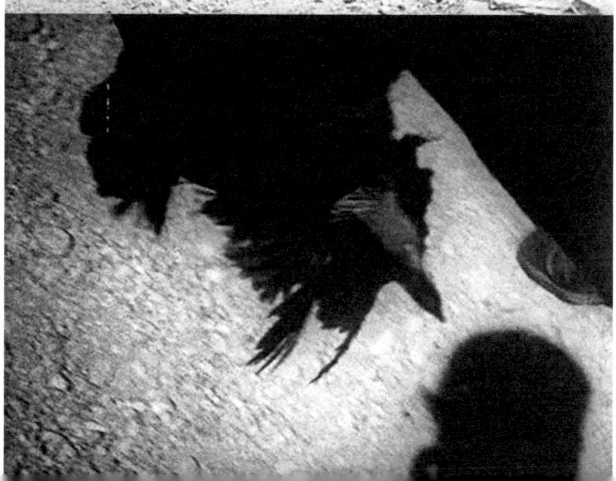

23’43”
the ‘main course’?

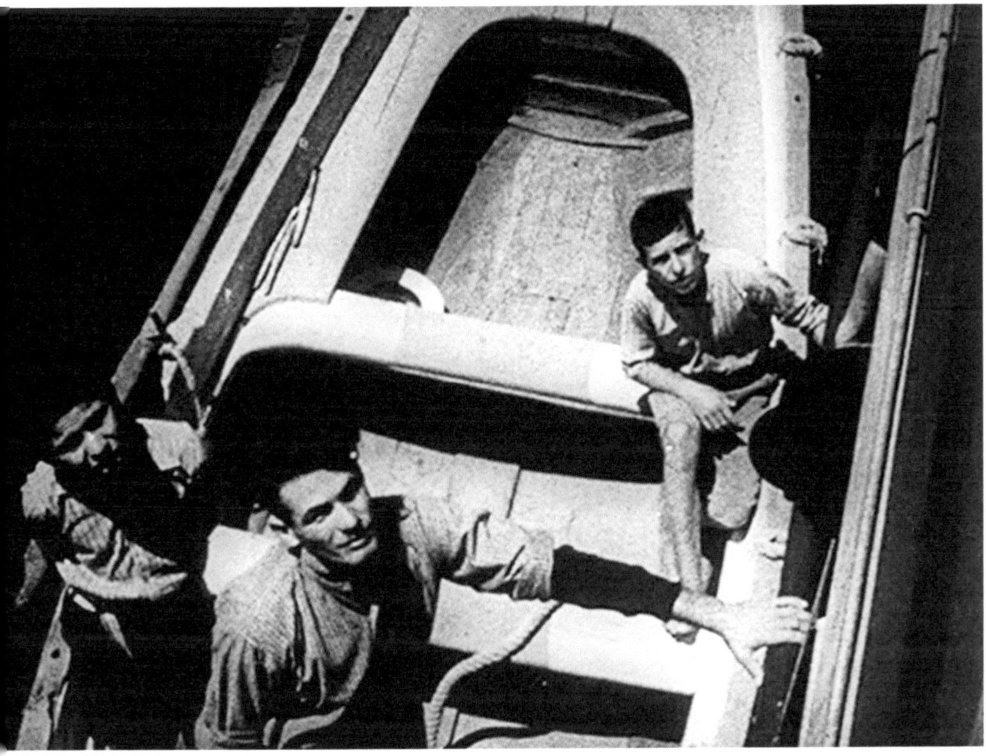

22'58"

island boatmen offer to take the cruise party ashore

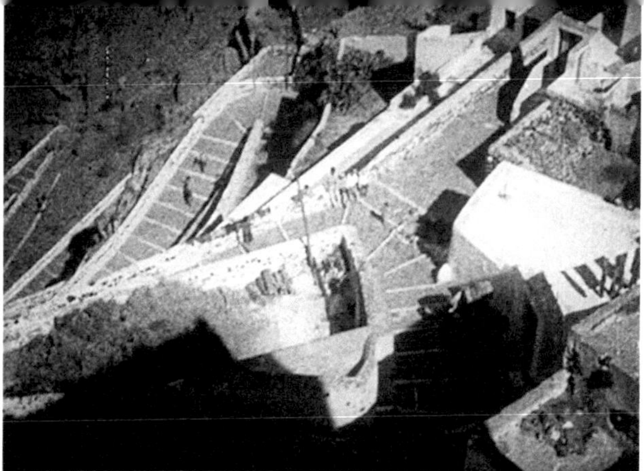

23’54”

Santorini:
summit of the *skála*

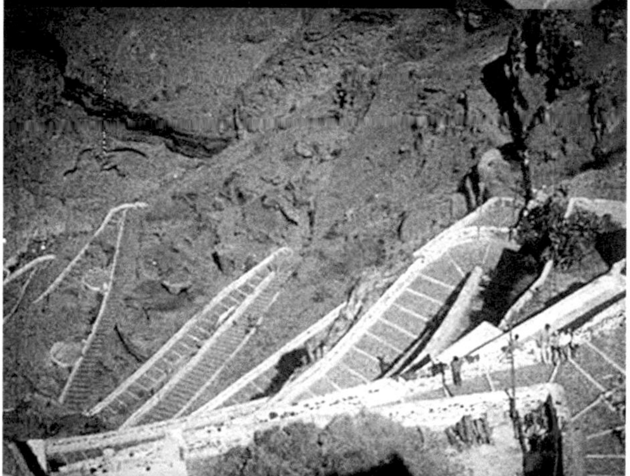

23’57”

the *skála*

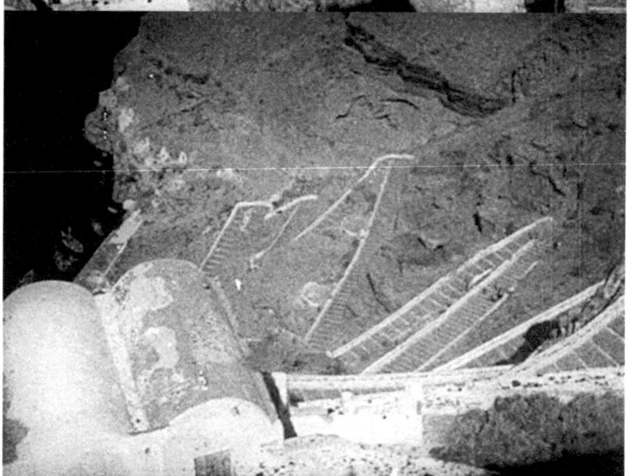

23’59”

the port of Fira

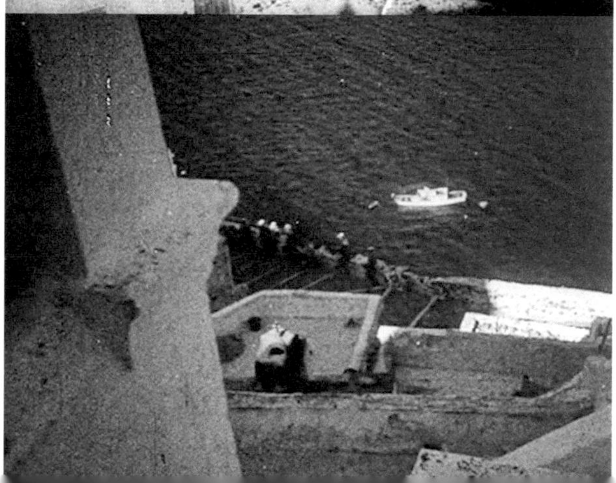

24’01”

Afros at anchor in the caldera

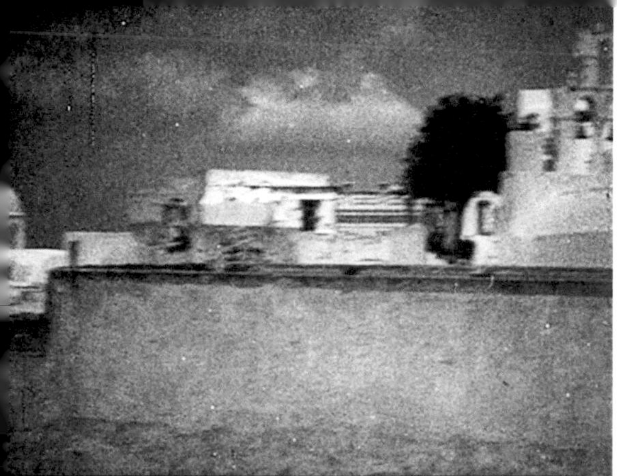

24’18”

‘pan’ to tossing tree

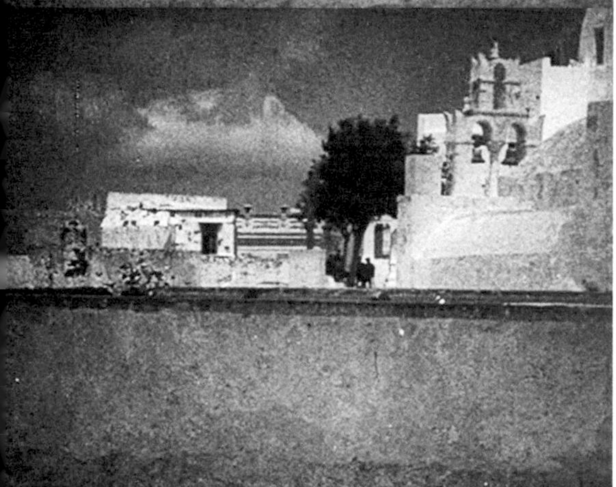

24’20”

tossing tree and belfry

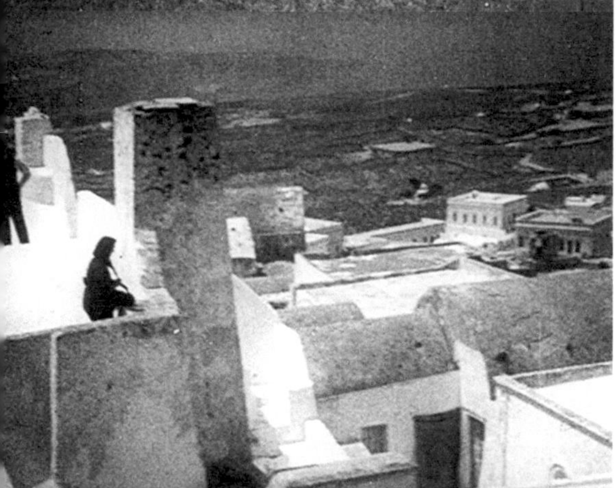

24’21”

onlookers on the roof

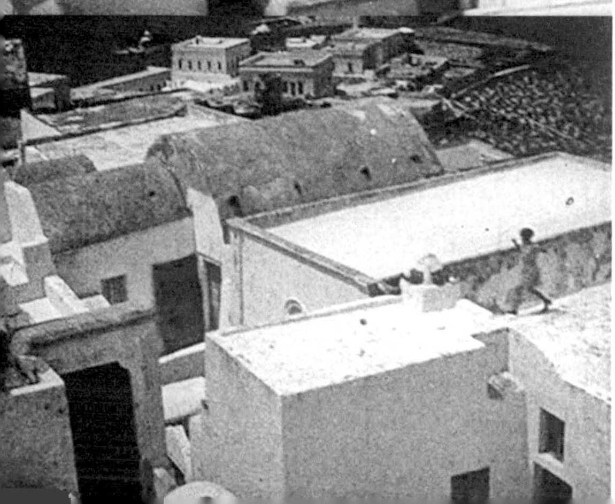

24’23”

opening of impromptu roof-top ‘performance’

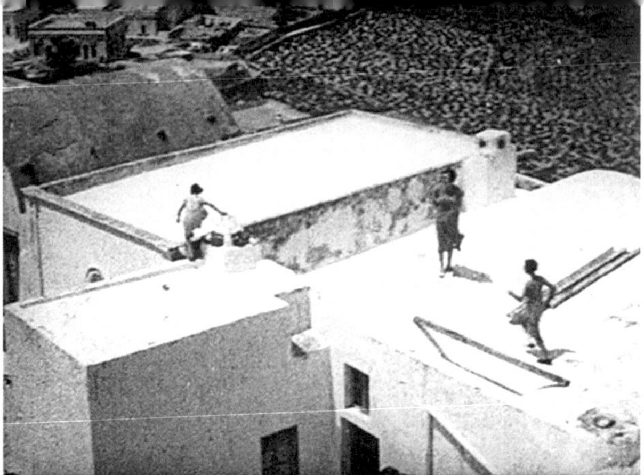

24’25”

‘performance’ continues

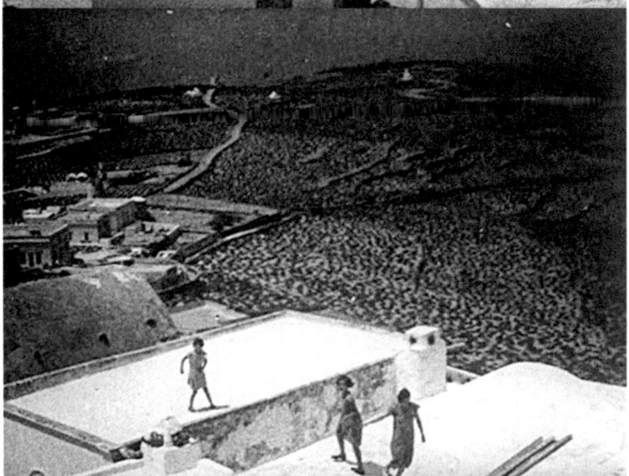

24’26”

conclusion of ‘performance’

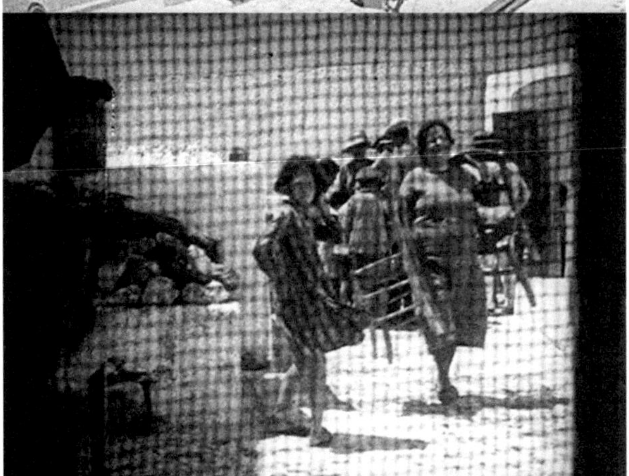

24’35”

inside the *taverna*

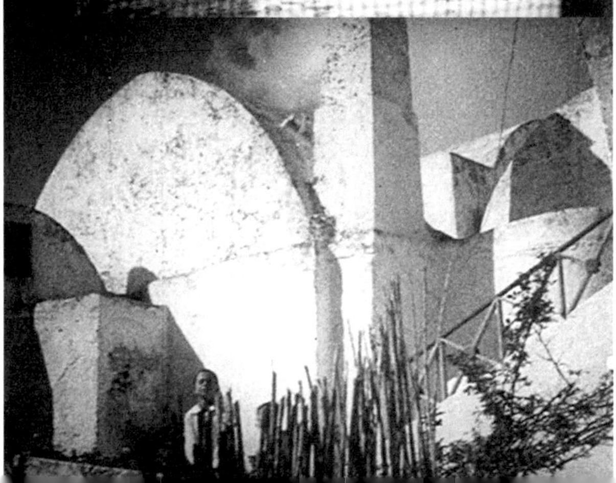

24’46”

bakery and small boy

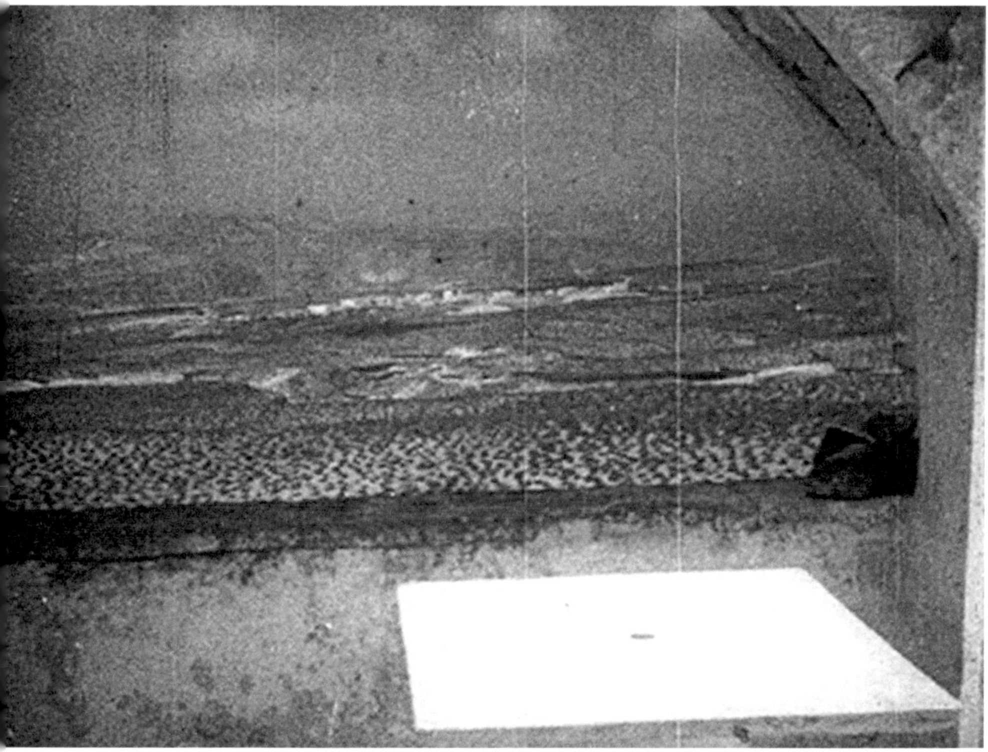

24’31”

‘white square’

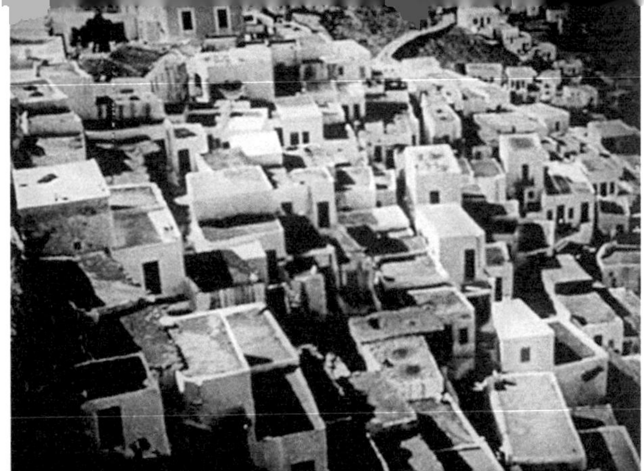

24’49”

rooftops of Fira

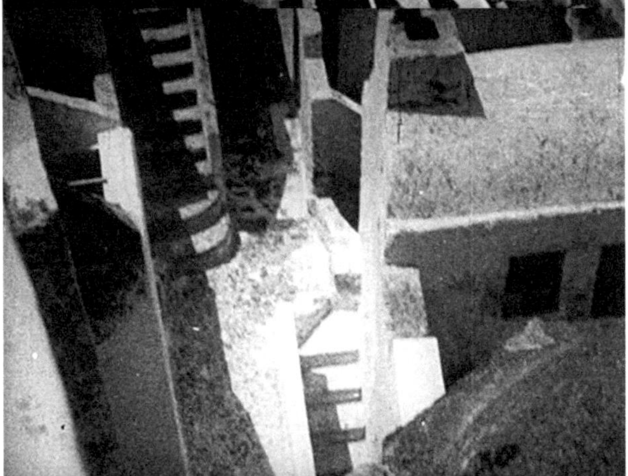

24’58”

beginning of ‘birds-eye pan’

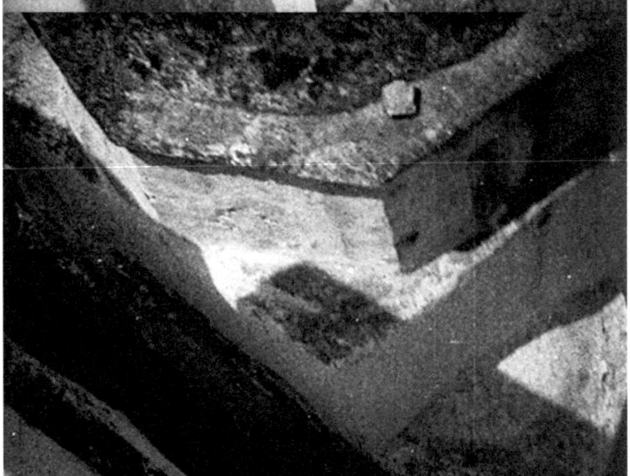

25’00”

‘pan’ continues

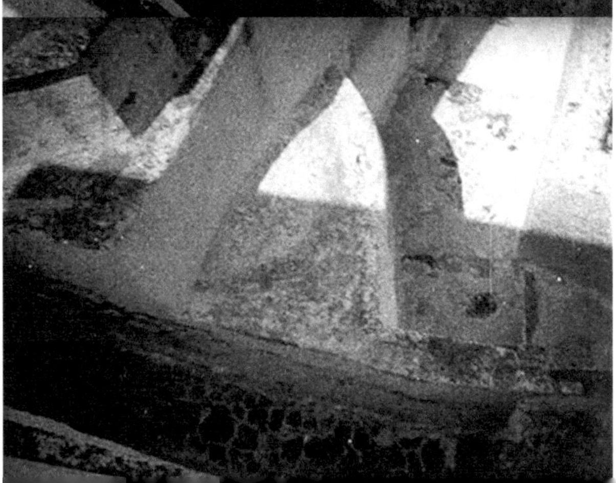

25’02”

‘pan’ continues

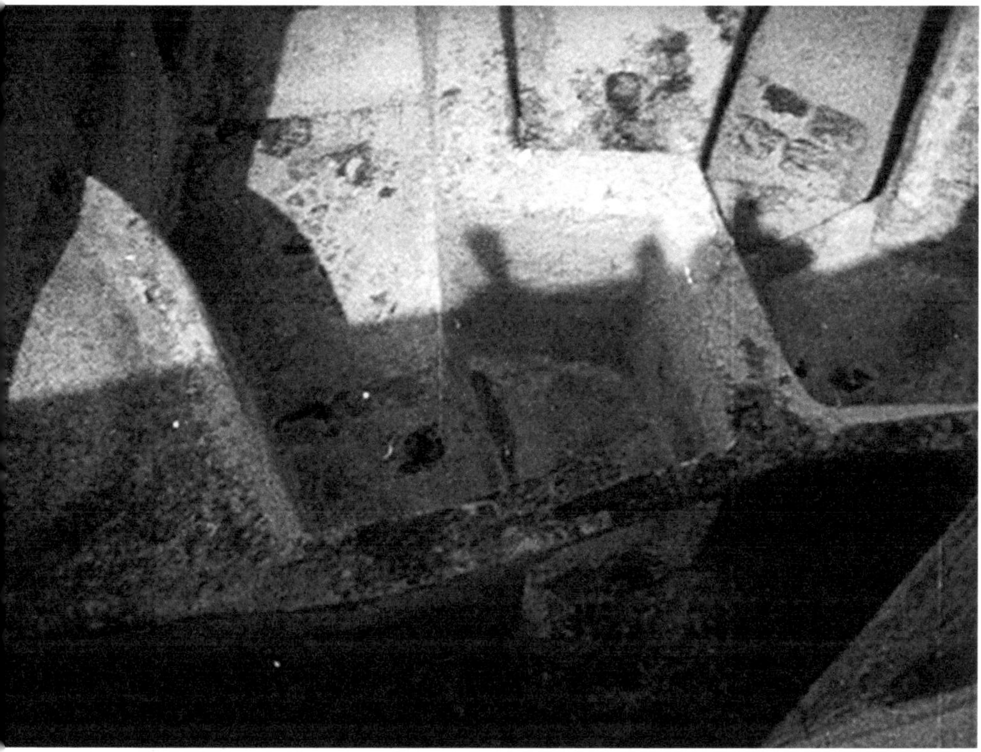

25'03"

conclusion: shadows of cameraman and friends

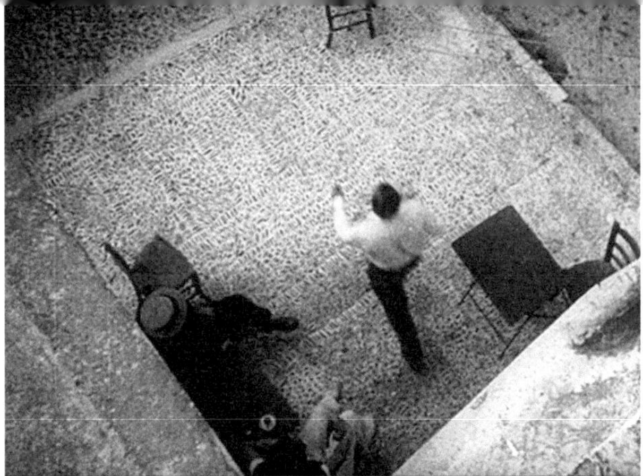

25’05”

‘birds-eye’ of *plateía* and hurrying man

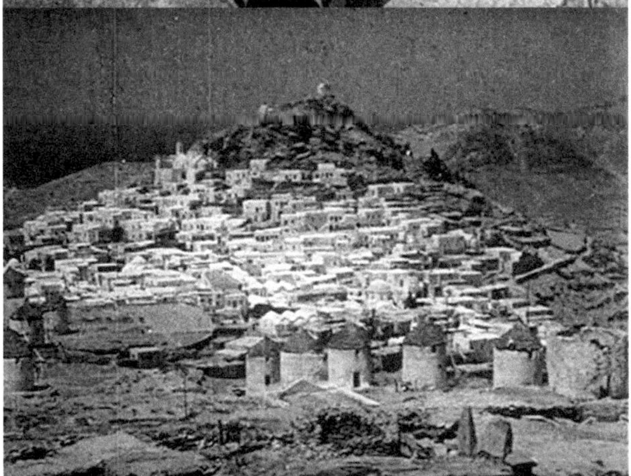

25’22”

Ios:
view of *chóra*

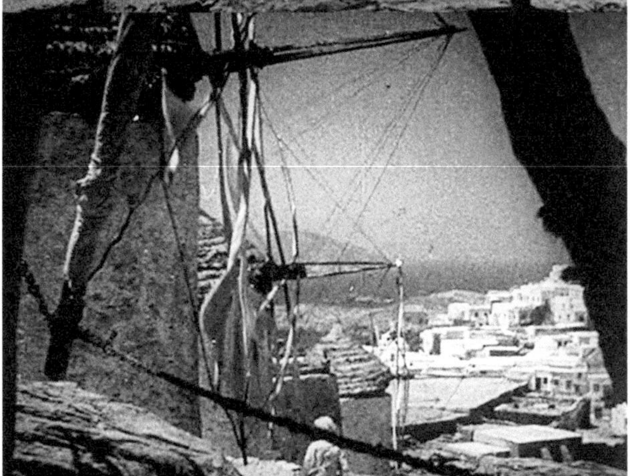

25’34”

windmill mechanism

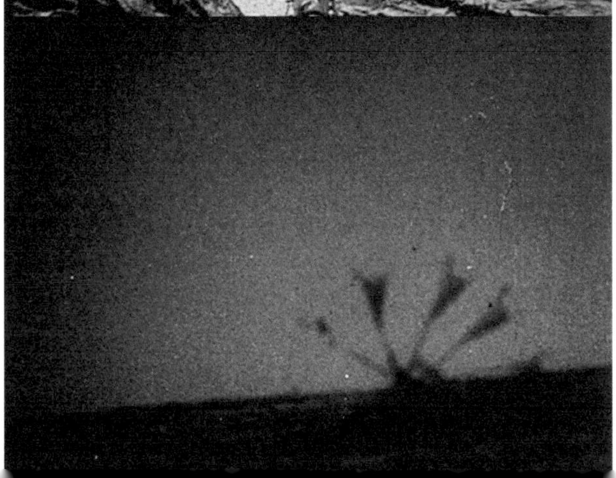

25’39”
conclusion of ‘film within’

V 'what's in a name?'

1 an air of unreality

Agros, however, translates as 'field': most unlikely name for a Greek boat, and ... 'converted English *collier* (?)'. Our curiosity about this suspected mistaken maritime identity took us to Ghika's palatial 1930s mansion on Kriezotou Street off Syntagma Square one September day in 2013. The maritime connection is not insignificant: Ghika's father had commanded the Greek fleet and was appointed Minister of Marine in the last Venizelos government and, in authentic Greek tradition, played a key role in no less than *three* coups, the last, which failed utterly, costing him his position in 1935.

Taking the elevator to the penthouse level we found ourselves in the painter's perfectly preserved studio, surprisingly constructed of *béton brut* and perforated concrete block—hinting not only at Ghika's admiration for Le Corbusier, but also the capabilities of the Hadjikyriakos family cement enterprise. In the adjoining archive the archivist assured us unequivocally that Ghika, whose memory was 'very reliable', had cruised the islands in 1933 on Andreas Embirikos's private yacht, and her name was *EROS.* As the primordial goddess of Love celebrated by Diotima—her panegyric in turn memorably recounted by Socrates in Plato's dialogue—it seemed a plausible name for an epicurean's yacht. In that instant, we saw the possibility of a far-from-peripheral project: the cruise of *EROS* as enlightened twentieth-century *Symposium* with far-reaching ramifications, against the louring backdrop of 1930s Europe.

In the disturbing reality of today's Athens an air of *unreality* evocative of the inter-war period clings to the relics of Ghika's aristocratic world. What if he was re-imagining the outrageous Embirikos through the kaleidoscopic spectacles of his later surrealist poetry and novels; in particular the eight volumes of his untranslated 'meganovel' *o Megas Anatolikos*—so explicit that he rivals the Marquis de Sade at his most inventive? Not forgetting that the yacht-owning surrealist poet would also become Greece's first psychoanalyst, specialising in sexual disorders. Or, was it possible that Ghika's memory was activated by free association—coloured more by the frisson induced by certain scenes in Moholy's 'film within' than by direct experience of the events? If Moholy's imagery had produced this effect on Ghika's subconscious, perhaps it had also stimulated our imagination; if we were going to aim for academic correctness and stick to the facts, the most that could be stated with certainty is that the events of August 1933 had been recorded by Moholy and Giedion. However, photography and film, as Moholy had pointed out with reference to his unconventionally framed shots, had the ability to distort perceived reality, thus equipping the viewer with a more intensified vision of truth—or losing it altogether, along with the editorial 'cuts' of unreliable memories.

At all events, higher-resolution reproductions and closer study of Le Corbusier's handwriting revealed that he had recorded the name of Embirikos's yacht as *Afros*—one of a number of onomatopoeic names for different states of *i thálassa:* the sea. *Flísvos,* for example, is that gentle breathing sound made by the ripples of a calm sea as they lap a beach and recede, while *áfros* is the violent 'sea-foam from the burst of waves'. In Giedion's account,the *vapeur* is sarcastically dismissed as 'ex-English coal barge',[61] and we're left wondering which aroused his scorn most: its former function—or nationality? Moholy's letter goes some way to explain the 'nutshell's' shortcomings: out of the thirty or so on board, *there is sleeping space in the cabins for 6 people, all of the others must sleep on deck, or in the saloon (3 people).* When we remember that there were at least nine women on board, many of whom—Carola Giedion-Welcker, Yvonne Zervos, Antigone Kotzia (Ghika's wife), for example—were writers and artists in their own right, and that they enjoyed the privilege of sleeping in proper bunks, it is perhaps not surprising that there should have been a degree of discontent among the males. Is it likely that Embirikos bedded down on deck—especially since he was accompanied on this romantic trip by his 'companion' of the day, the Belgian-born Marguerite Antoinette Jeanne Marie Ghislaine Cleenewerck de Crayencour, who would become a successful novelist under the anagrammatic *nom de plume* Yourcenar?

Can we be certain, though, that the future literary colossus and member of the Académie Française was one of the party, as anecdotal evidence in Greece suggests? There's good reason to believe that she knew Embirikos in Paris before 1933,[62] and, as avid traveller passionate about Greece, she surely would have accepted an invitation from Embirikos to join the elite company on a once-in-a-lifetime cruise. And from Embirikos's point of view, what was a private yacht for if not to transport one's closest friends to exotic locations?

We'll probably never have a complete manifest of the assorted 'personae' who boarded *Afros* for the Aegean cruise. Giedion—writing, or at least publishing, his account sixteen years after the event—describes them thus:

> It was a mixed and merry company of some twenty painters, architects, poets, musicians, and writers who met at lunch in Piraeus and then embarked together. Among the party were Fernand Léger, Moholy-Nagy, the surrealist painter Kurt Seligman, Le Corbusier and his brother the musician Jeanneret, Christian Zervos, Jean Badovici, the Dutch town-planner van Eesteren, one or two French men of letters, a few of the best Swiss architects, and a well-known French physician.

The normally fastidious historian has either forgotten the names of the anonymous 'painters, architects, poets, musicians, and writers' or he is being selective. And, how did he arrive at his order of precedence for those names he did mention? Even Plato, whose account was admittedly fourth-hand, omitted to name all the guests at his famous *Symposium,* devoting considerably more space to the revered Socrates and treacherous Alcibiades than the others—celebrated playwrights and philosophers.

From Moholy's viewpoint, writing a few days after the event: *25 chosen guests of the congress, mostly french, who like to keep to themselves, and several swiss, dutch and greeks + me,* seemed an adequate reckoning, their names a mere detail. His mind was clearly on more compelling matters; thus, it is interesting to speculate whether he was in Shakespearian mode when imagining the vessel to Sibyl as a *nutshell*—the infinite space of the Aegean Sea and islands conjuring up a network of meanings and possibilities at a time when he is himself entangled in Hamlet-like prevarication over the couple's future in an increasingly claustrophobic and menacing Germany. When it came to names, whether of boats or people, if there had been a category of *personae*—alongside Yourcenar and the poet Gaston Bonheur—who would achieve success after inventing their own names, it would also have to include Le Corbusier and Moholy.

2 infinite space: Le Corbusier's revolutionary project goes up in smoke

There is another name in the *carnet* that has long perplexed the forensic experts, particularly in view of the care with which Le Corbusier noted it. It appears diagonally opposite *Tombros*—but, who was *Papatsatos?* It turns out there was no such person; and the truth, in this case, really is stranger than fiction. In writing that 'the cost of these congresses of modern architects [...] are practically non-existent', Le Corbusier was being disingenuous. Had they wished to do so, the Soviet authorities could easily have concealed the cost of promoting the fourth congress in

Moscow. However, in cash-strapped private-enterprise Greece this was not possible; a sponsor with deep pockets had to be found: perhaps, appropriate to an architectural congress, a representative of the concrete industry. Instead, the Papastratos Cigarette Manufacturing Company, FIG. 23 which had a virtual monopoly in Greece, stepped forward at this point.[63] Surely not a coincidence when we consider that Le Corbusier, as Moholy's film reveals, was a serious smoker, his determination to extract one last 'drag' from each minuscule butt-end betraying a profound state of anxiety, at least on this trip. It happened that Sotiris Papastratos, proprietor of the company, was an enthusiastic supporter of modern architecture and having recently commissioned a state-of-the-art cigarette factory in the 'functionalist' style in Piraeus, he would go one better and have Le Corbusier build him a villa on the coast nearby.

Le Corbusier had met with Papastratos privately the day before CIAM, as a group, had visited the new factory; however, he had failed to note—or had misheard—his new client's name. No doubt he was turning the new commission over in his mind as the *Afros* steamed east. His last substantial villa had been the Villa Savoie at Poissy, completed in 1931—a 'type' that could very well be appropriate to a coastal site with views to distant islands: a luxurious suite of rooms partially surrounding a courtyard—in essence the ancient Greek house—and all elevated clear of the ground on pilotis. But he had no interest in repeating himself and was, perhaps, also aware of complications. There was, for example, the need for anti-seismic design: *Attention / tremblement de terre / system Japonais / Périclés me / renseignera*—and 'Pericles Paraskevopoulos Engineer, Athens Polytechnic', spells out his name on the same page.[64] Something altogether more elemental was called for.

The hastily drawn sketch-plan[65] perhaps offers a clue to his thinking about the Papastratos villa. His work was always

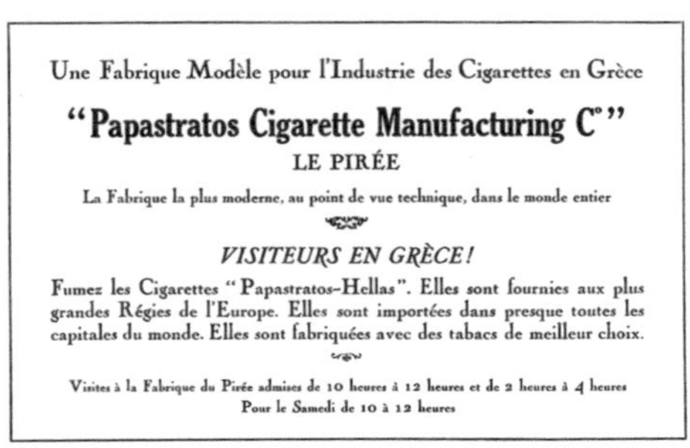

23 Advertisement from the journal *Voyage en Grèce* urging visitors to Greece to smoke Papastratos-Hellas cigarettes—and while they're there to also visit the factory: 'the most modern in the entire world from the technical point of view'. The Papastratos company sponsored CIAM 4 events in Greece.

characterised by *expanding horizons,* frequently achieved—as did that other revolutionary thinker, Copernicus—by inversion; his 'five Points towards a New Architecture' of 1926, for example, invert every aspect of the traditional house. It appears that as the *Afros* cruised eastwards towards the sunrise, a contrarian thought from several years earlier re-entered his mind: *the idea returns / of the / house / in Brittany / of 1924 / proceeding from 1 / central core.*

In the archives of the Fondation Le Corbusier there is a wonderful sketchbook from a vacation the architect spent in Plougrescant, Brittany, in 1924. In a series of some eight sketches, he lovingly analyses the robust stone architecture as it fits so naturally into the landscape. These are the sort of images that Pikionis would have shown to his students, having a strong affinity to his own sketches of the Rhodakis house on Aegina.[66] It is an architecture that could be called 'vernacular'; however there are places on this earth—like Brittany and the Aegean islands—where the *natural* architecture of ordinary people attains an altogether different level. In the lower left-hand corner of one of Le Corbusier's 1924 drawings,[67] there is a 'thumbnail' sketch plan. FIG. 24 It consists of a cellular structure of thick stone walls, like the Breton houses, surrounded on all sides by a glass membrane: *verre tout le tour.* Perhaps he imagined building himself a house there on the Breton coast, with sturdy stone walls enveloping *chambres* surrounded by a sunny glazed ambulatory and infinite oceanic space beyond. The idea returned to him on the *Afros,* triggered by the island architecture that also moved Moholy, and he realised that here was an entirely new 'type'—inverting the Greek island vernacular just as he had proposed in Brittany nine years earlier. A glass pavilion raised on *pilotis* requiring *circulation verticale* with, at its core, a series of protective spaces for night-time use—or when the *borías* howled.

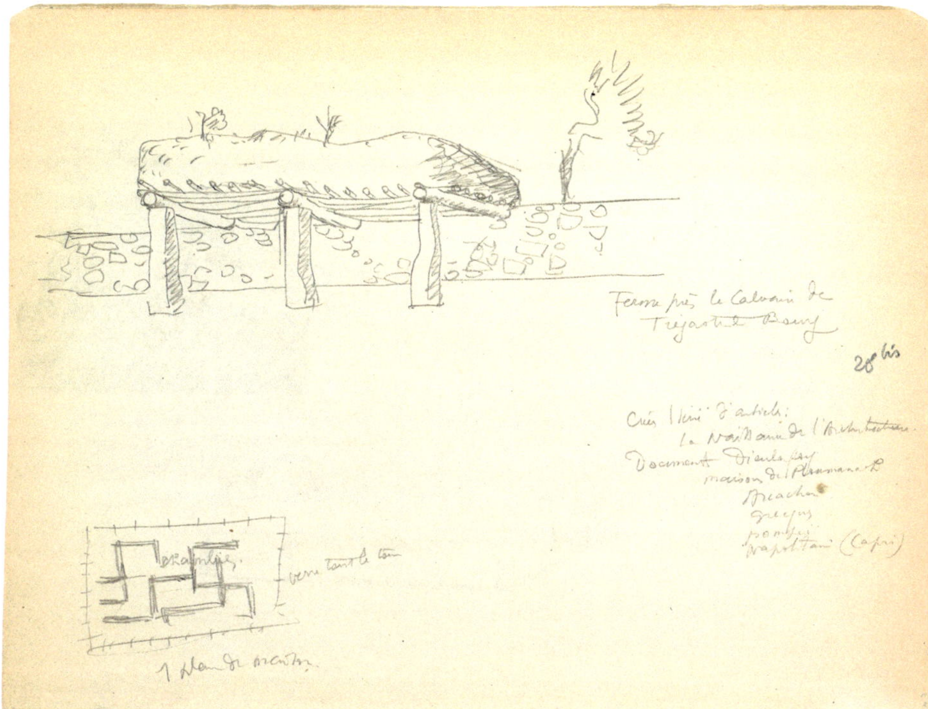

24 Page from Le Corbusier's sketchbook from his 1924 vacation in Plougrescant, Brittany, in which he lovingly analyses the robust stone vernacular architecture as it fits so naturally into the landscape. Reflecting on this, the idea of a radical new house type occurs to him, which he rapidly sketches in the bottom left hand corner. He imagines the *chambres* as a labyrinthine cluster of cells enclosed by thick stone walls, the whole assembly to be wrapped in a glass membrane: *verre tout le tour.*

Unfortunately, as with so many of Le Corbusier's revolutionary concepts, the Papastratos villa would come to nothing. Zervos, acting as go-between, reported that Greek construction costs were so low that 10 per cent of a million drachma construction budget at the 1933 rate of exchange—the drachma had been devalued by 75 per cent the previous year—would pay only a fraction of the fee in francs needed to cover the overheads of Le Corbusier's Paris studio.[68] Some years later the Greek government delivered the coup de grâce to the project by expropriating Papastratos's parcel of land.

3 Serifos: a denuded island blessed with *glorious architecture and wonderful smiling faces*

As the sun appeared above the horizon from that magical quarter
22'32" known to the Greeks as *anatolí*, the *Afros* entered the bay of Serifos. Moholy films the passing coast line, allowing a bare foot in close-up to intrude on his frame, a second or so later pulling focus to reveal the austere white *chóra* perched high up on the naked mountainside. It exhibits the quintessential Cycladic siting of an island capital elevated for optimal long-distance view and defence—originally against attacks by pirates. At one time rich in iron and copper, the island now fits Giedion's description: all traces of the aboriginal forests having long since disappeared, and there can be no doubt that the standard of life here is 'shockingly low'. Perhaps this is why the solemn Ghika, his vision coloured by inborn metropolitan tastes, remembered it thus: 'We put [...] into port at the beautiful and calm Seriphos; FIG. 25
however despite gallant efforts on the part of Ioannides it was not possible to find anything to eat but one hen.'[69] A negative 'review' that appears to be contradicted by Moholy's generous
22'40" Kinamo and letter in which he tells Sibyl that the island *presented glorious architecture and wonderful smiling faces*. Moholy films the friendly island boatmen as they row out from the beach to

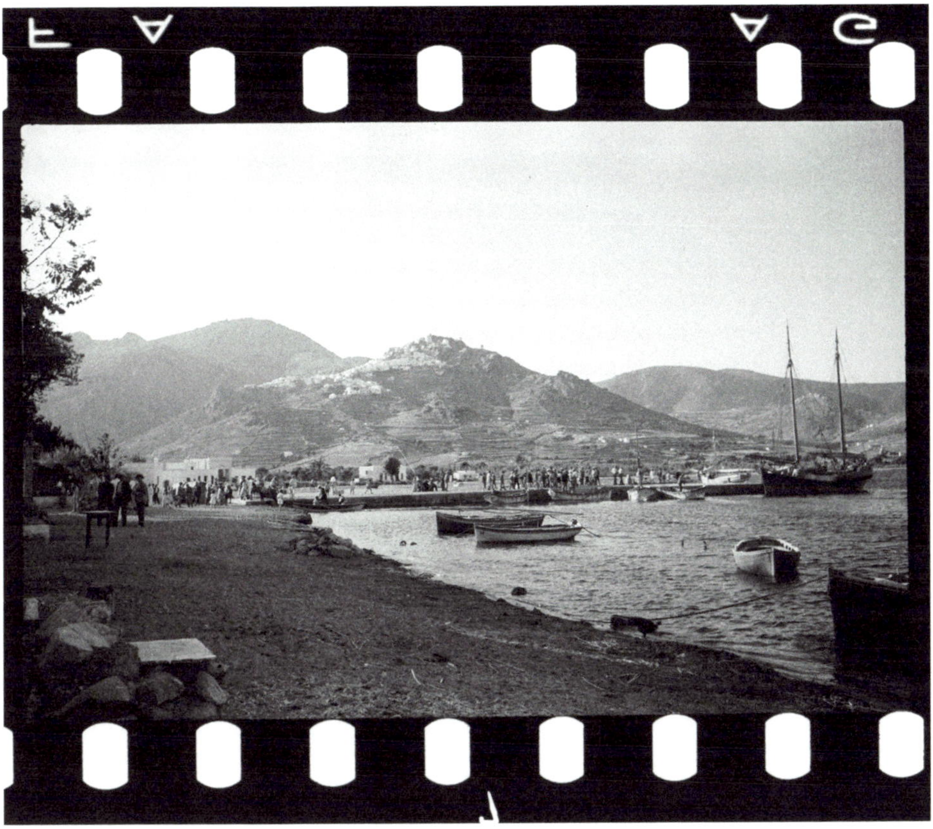

25 Serifos. The cruise party wait to be rowed out to the *Afros* on Sunday evening. In the background, the hilltop *chóra* Photo by Carlo Hubacher

meet the *Afros,* which has anchored in the bay. Léger hesitantly climbs over the rail into the islander's unsteady wooden boat, to be rowed ashore; and it was there, Ghika tells us 'that while stepping with one foot on to the ladder of the boat and going to put the other to balance and grab hold of the railing, my wife slipped and fell into the sea. But like a true knight, Heracles Ioannides dived into the sea, pulling her out.'

23'02" Safely on terra firma, Moholy films a sequence of shots of rough unmade streets in the elevated *chóra,* the steep rocky *monopáti* that connects it to the beach-side settlement of Livadi, puppy dogs play-fighting in the shadow of a wall and—this being Sunday—the village children trooping up the hill to church in their 'Sunday best'. Moholy's visual essay on Serifos life concludes with a small family group of villagers and two small barefoot boys,
22'35" followed by a laden donkey, striding down the rocky *monopáti* dangling several roosters by their legs. This is surely the cruise-party's 'dinner'—Moholy highlighting the irony by focusing on a close-up of one of the roosters, its motionless head pointing earthwards. Could this be the 'one hen' Ghika remembered many years later, in the process demonstrating once again how Moholy's often-startling imagery works on the unconscious, provoking reality-distorting memories to float involuntarily to the surface?

4 *pleonasmós:* increasing sense of 'otherness'—a nocturnal discussion on art, psychology and multiple identities

While verdant Aegina and Poros present the illusion of being securely attached to the European continent, this reassuring feeling is banished by the arid stony world of Serifos—notwithstanding its 'glorious architecture and wonderful smiling faces'. Leaving that island after sunset, the *Afros* sailed south-eastwards—down past Sifnos, between Ios and Sikinos, towards Santorini—with each nautical mile covered, the feeling of expectation would have increased, the sense of 'otherness' intensified.

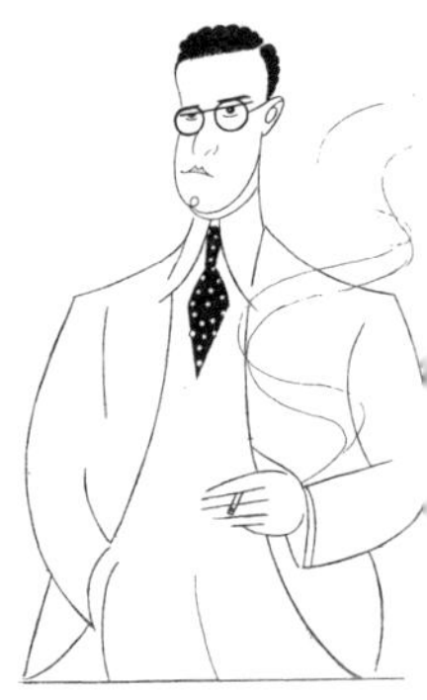

26 César Abin, 1932 caricature of the painter Ghika (Nikos Hadjikyriakos-Ghika). From *Leurs Figures*, with commentary by Maurice Raynal

The legendary exploded island was Zervos's goal: a letter he had written from Paris on Valentine's Day 1931 urges Giedion to join him on a cruise of the islands which are otherwise difficult to reach, and where 'one could take, above all on Santorini, magnificent photos of the houses'.[70] Giedion had ignored the offer at the time; however, the Russian *Nyet!* coming abruptly out of the blue in April 1933 had ultimately provided the pretext.

Any point on the periphery can be perceived as the centre of another circle: an adage that particularly holds true for the inhabitants of the islands. Naxiots, for example, regard their island as the centre of the universe and nearby Paros as a foreign land; naturally, the Parians return the compliment. Similarly, while Greece itself appears remote from the metropolises of northern Europe, there was a brief moment when she was recognised as a thriving centre of artistic invention, Le Corbusier, for one, taking the Greek artists seriously. We have already seen how he paid his respects to 'Ghika from here—one of the painters who is making a name for himself'—in his eulogy to Greece delivered to CIAM and its guests. Ghika, in turn, deserves to be heard; **FIG. 26** his *Memoirs of Le Corbusier* providing a colourful springboard for a discussion of the Parisian *avant-garde* in 1933:

> I met Le Corbusier in 1932 in Paris, at a time when I was feeling bleak and disappointed. I knew him only by name, but I held him in high regard so was stunned when I suddenly received his letter. For a long time I couldn't believe it, similarly I couldn't believe what flattering remarks he had written to me. 'I have just arrived back from a tour of Holland where I have seen Rembrandts and Vermeers, and I fell upon a showcase of your works. I congratulate you, so I would love us to get to know one another.'[71]

Le Corbusier had bought one of his paintings, *The Gondola* of 1931, **FIG. 27** like much of Ghika's work of this period, semi-abstract and evidently inspired by the Purism advocated by Ozenfant

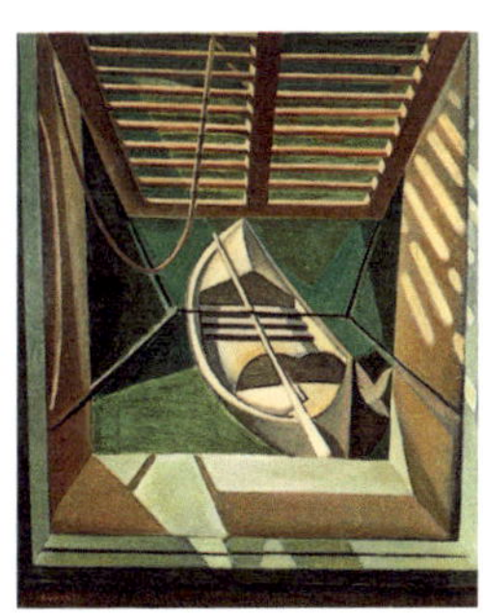

27 Ghika, *The Gondola*, 1931. Oil on canvas 81 × 65 cm. Le Corbusier bought this painting for his collection before meeting Ghika for the first time in 1932.

and Jeanneret—the uninvented name he retained for that half of his life—notably in *La Peinture Moderne* of 1925. Ghika continues,

> We became firm friends seeing each other almost every day. We ate at the same restaurant, the Petit Saint Benoit, at the same table. We exercised together and played basketball; he told me that it was the reason why he could scarcely see out of one of his eyes. He gave me all his books [...] however, most precious of all was his company. From him I learnt thousands of things of which I was unaware; architecture, sculpture, painting and lithographs. Most significant was our exchange of thoughts, our criticism of works of art we saw together, along with the ones we knew. He sought out my opinion and I asked for his. From time to time I made a critique of something he had done; naturally he was disconcerted. In the end, however, he would accept my opinion. I am sure he admired me as an artist, for he loved art even more than he loved architecture.

Ghika hints at Jeanneret / Le Corbusier's crisis of identity at that time: was he not, primarily, *an artist*? Not an insignificant question when it is considered that great architects and theorists—Adolf Loos and Mies van der Rohe, to name but two—had insisted that architecture is emphatically *not* an art. To demonstrate the dilemma, Ghika relates how Le Corbusier

> separated his life into two. All morning he painted at home in Rue Jacob, then all afternoon he was an architect. One morning he was preoccupied with his painting, unkempt and in his slippers, when the doorbell rang. Thinking it was the caretaker he went to open it; standing on the threshold was a serious well-dressed gentleman who politely asked: 'Does the architect Monsieur Le Corbusier live here?' 'No sir,' he answered, 'the painter, Jeanneret lives here.' 'Do you perhaps know how I could meet Monsieur Le Corbusier?'

> the visitor asked him again. 'Yes,' Le Corbusier responded, 'This afternoon at 35 Rue de Sèvres.' When he went there that afternoon he was somewhat puzzled to see Monsieur Jeanneret groomed and well-dressed in a bow tie greeting him as Monsieur Le Corbusier.

During the years before his move to Paris, Ghika made a series of pen-and-ink drawings titled *Refugee Huts* in the shanty towns that had sprung up around Athens in the aftermath of the exchange of populations. Like Le Corbusier's drawings of Breton cottages, these betray a striking affinity with the drawings of vernacular architecture made around the same time by Pikionis and pointed to the direction Ghika's work would take—albeit leavened with surrealist influences—after his return to Greece at the end of 1934. But this is to jump ahead: in August 1933, Ghika is still a member of Zervos's ex-patriot circle dedicated to abstraction. He briefly achieves recognition on the international stage with a show at Zervos's gallery, 14 rue de Dragon, alongside Hans Arp, Sophie Tauber and Jean Hélion, exhibiting *Objects in space*—quasi-surrealist visionary works constructed on the basis of abstracted everyday utensils.[72] Ghika's new friend Jeanneret / Le Corbusier, on the other hand, never accepted full-blown abstraction—dismissing the work of Mondrian and de Stijl, for example, as 'a negative demonstration [...] concerning itself exclusively with a few geometrical signs limited to the rectangle [...] a language so simplistic that it scarcely allows a stammer'.[73] For the source of this prejudice, we have to turn to the idiosyncratic and highly opinionated writings of Le Corbusier's collaborator (and financier) in publishing the review *L'Esprit nouveau* between 1920–25, Amédée Ozenfant. In this review and the subsequent book they had jointly authored, *La Peinture moderne,* the two artist-critics spelt out their formula for an art movement which was virtually restricted to themselves:

Purism. As Ozenfant is also a member of the ship-board group 'who keep to themselves', we have to imagine that their conversations ventured into dissections of rival Parisian art movements.

In the summer of 1933 the wider European turmoil finds an intensified reflection in the world of modern art; Picasso—in contrast to the rarefied and somewhat laboured constructions of the Purists—is now the prolific puckish sensation. His first major retrospective, including some 430 works—held in the Kunsthaus Zürich between September and November 1932—had been seen by tens of thousands and extensively discussed in the press; it had even engaged the attention of Carl Jung[74]. In Greece the atmosphere of radical change had been seized on by Tombros, who had returned from Paris in 1928 intent on fomenting an artistic revolution in his own country. His inspiration was the Italian poet and author of the 1909 Futurist manifesto, Filippo Tommaso Marinetti, who had delivered a series of lectures in Athens to coincide with an exhibition of Futurist *aeropaintings* in February 1933.[75] These lectures had generated a spate of polemical articles in the press, those in favour regarding Marinetti's advocacy of 'Italian-ness' and connections to Mussolini's regime as a promising path towards a parallel 'Greek-ness', which would be adopted three years later by the dictatorial Metaxas regime. Tombros concentrates his enthusiasm for change in a new review, *20th Century,* FIG. 28 bringing out the first issue in French to coincide with the opening of CIAM 4. The issue is lavishly illustrated, and he has succeeded in attracting substantial essays from Le Corbusier, Sigfried Giedion and Christian Zervos; thus we may imagine that *20th Century,* as 'the journal of the congress', generates some lively debate on board the 'nutshell'.

In his editorial titled 'Why I am bringing out a periodical', Tombros somewhat obliquely introduces the Western visitors to the corrupt Byzantine politics of his homeland, simultaneously appealing to those in power to open their minds to the progres-

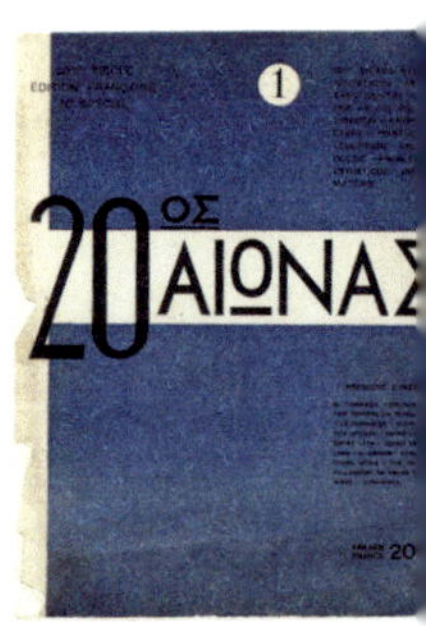

28 Cover of the first issue of Tombros's journal *20th Century,* published in both French and Greek to coincide with CIAM 4

sive influences of CIAM. He laments the 'suffocation' of creative work due to the 'lack of a dynamic atmosphere of encouragement under state control'; nevertheless it is clear that he expects the revolution to be brought about by a revitalised state—no doubt along Italian lines. While Marinetti's 'Manifesto addressed to the youth of Greece' had urged a rejection of the country's fixation on archaeology, in the process deflating the monumentality of the Parthenon, it is interesting to note that Le Corbusier—who is at this time actively wooing the Italian regime[76]—clings doggedly to his faith in the Periclean masterpiece. Le Corbusier's two contributions to *20th Century,* 'Decisive Manifestation', and 'Greek Spirit – Latin Spirit – Greco-Latin Spirit', are romantic evocations of the heroic spirit: 'On the Acropolis, in the silent lap of a landscape risen from prehistory, rises a pathetic discourse, almost a cry, a brief outcry, violent, compact, massive, acute, trenchant, decisive: the marble of the temples carries *the human voice*'. He repeats his barb from 'Throwing Knives':

> In 1933 the USSR wanted to express herself: she would construct the Palace of all the Soviets, the Palace crowning the Five Year Plan. TRUTH, CLARITY, PURITY. No! / The USSR no longer had the clear consciousness of her spiritual destiny. She consulted the college of old men, and the old men said: 'You must go to Athens and Rome', immoderately discouraging parody! / Mussolini reconstructing Italy, having in that case the same sole occasion to forge a dazzling image of reborn Italy, decreed: 'We must look at Rome', pastiche and parody. / Thus, for the present, the two greatest human enterprises for a long time, aborted. / Rome copies Rome: pleonasm.

Pleonasmós: a Greek word that aptly encapsulates the extravagant tautologies indulged in by these 1930s rhetoricians somewhat inclined to repetition. No less wordy—nevertheless brimming with informative content—is Zervos's contribution to *20th Century,* titled 'Introduction to the Art of Today':

> People in general think that modern artists' only aim is to innovate at all costs, that they reject the past altogether and run vainly after phantoms of novelty which represent nothing and are nothing. / However, on looking closely at their works, one perceives that the freedom with which they use painting scarcely signifies abandonment to the impulses of chance, blind and disordered submission to all exterior influences but, on the contrary, submission to a rigorous order which comes from the grand tradition [...] the art of today is not an isolated phenomenon.

Zervos takes us on a meticulously researched and well-illustrated journey from the 'drama and reverie' of Delacroix, through the 'literary transcription' of Courbet, the 'bizarre and grotesque' fantasies of Daumier, to his ideal of the 'equilibrium of spiritual and material' in Cézanne, whom he sees as 'the great originator of the modern movement'. However, his lengthy discussion of nineteenth-century history is but a preamble to the cubists, for whom 'negation of atmosphere, [...] their reaction against the order of sensation, their attention to construction, gave [...] that aspect of absolute vigour, that continuous restraint of the impulses of the heart, that appearance of inhumanity necessary to save art from shipwreck'.

The ever-prescient Zervos may have raised an eyebrow or two on the *Afros* with this metaphor, perhaps even more so with his concluding sentence: 'But whatever has been written about it, the new order [...] is exclusively the work of BRAQUE and PICASSO, who are the incontestable masters of that new order.' How did this go down with the self-appointed 'masters' of Purism—Jeanneret / Le Corbusier and Ozenfant—not to mention their *compagnon* Fernand Léger? Zervos's definition of 'the Art of Today' eloquently illustrates Moholy's ironic remark to Sibyl about *chosen guests of the congress, mostly french, who like to keep to themselves,* since those other vital pioneers of modern art, Russians, Germans and Dutch—many of whom were Moholy's teachers and friends—are excluded from the pantheon. And if, as we believe, Jeanneret / Le Corbusier was, in both his *personae,* experiencing a crisis at this juncture, Zervos's pronouncement must have provoked some serious soul-searching.

Zervos had been responsible, at least in part, for a further provocation; and this may have been of more than passing interest to the would-be psychoanalyst Embirikos. In 1929 he had entered into an exclusive contract with Picasso under which he would publish an illustrated catalogue of all the artist's work. This would eventually run to thirty-three volumes and, Picasso being Picasso, it was anything but 'exclusive'—as Tériade would also publish luxurious albums of the Spanish master's work. Less than lavish, however, were two articles by Carl Jung psychoanalysing the master published at that time. The first, which has become notorious, was published in the *Neue Zürcher Zeitung* to coincide with the closing of the retrospective in the Kunsthaus. Jung disdainfully begins, 'As a psychiatrist, I almost feel like apologising to the reader for becoming involved in the excitement over Picasso. Had it not been suggested to me from an authoritative quarter, I should probably never have taken up my pen on the subject'.[77] But, take up his pen he does—and at considerable length: according to his diagnosis Picasso is 'a schizophrenic'. It seems that this disorder was much discussed at the time, avant-garde artists—though apparently not architects—being particularly fascinated by Jung's anti-materialist view that the individual is 'made up of many selves'. Zervos—to be thoroughly *au courant* and no doubt spotting a marketing opportunity—also commissioned an article from Jung. This appeared in issues 8–10 of *Cahiers d'Art* 1932 titled 'Picasso étudié par le Docteur

Jung'. Giedion, as a frequent contributor to the review, and resolutely clinging to rationalism, was scandalised, writing to Zervos in November 1932,

> You treat Jung like a great savant! He is only a banal man who wears a scientific mask and who looks for his victims among famous men. While Joyce was in Zurich three months ago, he showed us a letter from Jung where he seeks, with all means, to approach him. Joyce was warned to mistrust him![78]

Le Corbusier in his bow-tie-attired afternoon *persona* would surely have gone along with Giedion. He, too, had approached James Joyce at around this time[79]—and, among others, Josephine Baker, Antoine St. Exupéry, Fernand Léger and Philippe Lamour—but this was in yet another role: as property developer seeking purchasers for his apartment building under construction at Porte Molitor. Did he perhaps imagine the building as a modernist Parnassus? The peripatetic Irish writer, already eleven years into the seventeen it would take him to concoct *Finnegans Wake*—the most fissiparously ramified avant-garde masterpiece of all, which would become a source of fascination for Moholy[80]—was unimpressed, finding the prospect of being a close neighbour of both Le Corbusier *and* his authoritarian *guru* Dr Pierre Winter unappealing. For the Jeanneret of be-slippered mornings in the studio constructing Purist canvases, Zervos's declaration that Braque and Picasso were 'the incontestable masters of the new order' must have sounded like a provocation. The media of the day were obsessed with the multiple personalities of Picasso, not to mention the excesses of surrealism; thus it is probable that with Kurt Seligmann, the Swiss creator of 'sinister biomorphic paintings', also in the party, these matters were indeed under discussion during that nocturnal voyage south-eastwards. Le Corbusier would have felt compelled to make a counter-gesture, perhaps turning at this point to his *confrère* Léger for support.

Léger had acquired from his wartime experiences an enthusiasm for machinery which he had then celebrated in his paintings; the dynamic *Propellers* of 1918 being a prime example.[81] The two men did not have to look very far to see rising before them the unequivocally functionalist steel anchor-winch of *Afros* with its naked cogwheels and rusting coiled chain **FIG. 29** that tethered the vessel each time they went ashore. Le Corbusier's spirited 21 × 31 cm pencil-and-wash drawing of the mechanism titled *Cyclade 1933 L-C* has the appearance of being rapidly sketched *sur le vif*—that is, until we compare it with a near-identical sketch also in the FLC. The muscular tackle dominating the foredeck of what was supposed to be a luxury yacht clearly fascinated him to the point where he would transform it into a graphic *objet à réaction poétique.* As the only other sketches surviving from the cruise are those of Aphaia in his pocket *carnet,* it's possible that the image was not committed to paper until he returned to his Paris studio. At all events, its distorted form reappears as the dominant element in a 72 × 91 cm painting, signed *L-C '33* with the legend on the stretcher *Sur le navire Afros aux Cyclades / CIAM Athènes 1933.* **FIG. 30**

The canvas could not have been painted on the *vapeur* and must have been done in the studio following his return to Paris. One suspects that there is more to this painting—which has been suppressed in the Corbusian canon—than meets the eye; the contorted jumble of forms place it outside the mainstream of Jeanneret's 'post-Purist' works of that time. The centre ground is occupied by the winch, transposed directly from the sketch; rendered in shades of blue-grey, the mechanism appears to lunge out of the canvas towards us. Equally dominant on the picture plane are three women: a grotesque nude to the left, her body daubed a lurid sienna, and two clothed women, the flesh of one tan, the other a drab shade of green suggesting putrefaction. Groupings of three women inevitably evoke those *Three Graces*—

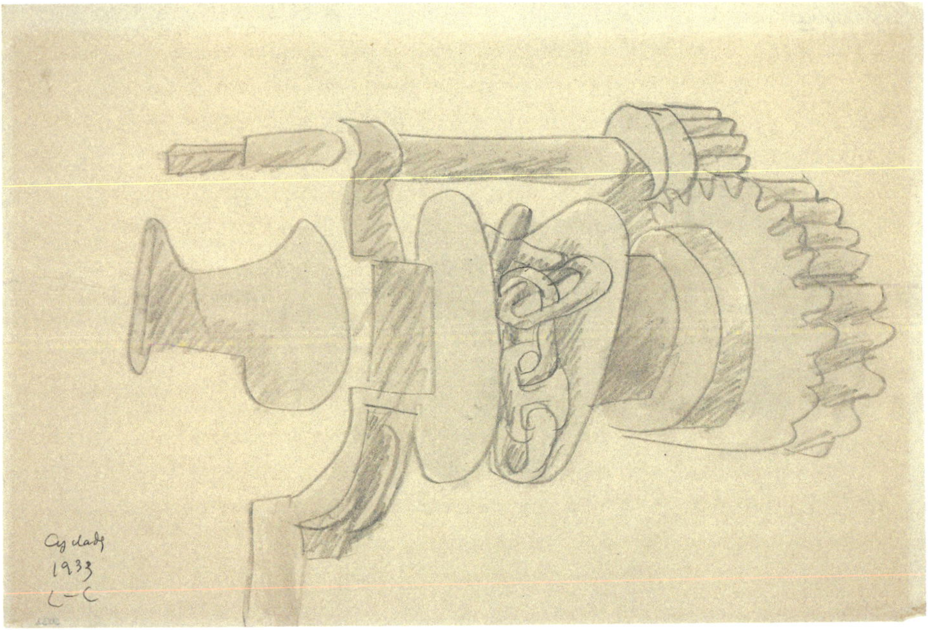

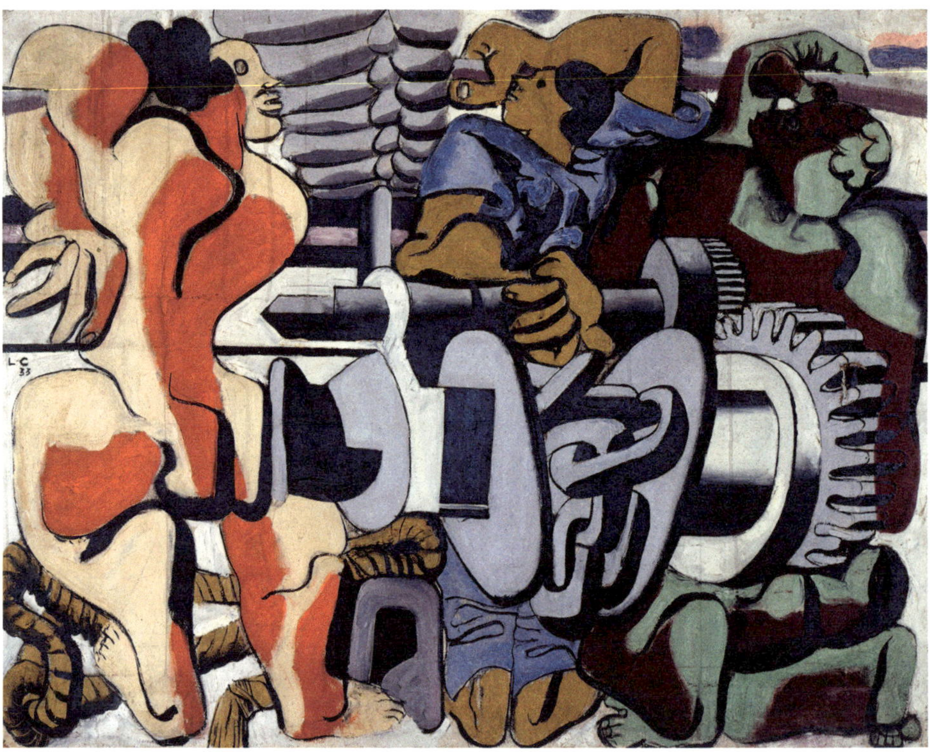
LC
33

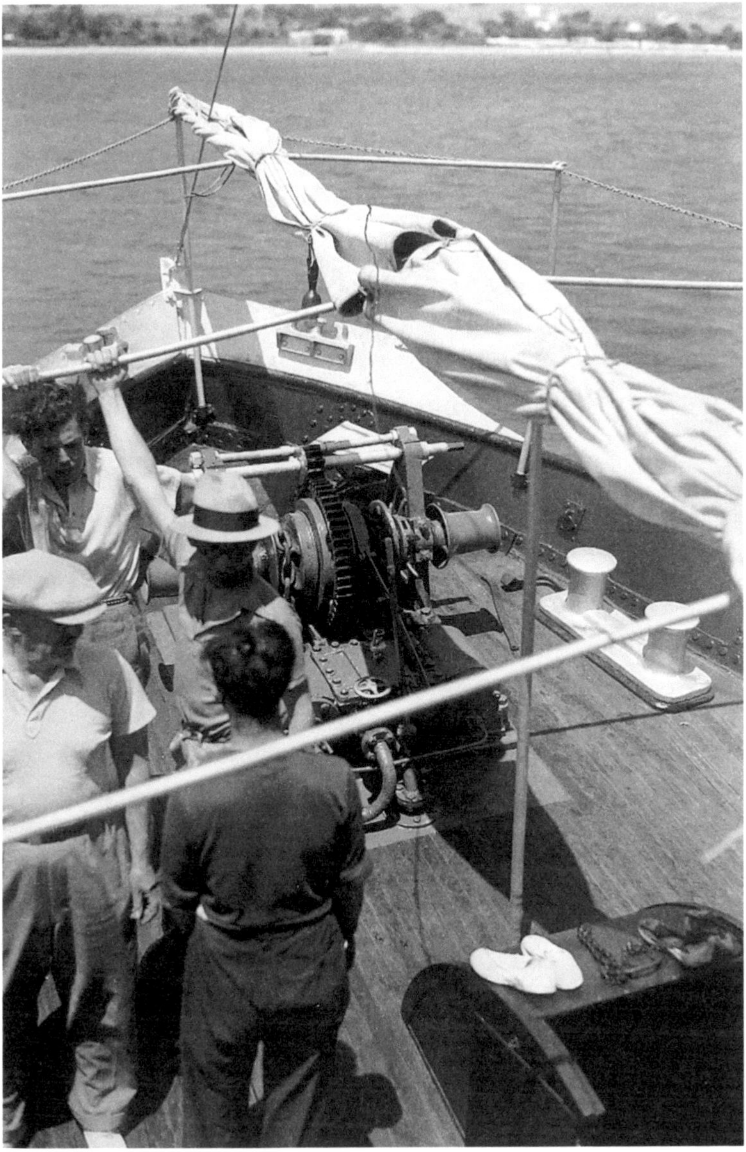

29 Le Corbusier, pencil-and-wash sketch titled *Cyclade 1933 L-C*, in which he abstracts the prominent anchor winch on the foredeck of *Afros.*

30 Le Corbusier, *Sur le navire Afros aux Cyclades / CIAM Athènes 1933.* Oil on canvas 72 × 91 cm. Painted in the weeks after his return to Paris, Le Corbusier's enigmatic 'three women' could be interpreted as his 'response to the spirit of the times'.

31 The French 'who keep to themselves' on the foredeck of *Afros* approaching Serifos. Le Corbusier in prototypical *Modulor* stance with Bonheur, Léger and Badovici (back to camera). Clearly visible are the anchor winch and furled canvas awning, both of which appear in Le Corbusier's painting *Sur le navire Afros aux Cyclades / CIAM Athènes 1933.* Photo probably by László Moholy-Nagy

mythical daughters of Aphrodite and Dionysus—who have, in various guises, provided subject matter for artists since at least the time of Homer. On board the *Afros* they appear painfully crushed by the weight of the winch while clutching at the vessel's railing; above their heads we recognise the ruffled folds of the furled canvas awning that can be seen in the photo of the vessel's foredeck. FIG. 31 The title suggests that the *L-C* who signs this tormented work wishes to immortalise an event that occurred on *Afros* during those four days and nights. Could it have been the epiphany that he would so forcefully articulate some months later in *Point de Départ*? 'The insatiable machine dominates us; it is preparing to make a banal sub-species of us.'

With the bizarre style and subject matter in mind, we might conjecture an impassioned debate—perhaps involving Zervos, Tériade and Maurice Raynal—about Picasso's stylistic convulsions. The Spanish artist's *Three Women at the Spring* painted in 1921,[82] was being discussed around that time as the prime exemplar of his 'neoclassical' style, for which he claimed a Hellenistic pedigree. Viewed with fresh eyes in the playfully luminous ambience of the islands, however, the sombre classically draped rotundities of Picasso's version of 'Greekness' would have appeared absurd. Did Léger at this point suggest a provocative *riposte*? And, apropos, he had himself in 1921 painted a very substantial *Three Women*,[83] which he regarded 'as one of the [...] masterpieces of his entire career [...] the premier example of his response to the spirit of the times'.[84]

Sur le navire Afros aux Cyclades is perhaps, Jeanneret / Le Corbusier's graphic response to the disturbing dilemmas undermining the spirit of August 1933. He has deviated a long way from Ozenfant-approved Purism, his three despairing 'graces' suggesting an *Ubu-esque* parody of Greek tragedy. And, if Dr Jung had confidently diagnosed schizophrenia in the case of Picasso—whose divergence from *Les Demoiselles d'Avignon* to *Three Women at the Spring* was purely a matter of painting style—what would he have made of a mind that could switch in short order from the rationalist geometrically ordered *Ville Contemporaine* to the disordered surrealist nightmare of *Sur le navire Afros*?

Le Corbusier had launched his CIAM 4 adventure by admonishing all and sundry thus:

> ... in the name of this harmony it is necessary in the whole world, without failure and with a courageous heart, to harmonise. This word veritably expresses the raison d'être of the present times. / And to be urgently imbued with that notion: to harmonise modern times. To find anew that quality of men: the 'harmonisers' of today. To discover that in the present calamity the key which will open the door through which will be expelled all disorders and woes, is harmony.[85]

He went on to extol the Acropolis as the epitome of that harmony. By contrast, in his melodramatic 'three women at the winch' he appears to be unmasking the 'disorders and woes' of the present.

VI from magical caldera to the island of exile

23'45" 1 *Santorin*

Any disharmony lingering from the night voyage would have been dispelled by the sheer delight of entering the magical caldera at the heart of this strange ring of islands before dawn. FIG. 32 Thus begins the epiphany Zervos has been planning for the Westerners since his own visit during the filming of *Le Voyage aux Cyclades* two years earlier. While the film and coverage of that visit in the pictorial review *VU* had followed the conventions of travelogue reporting, Moholy refuses to make any such concessions—preferring to surprise his audience from the outset with unforeseen viewpoints. Contrasting the monstrous volcanic spectacle with 'beautiful and calm Seriphos' and its *glorious architecture and wonderful smiling faces,* his ironic introduction to Sibyl leaves us in no doubt where his sympathies lie:

> *of course, people belong to all these things. where there are few visitors, there they are simple and warm-hearted, without greed. pierre jeanneret, who was in the peloponnese, told of a shepherd, who had served him with goats milk and cheese, and whom he wanted to pay, did not want to accept money from him. 'money brings misfortune,' he said, and this shepherd was formerly a waiter in america. the island of santorini, which has a lot of visitor traffic, presented different customs.*[86]

Already, by 1933, the Santorinians had become accustomed to the visits of cruise liners; thus images of the island's unique topography and architecture were not totally unknown in the outside world. Moholy deliberately avoids travelogue clichés, while Eli Lotar in his 1931 *VU* coverage FIG. 33 had been obliged to engage the interest of a wider audience; one photo in particular capturing the chaos of the tiny port in which—with multitudinous donkeys, mules and cloth-capped muleteers jostling for business—one can almost smell the aroma of dung. Moholy goes further, his sympathies with these placid beasts of burden clearly formed by his rural background in eastern Europe:

> *when we arrived* [...] *we—20 to 25 people—were overrun by c. 200 mule drivers in order to force us into the saddle. the city of tiros* [sic] *lies up on the mountain, and most tourists ride up there on the stairs. it is amazing what these animals are able to accomplish. in the most difficult places, steep, rocky, slippery, they trot—most of them stubbornly in front of their drivers, who are shouting fiercely and beating them with heavy sticks.*

As the mules finally gained the summit of the switch-back *skála* FIG. 34—in reality a roughly cobbled stepped ramp rising 260 metres—a dreamlike urban landscape was revealed to the visitors. The characteristic Santorini houses readily became 'magnificent photos' because, in Zervos's terms, they appeared 'archaic [...] in tune with contemporary sensibility'.[87] Following 23'48"
the title *Santorin* we have flown to a perch above the famous caldera whence we are looking down on the islanders on their rooftops—and beyond to the spectacular *skála* descending to the port. Thus, one of Moholy's longest sequences echoes a Lotar shot of two years earlier, culminating in a meditation on the diminutive white *Afros* anchored far below—as if to emphasise the perilous fragility of the *small nutshell.* 24'01"

Giedion, in documentary mode, records the cruise party's first sight of the island:

> Dawn revealed the summit of Santorin—its white-washed houses trailing like a drift of last year's snow along the edge of its precipitous cliff.... When we climbed up to those houses, Moholy pointed out (that) they merged so plastically into one another that the children were playing on their

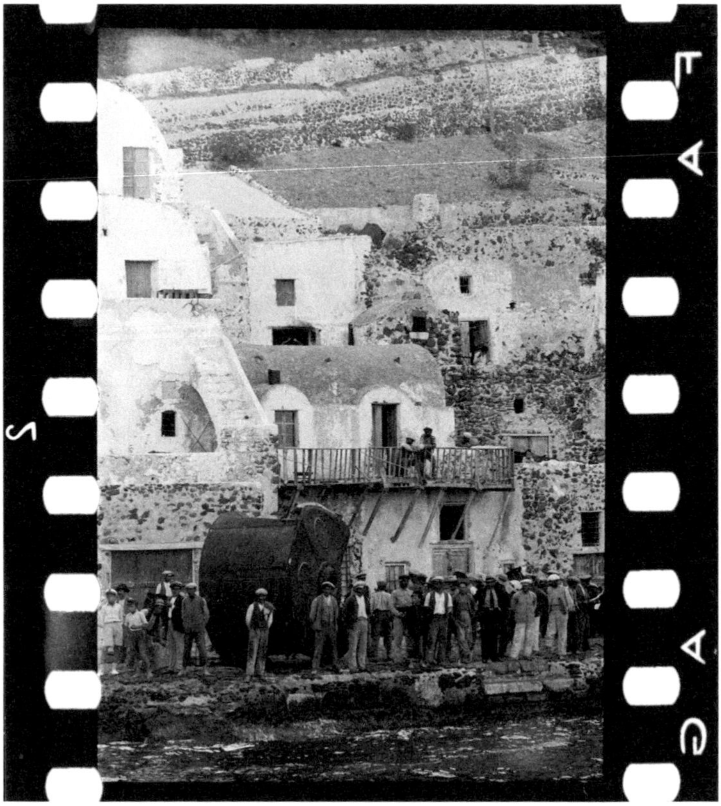

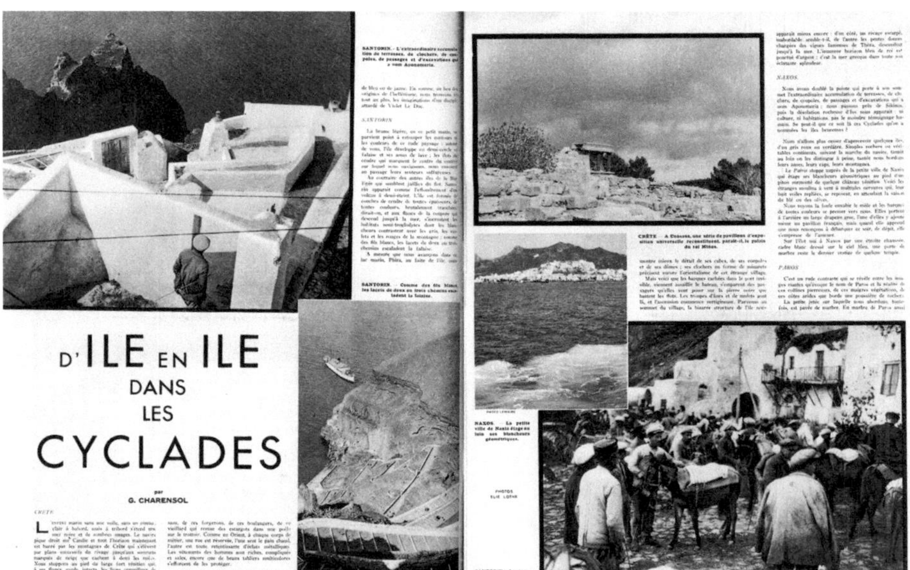

D'ILE EN ILE DANS LES CYCLADES

par G. CHARENSOL

N° 180 VU P. 2102

N° 180 VU P. 2103

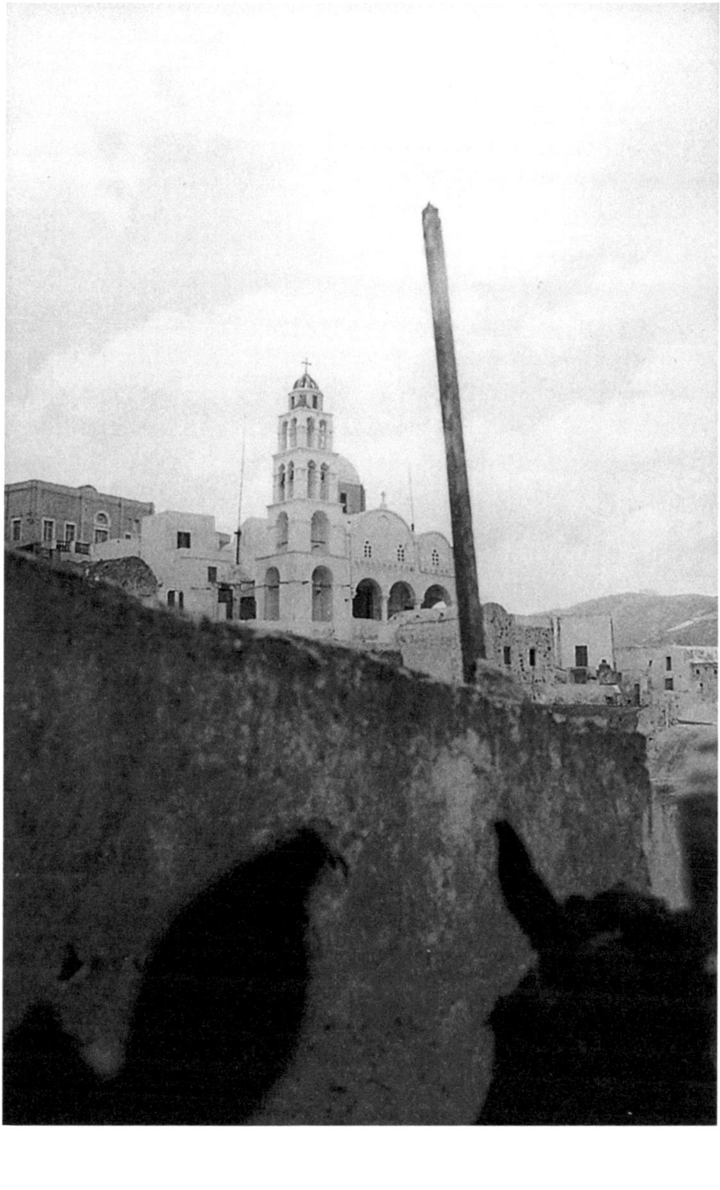

32 Santorini. Approaching the port of Fira at dawn. Photo taken from the *Afros* by Carlo Hubacher

33 *VU,* 26 August 1931. This popular pictorial review published a two-page spread—'from Island to Island in the Cyclades'—with photographs of Santorini and Naxos taken by Eli Lotar while filming *Le Voyage aux Cyclades.* This feature thus commemorates one of the earliest *Patris II* cruises. The ship can be seen in the lower photo, anchored close to the port far below in the caldera.

34 Santorini: approaching the summit of the *skála.* This perilous 'quixotic' shot taken from mule-back featuring the beast's ears in close-up is believed to have been taken by Giedion. On the skyline is the Byzantine-style cathedral of Fira.

> neighbours' flat roofs and how, being built up a steep slope in graduated steps, every house enjoyed a free and uninterrupted view over the sea.[88]

The two friends would have been interested to know that the flat roofs of Santorini have a multiple purpose: in addition to providing playgrounds and performance stages for the children, they are water-collectors during the rare rains, and floors for drying grapes in summer. Then there are the vaults: unique to this island, their form a direct consequence of the cataclysmic eruption of c. 1600 BCE that shattered the formerly round island of Strongyli, creating the spectacular caldera. Lacking timber, the islanders discovered that the volcanic products pumice and pozzolan could be combined to create extremely strong monolithic lightweight vaults. The lightness also registers in another, more poetic, dimension, as the half-cylinders are particularly responsive to the intense light which appears to flow unimpeded across their smooth, shadow-free surfaces.

That the technically-minded Western architects attempted to penetrate the mysteries of Santorini vault construction seems to be demonstrated by Le Corbusier's cryptic note on the *Tombros* page of his carnet: *materials: pumice stone of / Santorini / + earth of Santorini, which makes / hydraulic mortar.* Over the centuries the islanders had evolved a sophisticated method in which a 20–25 cm thick 'shell', consisting of pozzolan mixed with slaked lime and containing small pumice stones, was poured over a temporary formwork constructed of recycled timbers and a mat of branches topped with a sacrificial layer of plaster. Once hardened, the exterior of the vault would receive a fine coat of plaster capable of shedding the rare rainfall, every drop of which would be collected in underground cisterns. The soft volcanic material of the island encouraged the excavation of further subterranean vaults and the creation of a complex range of walls, ovens and chimneys; evidence that the island builders had exploited the unique topography and construction to 'create a built environment with an unusual freedom of expression'.[89]

Something of the sense of wonder aroused by a first encounter with this free architecture is evident in Moholy's 'film within'. The pure, white plastic forms created by the inventive islanders are contrasted with the violent, often hellish, black volcanic rock formations, reminding us that the gods have at intervals wreaked a cruel revenge. Moholy, though, is not content to merely conjure images, his didactic instincts prompting him next to pan over a group of elegant neoclassical houses set against a background of cultivated landscape. Neoclassical houses and churches with elaborate belfries signify the wealth of this island: vast quantities of pozzolan were mined here for the construction of the Suez canal, while the excellent wine—also a product of the volcanic soil and unique cultivation methods—was exported to pre-revolutionary Russia, whence precious straight timber was imported to build the fast sailing ships of the islanders' merchant fleet.[90]

Something catches Moholy's eye, and he abruptly swings **24'15"**
the Kinamo around to focus on a composition of two domed churches with belfries standing above a high retaining wall. A tree—a rarity on the island—has attracted his attention; a group of islanders, in silhouette, chatting in its shade. The agitation of the tree, its leafy branches tossing, triggers an involuntary memory; a similar image occurs in a dream sequence in Vertov's 1929 film *Man with a Movie Camera*. FIG. 35 Against the serenity of the island scenario, the ominous shot reveals a Moholy freed from documentary responsibilities: feeling under no obligation to film the CIAM *personae,* he focuses instead on a range of extraordinary places—the children and adults who 'belong to them'—and the effects of the ineffable Greek light.

We are now three minutes into the 'film within' and Moholy **24'20"**
is in another part of the town. He composes a tableau of rooftops

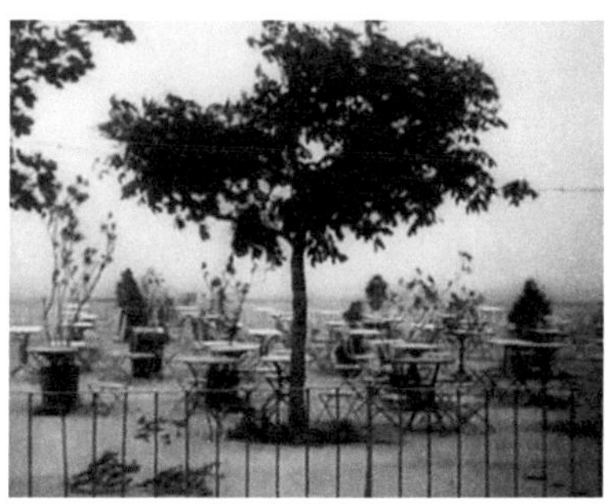

35 Still from *Man with a Movie Camera* by Dziga Vertov, 1929. Tossing tree from the dream sequence, which may have been the subliminal prompt for Moholy's shot on Santorini.

and countryside beyond; below him to the left is a flat roof, on which stands an elderly man in shirtsleeves and waistcoat, accompanied by a woman with scarf tied around her head, her hand resting on the parapet; the sober black dress and headscarf are in stark contrast to the gleaming whiteness of the architecture. While the man appears to be keeping an eye on Moholy, the woman in black is more interested in an event unfolding on rooftops further below. A horizontal pan and diagonal tilt down to the right reveals what it is that has caught her attention: a lissome girl in short cotton dress enters the frame running across the flat unguarded roofs until she effortlessly leaps across a narrow gap from one roof to the next. The girl's youthful mother enters the frame, pausing on a vaulted area of roof; then a second girl appears—as slender and athletic as the first—skipping onto the 'roof stage' from the right, whereupon the first girl springs gracefully onto a third roof. Has Moholy somehow contrived a spontaneous and daring 'dance performance' to dramatise the unique ambience of this island? Is it possible that the three dancers are blissfully unaware of Moholy and his whirring Kinamo—surely, by now, everyone in town has heard about the bemused *xénoi* who rode up the *skála* on mules from the little white steamer early this morning? The 'performance' ceases abruptly and all three turn their faces towards the cameraman—the entire shot has lasted a mere six seconds.

If Le Corbusier had witnessed the event he would have instantly recognised it as a demonstration of the most poetic of his 'five points of a new architecture': liberation of the roof plane. Moholy may, in turn, have relived his experiences in the revolutionary theatre of Erwin Piscator—in particular his ingenious multi-level stage set for *Der Kaufmann von Berlin* of three years earlier. While the rooftops of Santorini evoke innocent unrestricted play under the open sky—an unconscious 'modernism' that has been established here for centuries—the Berlin performance had provoked a sinister eruption. In Sibyl's account, 'The curtain had not yet fallen when one of the most violent battles in Berlin's history broke loose. Nationalists and Socialists in the audience attacked each other with fists and boots.'[91]

The rooftop sequence demonstrates the approach to film *as theatre*—exemplified by his friend Sergei Eisenstein—that Moholy has resolved to move beyond. Film *as light* is the abiding theme of his theoretical writings of the time and key to the experimental 'film within'; the Santorini sequences, in particular, represent an important landmark in the transition to his concept of abstraction. Thus, the vision of an as-found 'new architecture' is followed closely by another memorable revelation: intrigued by the geometric disposition of crops in the striated treeless landscape dotted with isolated vaulted churches, Moholy focuses through **24'29"** a round stone arch. To the right of the opening, a square white slab—a marble table top perhaps—catches his eye; the camera dwells on it for second or two. The radiant shape has a particular significance for Moholy, whose penetrating eye picks out this suprematist symbol of 'the end of painting'. It's as though the fabled island is *itself* addressing the photographer directly and 'calling the shots'. Giedion writes that he and Moholy had registered an equivalent serendipitous event on the Athenian Acropolis a few days earlier when the damaged column fragments

> ... involuntarily carried my mind back to the rocky cliffs of Belle Isle, the island off the coast of Brittany, which stands far out in the Atlantic.... I had watched Moholy taking a photograph from an upper window which intentionally destroyed the perspective of the hotel's terrace and flattened out the objects on it as happens in a bird's-eye view. FIG. 36 As [...] subject in the conventional sense, it was nothing much: a monotonous expanse of cement paving, a stretch of balustrade, a few chairs, a rectangular map spread on a round table with a young friend of ours in front of it. But to the best

> of my knowledge, this was the first time a camera had been used in such a manner with a serious purpose.[92]

The disturbing image had been featured in *Malerei, Fotografie, Film,* the first book to be published under Moholy's name, but which was in fact written in collaboration with his first wife Lucia[93] and published as volume 8 in the 1925 *Bauhausbücher* series. The authors defined the image as a 'faulty' photograph: 'a view from above, from below, the oblique view, which today often disconcert people who take them to be accidental shots', yet nevertheless effective because the camera 'reproduces the purely optical image and therefore shows the optically true distortions, deformations, fore-shortenings ... whereas the eye together with our intellectual experience, supplements perceived optical phenomena by means of association and formally and spatially creates a *conceptual image.*' After a hundred years of photography and two decades of film, the objectivity of the camera image abolishes time-honoured 'pictorial and imaginative association pattern which has remained unsuperseded for centuries.

His eagerness to find equivalent 'faulty' shots must have intrigued those members of the cruise party who observed him at work with the Kinamo. Le Corbusier, who limited himself to buying two tourist postcards on Santorini, would take up photography again later in the 1930s—not with a conventional camera, however, but by using the 'stop-frame' function of a movie camera to create stills in a mode not unlike Moholy's.[94] Thus it is interesting to speculate whether the two men did discuss these matters on the island—especially since there was serious debate around this time as to whether photography *could* be considered an art. As we have seen, Le Corbusier was sceptical—remaining committed to the traditional conception of easel painting that Moholy had dismissed in numerous theoretical writings. Artistic differences apart, Moholy evidently held the

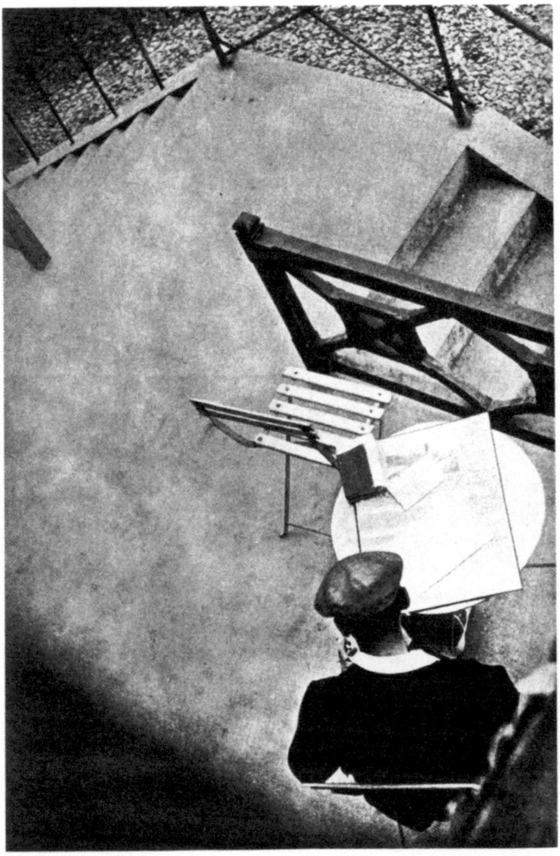

Aufnahme von oben Foto: **MOHOLY-NAGY**

Der Reiz der Aufnahme liegt nicht im Objekt, sondern in der Sicht von oben und in den abgewogenen Verhältnissen.

12* **91**

36 'Photograph from above'—the celebrated 'faulty' photo taken by Moholy on Belle isle, Brittany, and first published in the second, modified edition of *Malerei, Fotografie, Film* from 1927, Vol. 8 of the Bauhausbücher series, p. 91

architect in high regard: he had included an image of the Maison La Roche in his second book *Von Material zu Architektur* and, in a letter written to Sibyl from the chateau of La Sarraz in July 1932,[95] he mentions being delighted to go 'AWOL' with Giedion from Mme de Mandrot's claustrophobic exclusively male gathering to admire *la petite maison*—Le Corbusier's house for his mother at Vevey.

If a discussion with Le Corbusier on art theory prompted by the distinctive island aesthetic *did* take place, perhaps it was in the Fira taverna which appears next in the edited sequence. Moholy shoots from a dark interior through a square-mesh fly-screen out onto an intensely-lit street scene; a small boy presses his face to the screen to watch the cameraman at work while a stout woman carries several chairs towards us, suggesting that this is extra seating for the party. Our expectations of witnessing an anecdotal sequel, though, are abruptly dashed as Moholy cuts to a continuation of his visual explorations. After another sweeping shot over the rooftops and the *wonderful, simple, white architecture,* the film-maker finds the quintessential

24'53" 'bird's-eye' viewpoint.

Once again he is high up on a rooftop, this time leaning over the parapet and tilting his camera down to frame a section of narrow street that at first seems undistinguished. As he slowly pans down and to the right, details begin to emerge: external stairs, vault, squat chimney, wall planes, a roughly rendered dome on an octagonal base. He continues the slow pan for some eight seconds, culminating in an abstraction of street in shadow, walls, radiating terraces, jagged diagonal steps, each frame a perfectly composed abstraction. Finally, the wall's deep shadow slices the frame diagonally: projecting above it the shadows of three heads; that on the right—head and shoulders hunched above the parapet—is the cameraman. It must have amused Moholy, as master of irony, to contrive this slow build-up to his sole 'appearance' in the CIAM film—as a shadow. This strange image also resonates and brings to mind a fuzzy reproduction in the first, Spring 1934, issue of Neptos's travel journal *Le Voyage en Grèce.*[96] A vertiginous composition of dark, narrow streets, stairways, lofty weathered vaults and—nestled in the shadows—a coarse rendered dome. FIG. 37 Breaking the skyline, silhouetted heads and shoulders—a pair to the right and a threesome to the left—all appear to be watching the photographer below. So idiosyncratic is this 'worm's-eye' that the credit *Photo: Moholy-Nagy* seems entirely plausible. It is, though, proof of the difficulty of attribution.[97] Since Moholy's still camera (or, rather, the one he had borrowed from Lucia) had been stolen along with his suitcase, Giedion had offered him the use of *his* folding camera. However, the 'film within' tells us that it can only be Moholy—clutching the indispensable Kinamo—who is peering over the parapet to the left of the group. The haunting image is evidence not only of the close and enduring collaboration between the two men, who had been friends since 1925 and had together conceived the didactic 'Room 1' at the 1929 *FIFO New Vision* show in Stuttgart and Berlin, but also of Giedion's own photographic skills. However, in the mind of Tériade, who was artistic consultant to the journal, there was only one *serious* photographer on the cruise.

We have a sense of things drawing to a close; Moholy, **25'03"**
though, is reluctant to leave the island without filming one more 'bird's-eye'. He is on a rooftop overlooking a room-size *plateía*—elegantly paved with an intricate grid of fine pebbles which he frames diagonally—zooming in to reveal a black metal *kafeneíon* table and four or five chairs strategically placed to the right of the frame. Two men attired in dark jackets and hats relax over their coffees at a table in the shade just inside the frame to the left. As one of them slowly crosses his legs the serenity of the scene is shattered when a third man, bareheaded and in white shirt, abruptly emerges from the building under

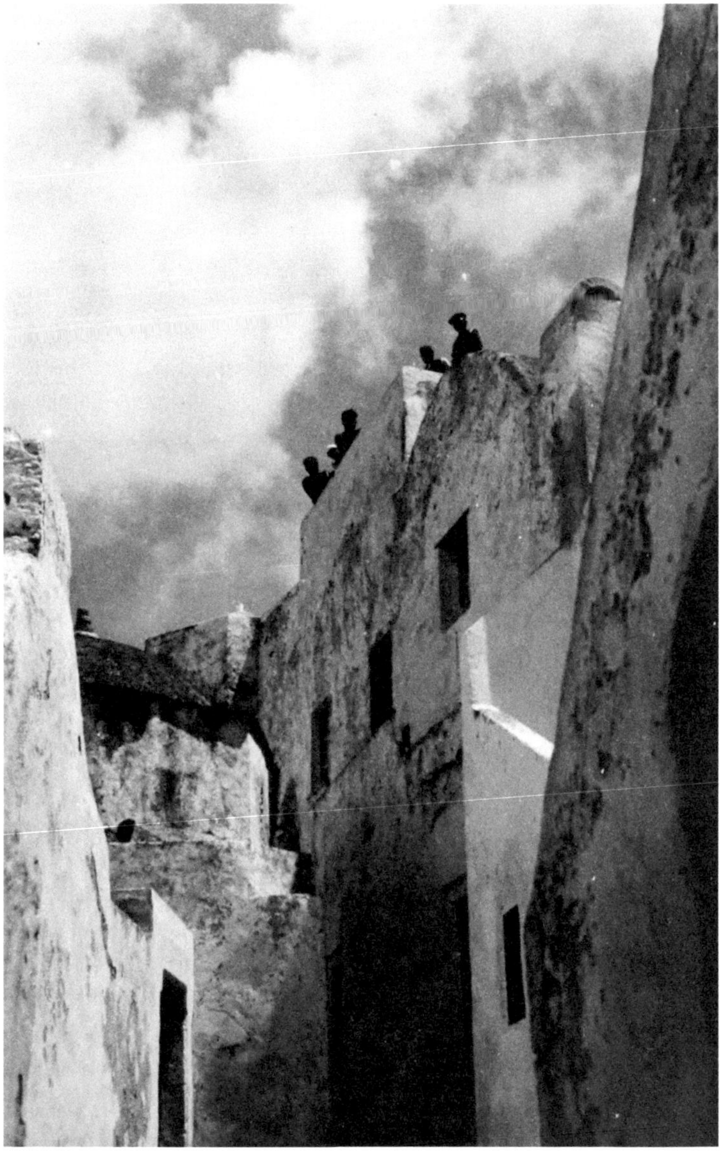

37 Street in Fira, Santorini. Silhouetted on the skyline to the left is Moholy in the process of filming the long 'bird's-eye' pan. Photo by Sigfried Giedion

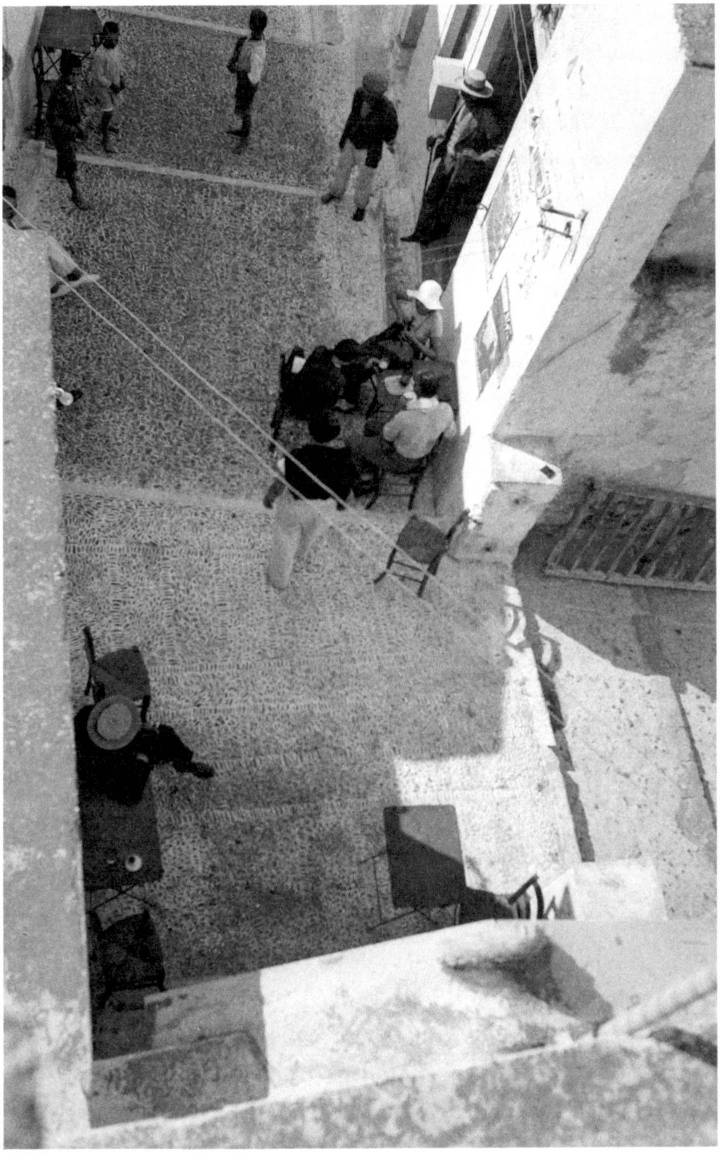

38 Santorini. 'Bird's-eye' of small *plateía* in Fira—members of the cruise party relax outside a *kafeneíon*, while islanders look on. Photo probably by Sigfried Giedion, who was sharing his camera with Moholy

Moholy's feet and strides rapidly across the diagonal frame. Of less than two seconds' duration, the shot exemplifies Moholy's telegraphic mastery of atmosphere: simultaneously jolting our perceptions of space and the passing of time.

Further emphasising, by contrast, the distinctive quality of Moholy's filming on the island is a still photo taken from the same viewpoint and apparently close in time. FIG. 38 The 13.5 × 8.5 cm contact print once again raises the question of attribution. It is orthogonally framed and includes much more of the urban space—so gracious in those days before the venalities of mass tourism swamped the island. Now we can see that a number of islanders are clustered in the background, watching the visitors as they relax outside the *kafeneíon* which the white-shirted man has just entered. The photograph mimics the mode of Moholy's first 'bird's-eye'; however, the more orthodox framing and orientation place it firmly in a documentary context.

Relaxed conversation in the shady *plateía* reminds us that it's late afternoon and Santorini is at the southern extremity of the Cyclades; the urgent pace of the white-shirted man insists that it's high time they resumed their voyage. The *personae* must reconvene and wend their way down the *skála*—close to six hundred cobbled steps deep in mule dung—to the port, where they once again board the waiting *vapeur.*

2 'the plastic feeling' contributes to a change of sensibility

Though it is sheltered down here, the image of the tossing tree returns to haunt Moholy as the vessel sets off on its slow progress across the caldera; the sulphurous blackened lava pile of the dormant volcano further hinting, as they pass by, at the possibility of setbacks ahead. As the *Afros* headed towards the open Aegean, leaving behind the surreal fractured island arranged like a necklace around its breathtaking caldera, the *compagnons* perhaps sensed that forthcoming ports of call would be an anti-

39 *Cahiers d'Art* 1–4 (1934) cover

40 *Cahiers d'Art* 1–4 (1934). First page of article by Panos Djelepy, 'Houses of the Greek Archipelago Observed from the Point of View of Modern Architecture' illustrated by a photograph of Pyrgos, Santorini, by Sigfried Giedion

climax. Zervos had been determined that they should experience Santorini at all costs, while the assertive Professor Anastasios Orlandos—Dean of the Athens Technical School—had insisted in his opening address to the Congress that the visitors from the West would find true enlightenment and confirmation of a pre-existing 'modernism' on Delos and Mykonos.[98] Zervos was right in thinking that the popular architecture of those islands they did succeed in visiting would profoundly move the visitors; but how to explain this effect and—more importantly—ensure its survival and wider influence?

To keep that feeling alive in difficult times, Zervos would go to considerable lengths to publish testimonials to the Cycladic experience as soon as practically possible after the cruise. Early in January 1934 he published his sumptuously illustrated volume *L'Art en Grèce.* Then, in *Cahiers d'Art* FIG. 39—and more directly relevant to the popular architecture of the islands, thus offering a clue to how the cruise party perceived it—an essay by the architect Panos Djelepy titled 'Houses of the Greek Archipelago, Observed from the Point of View of Modern Architecture'. FIG. 40 Consistent with the Functionalism of the Westerners, Djelepy writes:

> From our point of view, the house should respond strictly to the needs of the occupant. In the same way, for the inhabitants of the Greek archipelago it is the indispensable dwelling place, not at all an object of refined aesthetics.

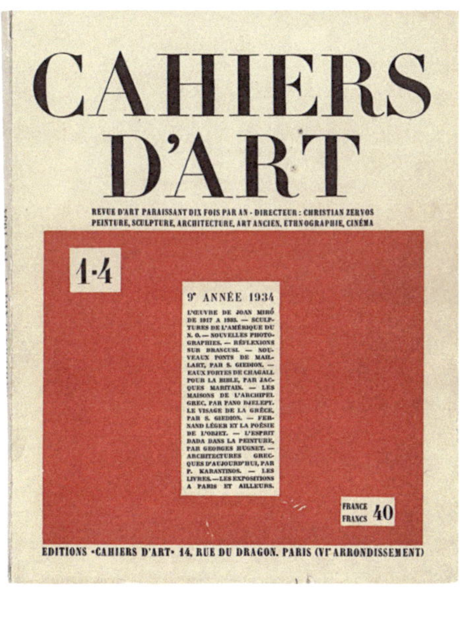

CAHIERS D'ART

REVUE D'ART PARAISSANT DIX FOIS PAR AN - DIRECTEUR : CHRISTIAN ZERVOS
PEINTURE, SCULPTURE, ARCHITECTURE, ART ANCIEN, ETHNOGRAPHIE, CINÉMA

1-4

9e ANNÉE 1934

L'ŒUVRE DE JOAN MIRÓ DE 1917 A 1933. — SCULPTURES DE L'AMÉRIQUE DU N. O. — NOUVELLES PHOTOGRAPHIES. — RÉFLEXIONS SUR BRANCUSI. — NOUVEAUX PONTS DE MAILLART, PAR S. GIEDION. — EAUX FORTES DE CHAGALL POUR LA BIBLE, PAR JACQUES MARITAIN. — LES MAISONS DE L'ARCHIPEL GREC, PAR PANO DJELEPY. LE VISAGE DE LA GRÈCE, PAR S. GIEDION. — FERNAND LÉGER ET LA POÉSIE DE L'OBJET. — L'ESPRIT DADA DANS LA PEINTURE, PAR GEORGES HUGNET. — ARCHITECTURES GRECQUES D'AUJOURD'HUI, PAR P. KARANTINOS. — LES LIVRES. — LES EXPOSITIONS A PARIS ET AILLEURS.

FRANCE FRANCS 40

EDITIONS «CAHIERS D'ART» 14, RUE DU DRAGON. PARIS (VIe ARRONDISSEMENT)

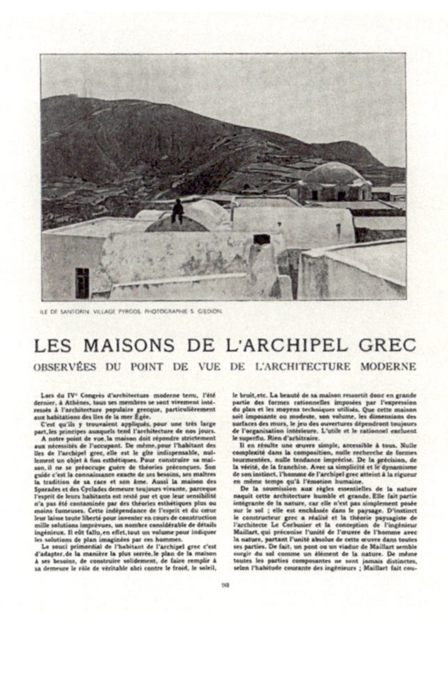

ILE DE SANTORIN. VILLAGE PYRGOS. PHOTOGRAPHIE S. GIEDION.

LES MAISONS DE L'ARCHIPEL GREC

OBSERVÉES DU POINT DE VUE DE L'ARCHITECTURE MODERNE

Lors du IVe Congrès d'architecture moderne tenu, l'été dernier, à Athènes, tous ses membres se sont vivement intéressés à l'architecture populaire grecque, particulièrement aux habitations des îles de la mer Égée.

C'est qu'ils y trouvaient appliqués, pour une très large part, les principes auxquels tend l'architecture de nos jours.

A notre point de vue, la maison doit répondre strictement aux nécessités de l'occupant. De même, pour l'habitant des îles de l'archipel grec, elle est le gîte indispensable, nullement un objet à fins esthétiques. Pour construire sa maison, il ne se préoccupe guère de théories préconçues. Son guide c'est la connaissance exacte de ses besoins, ses maîtres la tradition de sa race et son âme. Aussi la maison des Sporades et des Cyclades demeure toujours vivante, parceque l'esprit de leurs habitants est resté pur et que leur sensibilité n'a pas été contaminée par des théories esthétiques plus ou moins fumeuses. Cette indépendance de l'esprit et du cœur leur laisse toute liberté pour inventer en cours de construction mille solutions imprévues, un nombre considérable de détails ingénieux. Il eût fallu, en effet, tout un volume pour indiquer les solutions de plan imaginées par ces hommes.

Le souci primordial de l'habitant de l'archipel grec c'est d'adapter, de la manière la plus serrée, le plan de la maison à ses besoins, de construire solidement, de faire remplir à sa demeure le rôle de véritable abri contre le froid, le soleil, le bruit, etc. La beauté de sa maison ressortit donc en grande partie des formes rationnelles imposées par l'expression du plan et les moyens techniques utilisés. Que cette maison soit imposante ou modeste, son volume, les dimensions des surfaces des murs, le jeu des ouvertures dépendront toujours de l'organisation intérieure. L'utile et le rationnel excluent le superflu. Rien d'arbitraire.

Il en résulte une œuvre simple, accessible à tous. Nulle complexité dans la composition, nulle recherche de formes tourmentées, nulle tendance imprécise. De la précision, de la vérité, de la franchise. Avec sa simplicité et le dynamisme de son instinct, l'homme de l'archipel grec atteint à la rigueur en même temps qu'à l'émotion humaine.

De la soumission aux règles essentielles de la nature naquit cette architecture humble et grande. Elle fait partie intégrante de la nature, car elle n'est pas simplement posée sur le sol ; elle est enchâssée dans le paysage. D'instinct le constructeur grec a réalisé et la théorie paysagiste de l'architecte Le Corbusier et la conception de l'ingénieur Maillart, qui préconise l'unité de l'œuvre de l'homme avec la nature, partant l'unité absolue de cette œuvre dans toutes ses parties. De fait, un pont ou un viaduc de Maillart semble surgir du sol comme un élément de la nature. De même toutes les parties composantes ne sont jamais distinctes, selon l'habitude courante des ingénieurs ; Maillart fait cou-

98

> To construct his house, he doesn't preoccupy himself much with preconceived theories. His guide is exact knowledge of his needs, his masters the tradition of his race and his soul. Moreover the house of the Sporades and Cyclades still remains alive because the spirit of its inhabitants has remained pure, and their sensibility has not been contaminated by [...] hazy aesthetic theories. That independence of spirit and heart leaves them total freedom to invent [...] a thousand unforeseen solutions, and a considerable number of ingenious details.[99]

It is in his remarks on rationalism and the sculptural aspect of architecture that Djelepy is particularly prescient:

> There is no house of the islands, however unimportant, that has not been conceived and executed sculpturally. It is for this reason that even the most modest habitation never has a miserable appearance. If one closely examines the Parthenon, it is impossible to distinguish that which becomes sculpture in the construction of the monument and that which is properly architecture. The two arts are found to be indissolubly joined and combined in a feeling of intense plasticity. It is the same with the houses of the islands. Each appears to us as a sculpture. It is also noble architecture. To say which inclines to the one or other of the arts would be difficult, because it is difficult to decompose the plastic feeling into distinct functions as we do in our time, an epoch of cold rationalism.

In his analysis of the house types of the islands, Djelepy closely anticipates Le Corbusier's research into harmonious dimensioning systems which would culminate, in the late 1940s, in the discovery of *Le Modulor:*

> But that which astonishes equally in these houses, confirming the beauty of their facades, is the dimensions of the cubic masses from which they are formed and the relationships between the principal mass and the secondary elements all moulded in the same material. These concordances of mass create a sort of harmony between the diverse parts of the house, and also between the house and the earth.

No record exists of Le Corbusier's circumambulations on Santorini; he was, though, a keen walker and it seems reasonable to assume that he had at some point during the long day set off on a hike with his brother Albert and close friends Léger, Ghika and Zervos, the group that had accompanied him on his early morning *vólta* along the Piraeus dockside shortly after their arrival in Greece. The party from *Afros* had been put ashore at the port of Fira, capital 'city' of the main island: crescent-shaped Thera. Starting from the arrival point at the summit of the *skála,* the visitor's inclination is to continue higher: turning to the left and walking north, following the 'drift of last year's snow along the edge of its precipitous cliff'. In the distance shimmers the archetypal white-vaulted village of Oia on its headland; in those pre-vehicular days linked to Fira only by boat or the narrow cliff-top *monopáti.*

The architect had a long-standing interest in 'vernacular architecture and folklore'; on his 1911 travels he had sought out, sketched and photographed the cemeteries of the Levant.[100] Not far north of the neighbouring village of Imerovigli is the all-white walled cemetery; densely packed with elaborate marble memorials and presided over by an 'organic' vaulted church which could serve as the perfect demonstration of that sculptural-architectural ambiguity identified by Djelepy. If we are familiar with Le Corbusier's pilgrimage chapel of Notre Dame du Haut at Ronchamp in the Jura—completed in 1954 after a lengthy gestation—we may be struck by a correspondence. Characteristically coated in thick render and whitewashed as though 'moulded in the same material', the plasticity of the east wall of the Imerovigli church is particularly striking: simultaneously curved, angled and dipping earthwards, it is surmounted by an impressive spout-like gargoyle, the ensemble calling to mind the west elevation of the Ronchamp chapel.

On the evidence of his *carnet*—'stream of consciousness notes' and an uncharacteristic paucity of sketches—Le Corbusier was preoccupied on the island cruise, his mind perhaps wrestling with a number of crises. Nevertheless, with the passage of time the island experience contributed to a pronounced change of sensibility as his subsequent writings testify. The new way of thinking was further intensified during his wartime exile from Paris when he was thrown back on his own inner resources, becoming apparent to the architectural community at large with his radically rethought approach to architecture in the immediate post-war years. This was to be a less rational architecture composed in part of unprocessed materials and admitting 'flaws' in execution. Thus, the technological certainties of CIAM were undermined, setting off a reaction which would ultimately result in its dissolution in the late 1950s. No doubt a combination of factors underlay the transformation: compelling landscape forms, 'ineffable light' and profound shadows—not forgetting the people who, in Moholy's words, 'belonged to these things'. The simplicity of the houses and churches reflected the blunt, yet hospitable, character of the islanders who, at that time, still lived close to nature; mostly lacking monetary wealth and material possessions they were, nevertheless, defiantly alive—finding time to celebrate feast days with wild music, dancing and conviviality. As the so-called 'vernacular' seems to play a parallel role in relation to architecture as mythology does to history, it could be said that the diverse facets of island life and architecture combined synergistically with the creative energies of the open-minded visitors from the West. Having entered their subconscious, these influences would resurface involuntarily in other times and other places.

3 Ios: 'giant kinetic sculptures' and political realities—end of the 'film within'

As the *Afros* steamed past the clifftop village of Oia at the northern end of Thera, out of the sheltering caldera and into the open Aegean, she was abruptly confronted by the oncoming gale and cresting seas. The image of the agitated tree, its branches tossing, flashes through Moholy's mind, and he anticipates the adventure to come with a certain frisson: the smooth cannot be separated from the rough, after all, and there is poetic justice in the thought that the sublime idyll of the outward voyage will be balanced by an existential battle to make it back to the mainland and normality. Back, also, to the mundane realities of film-processing and editing, meetings and—no doubt—exile.

It's not as though this is a particularly sinister storm; in the failing light the skies are clear. Nevertheless, *Afros* is obliged to struggle against a cruelly relentless wind: the *borías* that barrels down the Aegean, sometimes for days on end, drawn southwards and up into the stratosphere by the furnace heat of the Egyptian desert. To reach Mykonos, they must pass by the west coast of Ios, then head due north through the strait between Naxos and Paros, a long perilous voyage in the teeth of the storm—something the islanders themselves would not have contemplated. For an hour or so, *Afros* struggles against the gale, but it lacks the power to tackle it head-on. It became obvious to all that their goal was unrealistic; the captain, who knew a thing or two about this sea—and his craft—decided to run for shelter. Thus, the party fetched up on seldom-visited Ios: famous as Homer's resting place. The island's harbour is a secure haven sheltered from the gale; however, at this point in the 1930s, as the *compagnons* would discover for themselves, its benign appearance concealed a sinister reality.

25'15" Waking on Tuesday morning there was, perhaps, the reassuring illusion that the wind had dropped; however, as they made their way in small groups to the crest of the steep hill above the port, the cruise party were quickly disabused. In Moholy's film, the title *Ios* is followed by a long panning shot over a terraced hillside to the white cubist *chóra* capped by a small domed church. Stretched across the frame is a row of at least ten squat cylindrical stone windmills with conical thatched roofs—each with its six 'arms' crazily turning, even though the triangular canvas sails are furled to next-to-nothing. As if these were not enough, he pans left to reveal yet more of the threatening anthropomorphic structures—why so many? He cuts to a close-up of one of the contraptions: it's as though we're about to be sliced by the 'arms' which, on closer inspection, are sophisticated structures assembled from slender wooden poles and fine tension wires. The creator of the *Light-Space Modulator* is clearly fascinated by these giant kinetic sculptures, heightening the tension further by revealing a young boy striding, apparently unaware of the danger, towards the flailing arms. At this point Moholy is either running out of film or is suddenly reminded of Cervantes's gesticulating giants; perhaps he stopped filming, feeling that—after
25'36" the riot of scything arms—there was nothing more to be said. He abruptly concludes his 'film within' with a solo mill, its slowly revolving arms silhouetted against the twilit sky. In a reversal of the bleached optimism of the opening, the screen goes black.

It would surely have come as a shock to Moholy, who had himself been forced into exile in 1920 after getting involved in revolutionary activities in Hungary,[101] that Ios was being used by an elected Greek government as an exile island. This little-known fact came to light when Carlo Hubacher's legacy of approximately 100 35 mm photographs taken on the cruise began to be catalogued in the gta archives in Zurich in the summer of 2014.[102] FIG. 41 Included in the sequence are two underlit interior shots showing a group of serious young men, some holding left-wing opposition newspapers. There are around eight in the first shot, FIG. 42 looking straight at Hubacher's Leica, while the second shot shows a group of fourteen men, five of whom are sitting on the floor, all facing away from the camera towards the left of the frame. Perhaps there is another photographer present; if it was Moholy, he may have decided that a record of the political internees was best left to be discovered in the cassettes exposed by Hubacher's penetrating Leica, since this disturbing situation would be considered beyond-peripheral to the CIAM agenda. The irony would surely not have been lost on the radical ex-Bauhaus teacher that many of these serious young men were also teachers—perhaps even from the impressive new schools that the Greek authorities had so proudly shown to the Westerners a few days previously.

Life, for the exiles, was blighted by boredom; thus, the unexpected arrival on the island of a party of cosmopolitan intellectuals must have been as welcome as manna in the desert. There were apparently few restrictions; an official 'blind eye' was turned if they organised classes and dramatic productions for the islanders—as long as they remained on the island and incommunicado with the rest of Greece. Hubacher was sufficiently moved by their plight and what it said about the state of democracy in the very country that had invented the idea, to make a record of the claustrophobic assembly. If Zervos, Tériade, Ioannides and Embirikos—all of whom are known to have been well to the left of centre on the political spectrum—took the discovery of the exiles as an opportunity to enlighten the Western visitors as to the *real* situation in their country, then perhaps this contributed to the estrangement (*la brouille*) between Le Corbusier and Zervos which is known to have begun at some point during the

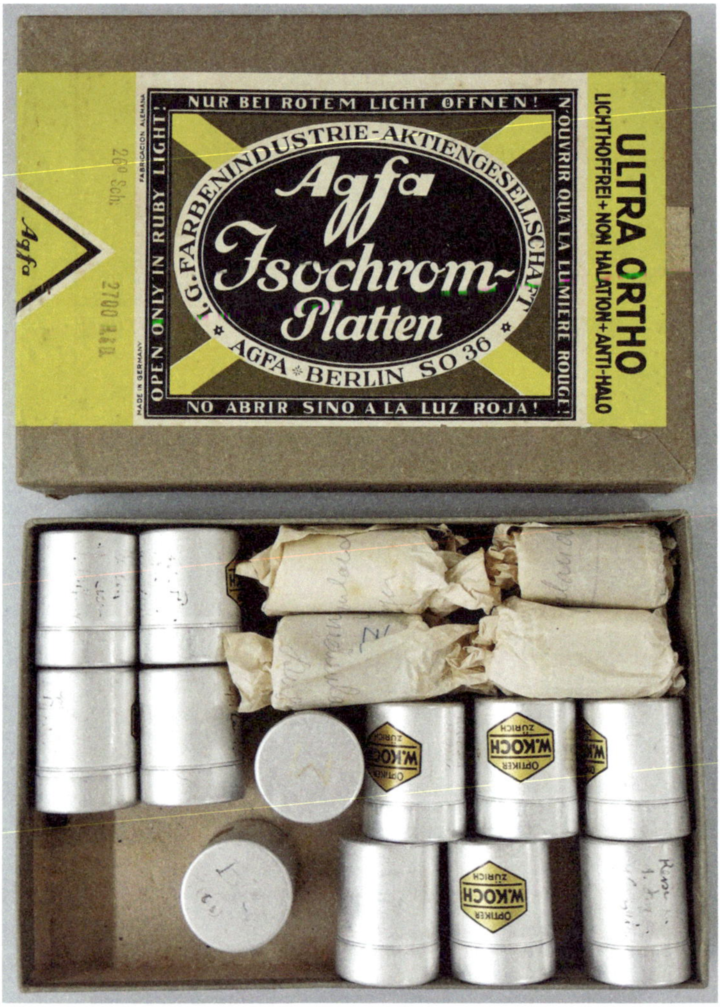

41 Box of Agfa Isochrom 35 mm cassettes used by Carlo Hubacher. Photo by Judith Levine

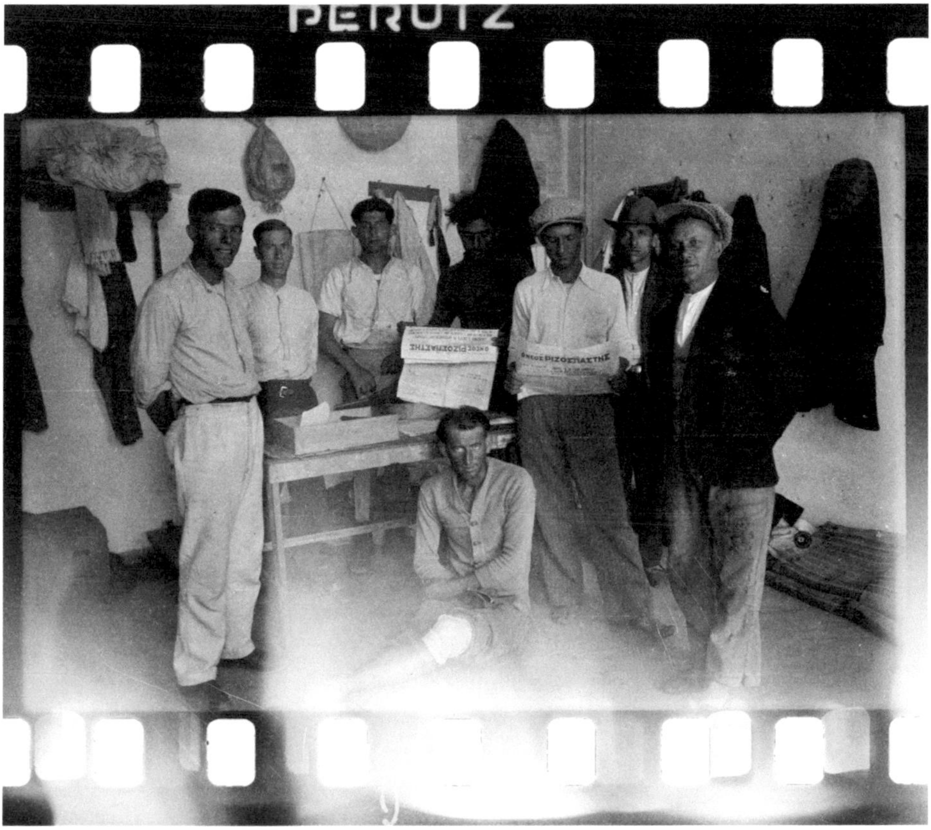

42 Ios. A group of left-wing political exiles, many of whom were probably school teachers.
Photo by Carlo Hubacher

Greek adventure.[103] In the months following the congress, financial embarrassments and complications with the Papastratos commission reduced correspondence between the two men to chilly formalities, the consequence being that while Zervos had given the Palace of the Soviets project a generous spread in *Cahiers d'Art* in 1932, he subsequently declined to publish Le Corbusier's work until their belated and half-hearted reconciliation in 1940.

As if the existence of the detainees was insufficient reminder of the sinister forces stalking the European continent, from which the cruise party were doing their best to distance themselves, the presence of Le Corbusier's adviser on all matters of urbanism must have compounded the disagreeable atmosphere. Dr Pierre Winter would surely have been regarded by many on board as a provocative presence, since both he and Le Corbusier had been closely associated with Georges Valois's right-wing *Faisceau* party formed in 1925 with an agenda based on hygiene, physical fitness and racial purity.[104] Declining to mention him by name in his memoir of CIAM 4, Giedion would refer to him only as 'a well-known French physician'. Perhaps the serried ranks of flailing windmills—so alarmingly captured by Moholy—reinforced Zervos's apprehensions about certain of Le Corbusier's theories. Since 1922 he had been actively promoting his 'Contemporary City' in any publication that would give it space; it was the lavish presentation of his proposed redevelopment of the heart of Paris at the 1925 Exposition des Arts Decoratifs that had brought the 38-year-old architect to the attention of the wider world. Le Corbusier describes his startling intervention in twentieth-century culture in apocalyptic terms:

> In 1922 I began to enter a dream which I can no longer leave: to live in a city of modern times! I made complete studies of a contemporary city of three million inhabitants. I created new dimensions, I perceived the essential joys:

> sky and trees as everybody's companions. Sun in the rooms, azure in the window, waves of green before me on waking in the city![105]

He would go to any length to publicise his utopian vision, which, he was convinced, would not only solve the functional deficiencies of the city but also improve the mental and physical health of its inhabitants, bringing in a regime of Harmony. The 'Contemporary City' was the basis of his interventions in the proceedings of the congress on board *Patris II* and since he knew precisely how it should be built, why waste time debating it further?

Giedion, as one of Le Corbusier's most devoted supporters, would also promote his urbanist theories in print. Working on an article for *Cahiers d'Art* in February 1932, he writes to Zervos, asking him at short notice if he can supply Atget photographs of the decaying *quartiers* of Paris or, failing that: 'Has M Lothar [*sic*] or one of your friends taken a photo of hovels around Paris? It should be: wooden huts, old packing cases serving as shelter'[106]—for Giedion an uncharacteristic choice of images, but presumably thought necessary to support Le Corbusier's thesis by contrast. Le Corbusier's theoretical city left nothing to chance; it had been worked out in great detail in terms of density, plot size, streets, traffic—and he meant it to be built exactly like that. As he wrote in *Urbanisme* in 1924, it should be organised as a mechanised industrial process directed by 'Ministries' having the authority of absolute monarchs of the past—as in the case of Louis XIV creating the Place Vendôme: 'The last great town planner in history,' when 'Paris was [...] nothing but an ant-heap, the fatal consequence of lack of order.... A network of overcrowded alleys.'[107] It had come to him, as he admitted, in a dream; nevertheless, he was insistent that 'we struggle against chance, against disorder, against a policy of drift and against the idleness which brings death; we strive for order which can be achieved only by appealing to what is the fundamental basis on which our minds can work: geometry'. And if the civil argument fails to impress the authorities, he will appeal to their horror of insurrection—and 'other': 'The city of to-day can no longer put up a military defence [because its gates—the railway stations—are in the centre]; its boundaries have become a confused and stifling zone comparable only to a camp of roving gypsies, who may have plumped their overcrowded caravans down anywhere'. We may imagine that Moholy, who had great respect for the culture of the *Roma*, was not overly impressed by this sentiment.

Zervos almost certainly had not fully grasped the seriousness of Le Corbusier's intentions until the two men found themselves in prolonged close company on the island cruise; now, in Le Corbusier's hectoring and appeals to Authority, he hears echoes of the crunch of jackboots as they advance inexorably across Europe. He is exasperated: as a Greek intellectual who has intentionally made Paris—at that time still centre of the universe of art—his home, he finds Le Corbusier's technocratic thesis supremely unappealing. Aside from his visceral resistance to the 'new political order' that implementation of the theory would require, Zervos regards the idea of starting from a scorched-earth *tabula rasa* ridiculous—perceiving the 'as found' fabric of Paris in the same sympathetic light as the cubists viewed the world of 'things'. As he would write of Max Ernst's *Jeu de constructions anthropomorphes* and the collages of Picasso and Braque: 'Since cubism we have often spoken of the beauty of the humblest or roughest [*frustes*] objects, of their plastic quality, of the possibility of expressing through them the dream which was uniquely the prerogative of the nobility.'[108]

We may imagine that as the day wore on the *compagnons* themselves began to feel like exiles; the tensions between them increasing as the urgency of rejoining the congress became more pressing. While the anxiety of van Eesteren and Giedion to regain control of affairs is palpable, Le Corbusier—mythologist and avid reader of Cervantes—must surely have been even more impatient to take leave of the island's woeful apparitions and once again brave the elements. Hubacher, meanwhile, continues to find engaging subject matter for his Leica among the smiling island children and gesticulating windmills. With his emphatic black screen Moholy signals that, for him, the carefree island adventure is at an end; documentary responsibilities reassert themselves, and he must conserve what film he has left for certain personalities and vignettes of life on the *Patris II* which have, so far, evaded the Kinamo. As the disconsolate group returned to the *Afros* that evening, the question was, *could* they make it back to Athens?

VII Moholy's letter to Sibyl

13 / VIII / 33

my dear sweet sibyl, h-a, i am all right, you must know letter writing on the boat demands a real decision, because in general one is extraordinarily focused animal-like on looking, loafing around and eating. but it is impossible that i do not answer your dear letters in detail, so love is the only force that drags me out of my passivity. the word 'passivity' doesn't apply to me at all, really. until now i've been working all day everyday. and yesterday it happened for the first time that i spent 3/4 hour in a deckchair without chasing after the various goings-on.

though actually this chase is worthwhile in itself; the day before yesterday i was able to show the—admittedly uncut—film in chronological sequence of shooting (apart from the island cruise, about which i want to tell you more later). people were delighted by the shots, understandably so, as the entire film is exclusively about 'family scenes', i.e., the congress at work, a bit on the passage through the isthmus canal and athens.

at the moment i'm taking a few metres of 'after' shots of heads that have not featured up till now etc; the island cruise—c. 130 m—hasn't been developed yet. early this morning on deck at half past six i filmed some of those in our group who, instead of being wrapped up in blankets, preferred*

**) the american speed of athenian development and copying was, of course, quite hard work but, in the end, people saw that i wasn't just running around mindlessly with my equipment*

13/VIII/33

meine liebe süsse sibyl, h-a, mir geht es gut, damit du es weisst.
das briefschreiben erfordert auf dem schiff einen wirklichen entschluss, weil man im allgemeinen ausserordentlich animalisch auf das sehen, herumlungern und essen eingestellt ist, doch ist es unmöglich, dass ich auf deine lieben briefe nicht ausführlich antworte, so ist die liebe die einzige kraft, die mich aus der passivität reisst.
das wort „passivität" passt eigentlich gar nicht auf mich, ich arbeitete bisjetzt die ganzen tage und gestern war es das erstemal, dass ich 3/4 stunde in einem liegestuhl, ohne den ereignissen nachzujagen, verbrachte.
an sich lohnte sich dieses jagen; ich konnte den (allerdings) ungeschnittenen-film in chronologischer folge der aufnahmen (ausser der inselfahrt, von der ich dir noch berichten will) vorgestern abend vorführen. die leute waren entzückt von den aufnahmen, was selbstverständlich ist; da der ganze film nur „familienszenen" enthielt, d.h. den kongress bei der arbeit, etwas von der durchfahrt im Isthmus-Kanal und athen. (bisjetzt nicht vorgekommene) jetzt mache ich einige meter nachaufnahmen von kippen etc. die inselfahrt – ca 130 m – noch nicht entwickelt *)
heute früh um ½ 7 nahm ich auf dem deck einige unserer leute auf, die es vorgezogen haben statt in decken

*) das amerikanische tempo der athener entwicklung + kopie hat mir ziemlich zu viel mühe gekostet. aber am ende sahen die leute, dass ich nicht nur [illegible]

to sleep in the open air.

incidentally, i have done this quite often myself on our island cruise, and if i could give a real portrayal, i would be very happy, because it was an unusual experience. imagine a small nutshell on a rough sea, manned by a captain, helmsman and several sailors, and 25 chosen guests of the congress, mostly french, who like to keep to themselves, and several swiss, dutch and greeks + me. there is sleeping space in the cabins for 6 people, all of the others must sleep on deck, or in the saloon (3 people). now look at the map of greece:

our journey began in piraeus with a calm sea to aegina; i rode up to the temple on a mule for the first time. we swam in a charming small bay and were viewed and greeted as miraculous creatures by the nicest, most naive inhabitants of the island. from aegina we went to poros, where we experienced the wonderful, simple, white architecture of the island by brilliant moonlight. the people white-wash their villages once a week; if emigrants from america, canada, etc. return on a wednesday, the playful young women, who are open to marriage, do not shy away from wielding the brush in the middle of the week. everything blazes with cleanliness. even the treads of the stairs are white, and on every tread there are only two specific places to step, hence permitted to become grey. the steps and large terraces are without railings, the houses are cubic, clear, sharp-edged, the

gehüllt, im freien zu schlafen.
das habe ich übrigens (selbst) ziemlich oft bei unserer inselfahrt
gemacht und (wenn) ich (darüber) die richtige schilderung geben könnte,
wäre ich ganz froh, weil das ein eigenartiges erlebnis war.
denk dir eine kleine nussschale auf stürmischem meere vor,
besetzt mit kapitän, steuermann und einigen matrosen, dazu
25 auserlesene gäste des kongresses, meist franzosen, die gern
untereinander bleiben und einige schweizer, holländer und
griechen + mich. platz zum schlafen gibt's in den kabinen
für 6 personen, alle andere müssen auf dem deck, oder im
salon (3 personen) schlafen.) jetzt schaue dir die karte von grie-
chenland an:
unsere reise ging (bei ruhigen see) in piräus an, nach ägina; das erstemal ritt ich (dort)
an einem maulesel zum tempel hinauf. wir badeten in einer
reizenden kleinen bucht und wurden von den nettesten, naiv-
sten einwohnern der insel, wie wundertiere besichtigt und
begrüsst. von ägina fuhren wir nach poros, wo wir im strah-
lendstem mondschein die wundervolle, einfache, weisse inselar-
chitektur erlebten. die leute (kalken) ~~streichen~~ ihre dörfer jede woche
~~[illegible]~~ einmal an; wenn auswanderer aus amerika, kanada
zw. schon (an) einem mittwoch zurückkommen, scheuen sich die heirats-
lustigen jungfrauen nicht, den pinsel auch in der wochenmitte zu
schwingen. alles blitzt vor sauberkeit, selbst die treppenstufen
sind weiss, und es gibt an jeder stufe nur zwei (bestimmte) stellen, die
betreten (also gran) werden dürfen. die treppen und grosse terrassen sind
ohne geländer, die häuser kubisch, klar, scharfkantig, die

numerous orthodox churches, like small baking ovens, according to old byzantine heritage in between. this white sharpness of the island architecture set with wonderful clarity on the hills, which we later encountered everywhere, was the greatest experience for me. also the vivid blue sea and the mostly red-brown, yellow-brown rocks.
of course, people belong to all these things. where there are few visitors, there they are simple and warm-hearted, without greed. pierre jeanneret, who was in the peloponnese, told of a shepherd, who had served him with goats milk and cheese, and whom he wanted to pay, did not want to accept money from him. 'money brings misfortune,' he said, and this shepherd was formerly a waiter in america. the island of santorini, which has a lot of visitor traffic, presented different customs. when we arrived after our visit to the island of seriphos, which also presented glorious architecture and wonderful smiling faces, we—20 to 25 people—were overrun by c. 200 mule drivers in order to force us into the saddle. the city of tiros [sic] *lies up on the mountain, and most tourists ride up there on the stairs. it is amazing what these animals are able to accomplish. in the most difficult places, steep, rocky, slippery, they trot—most of them stubbornly in front of their drivers, who are shouting fiercely and beating them with heavy sticks.*

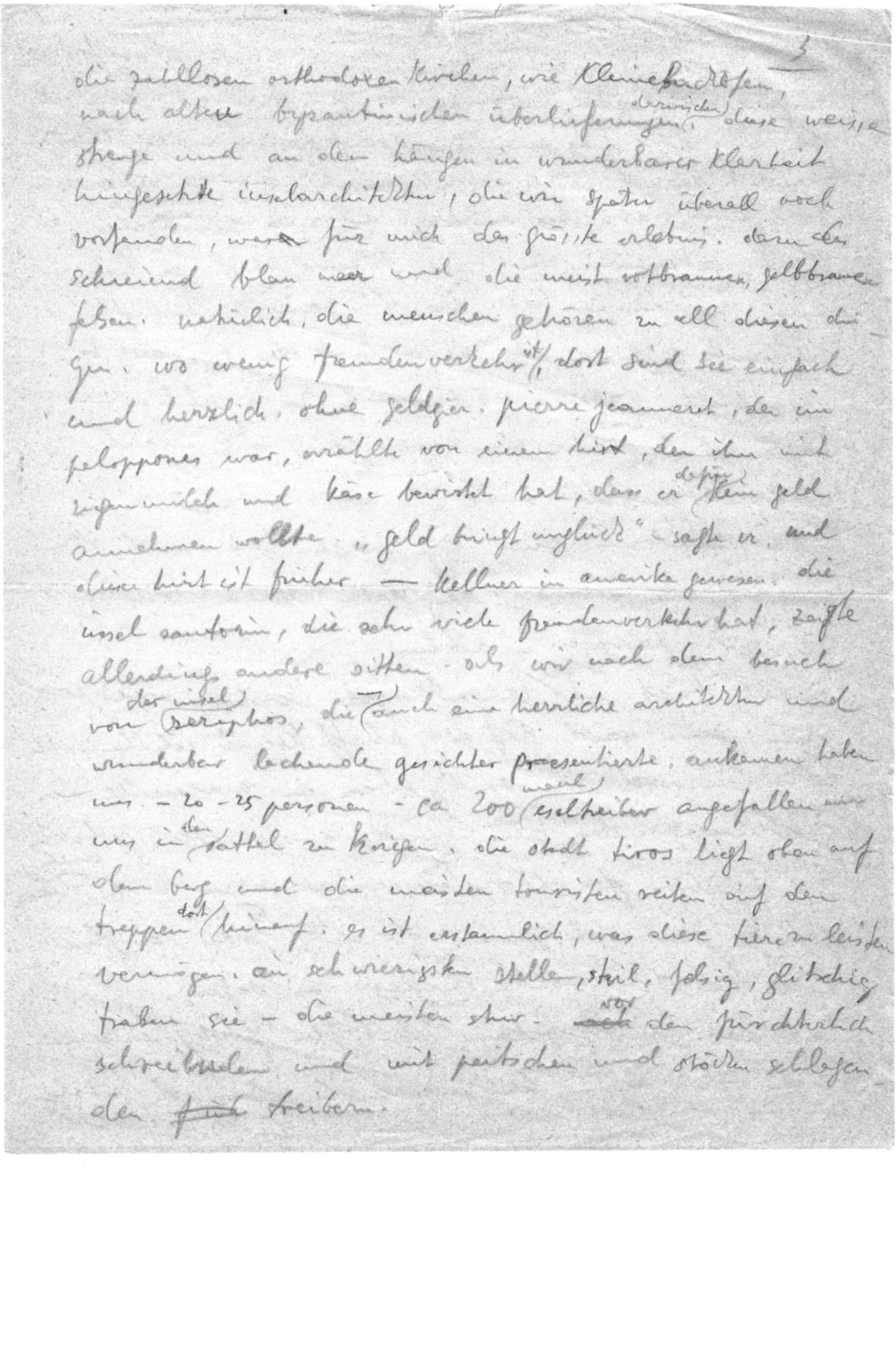

3

die zahllosen orthodoxen kirchen, wie kleine backöfen, nach alter byzantinischen überlieferungen, dazwischen diese weisse stiege und an den hängen in wunderbarer klarheit hingesetzte inselarchitektur, die wir später überall noch vorfanden, war für mich das grösste erlebnis. dazu das schreiend blau meer und die meist rotbraunen, gelbbraunen felsen. natürlich, die menschen gehören zu all diesen dingen. wo wenig fremdenverkehr ist, dort sind sie einfach und herzlich, ohne geldgier. pierre jeanneret, der im peloppones war, erzählte von einem hirt, der ihn mit ziegenmilch und käse bewirtet hat, dass er dafür kein geld annehmen wollte. „geld bringt unglück" sagte er. und dieser hirt ist früher – kellner in amerika gewesen. die insel santorin, die sehr viele fremdenverkehr hat, zeigte allerdings andere sitten. als wir nach dem besuch der insel seriphos, die auch eine herrliche architektur und wunderbar lachende gesichter praesentierte, ankamen haben uns – 20–25 personen – ca 200 maul eseltreiber angefallen, um uns in den sattel zu kriegen. die stadt firos liegt oben auf dem berg und die meisten touristen reiten auf den treppen dort hinauf. es ist erstaunlich, was diese tiere zu leisten vermögen. an schwierigsten stellen, steil, felsig, glitschig traben sie – die meisten stur – vor den fürchterlich schreienden und mit peitschen und stöcken schlagenden treibern.

but, dear, i didn't want to tell you so many geographical, ethnographical details. the entire letter—i can confess now at this point, is intended to describe my heroic deed—that i didn't get seasick. in short, at santorini a rather strong storm blew up, that had our little boat dancing around so much that the entire party became seasick. i—thanks to your despised vasano—survived two bad days and was one of the few that didn't get seasick.

from santorini we went to ios and from there to sounion, and then back to piraeus athens.

my letter should have been more long-winded as it will be now, but i couldn't finish it on-board ship and we have just arrived in marseille. getting on and off the boat belong to my most terrible memories, and also the present getting off just now is so tiring, that i am happy to just say adieu to you. on the boat (just now) i received a letter from mme de mandrot, that i should

aber liebe, ich wollte dir gar nicht so viele geographische, eth-
grafische einzelheiten mitteilen, der ganze brief – das kann ich
an dieser stelle nun eingestehen, darauf gerichtet, meine heldentat
– nämlich dass ich nicht seekrank geworden bin – zu schildern.
Kurz und gut, bei santorin ist ein ziemlicher
Sturm gekommen, der unser kleines schiff so hin-
und her tanzen liess, dass die ganze gesellschaft
seekrank geworden ist. ich – dank des von dir so
verachteten vasano – überstand zwei schlimme
tage und war unter den wenigen, die nicht
seekrank geworden sind.
von santorin sind wir nach ios und von
dort nach sunion gefahren, dann wieder
zurück piräus – athen.
mein brief ~~ist~~ sollte langatmiger werden, ~~als~~ er
nun sein wird. auf dem schiff konnte ich ihn nicht
beenden und wir sind eben in marseille an-
gekommen. das ein- und ausschiffen gehört
zu meinen furchtbarsten erinnerungen und auch das
jetzige verwundert einen derartig, dass ich glück-
lich bin dir noch adieu zu sagen.
Auf das schiff bekam ich (eben jetzt) einen
brief von mme de mandrot, dass ich noch

go to la sarraz for at least a week, but i prefer to stay in the area, although i don't have a penny left), because i would like to relax a bit. we will remain here today and possibly tomorrow, then we will tarry somewhere in the area with alvar aalto (from finland) and with s.g's. (of course, i will write you the address right away from the station). i can't write at all about business or studio matters, only one word about the american photo receipt: it's highly probable that it lies in the top or next to the top sheet metal drawer of the metal file cabinet near the studio door, or rather between the studio door and the drawing cabinet. all the photograph shipments are registered there. i believe this shipment went to pennsylvania, so pick out those papers!*

lucia—she wrote me to athens—would definitely like to speak with me before my return

**) i am awaiting a transfer here. hopefully it will work out*

wenigstens eine woche nach la sarraz fahren soll. aber ich ziehe es vor in der gegend zu bleiben, obwohl ich kein pfennig geld mehr habe*), weil ich mich etwas ausruhen möchte. wir bleiben heute und event. morgen noch hier, dann werden wir uns in der gegend irgendwo aufhalten. mit alvar aalto (aus finland) und mit s. g. s. (natürlich schreibe ich sofort von der station)

geschäftliches, ateliermässiges kann ich garnicht schreiben, nur wegen der amerikanischen fotoquittung ein wort; sie ist höchstwahrscheinlich in der obersten oder zweitobersten blechschublade des blechschrankes (neben der ateliertür, bzw. zwischen ateliertür und zeichenschrank. dort sind alle fotosendungen registriert. die sendung ist – glaube ich – nach pennsylvania gegangen, also diese papiere aussuchen!

lucia will mich – sie schrieb mir nach athen – <u>vor</u> meiner rückkehr unbedingt noch sprechen

*) ich erwarte hierher eine überweisung. hoffentlich klappt es damit

and suggested several different places for a rendezvous in different parts of the world (tyrol, ČSR, vienna; wherever i want).
i don't know at all if i should want this? i will go from here to sg.'s in zürich and will be back home around 1 sept. do you agree, my love? or should i come rather earlier? i need to know right away, how are you? the most reliable address for me is, and remains from now on until i tell you otherwise doldertal 7.

i kiss you, dear, sweet woman!

your

mü

till now, this journey—except for losing the suitcase—was wonderful, wonderful !!!

greet rose and marta, curjels and whoever else i should greet ..

und schlägt mir verschiedene rendezvous in verschiedenen weltteilen vor. (tirol, ČSR, wien; wo ich will.) ich weiss es gar nicht ob ich es wollen soll? ich fahre von hier nach zürich zu G.'s und bin 1. sept herum zu hause. bist du einverstanden liebes? oder soll ich schon eher kommen? ich möchte rasch wissen, wie es dir geht? die sicherste adresse ~~nachrichtenquelle~~ von mir ist und bleibt jetzt bis ich nicht anders mitteile doldertal 7.

ich küsse dich teuere, süsse frau!

dein

uri

dies reise war bisher – ausser dem kofferverlieren – wundervoll. wundervoll!!!

grüsse rose und marta, angela und wen ich grüssen muss.

VIII 'a good slice of art history might never have been written'

1 mythical immersion: Le Corbusier relives the tempestuous night voyage in Homeric terms

Perhaps a lull in the gale persuaded the captain to press on with the return; or was it that the sheltered port encouraged a false sense of security? However, no sooner had the feeble *vapeur* rounded the protecting cape than she was once again battling the *borías.* Extreme conditions which can be stomached in bright sunlight rapidly become woeful as the sun goes down. Writing about the experience in the comfort of his Zurich apartment some fifteen years later[109], Giedion remembered that

> the weather changed abruptly, and grew from storm to tempest. We made ourselves fast, but the waves crashed over the deck, drenching us to the skin and soaking our mattresses. The little ship could no longer answer the helm or reach the port we were making for. To avoid capsizing, we had to let it follow the wind. Through the howling gale I heard Fernand Léger, who was at the other end of the ship, bellowing like a lion at each fresh spasm of seasickness. My mattress was just above Corbusier's and throughout the night he kept repeating the same words: *'Ne me crachez pas dessus!'*

Having miraculously survived both Olympian expectorations and immersion in the realm of Poseidon, Le Corbusier would later relive the tempestuous night voyage north in Homeric terms. Perhaps he also recalled the legend of Theseus battling these seas as he fled Crete with his prize Ariadne—only to shamelessly abandon her to that notorious and disreputable deity Dionysus on the mountainous island glimpsed through the murk over to starboard: Naxos. Le Corbusier found in the turmoil, as he would later write,

> measure like the archer when he hits the bull's eye; measure, also, of the Cyclades pilot when the small regional storms blow up in full sun, blue sky, or full moon and sky full of stars; of those storms such as we had for two days when the three crewmen—pilot at the prow, captain on the bridge, helmsman at the wheel—played a game for the second watch, twice during forty-eight hours and without respite, playing 'chicken' with each wave.[110]

Afros lived up to her name *'sea-foam from the burst of waves'* with a vengeance; and as the waves broke over her, we imagine certain members of the company enquiring uneasily about her seaworthiness. Perhaps her master—who knew a thing or two, but out of loyalty to Embirikos refuses to say very much—lets slip that 'she' had had many lives:[111] built by the Norwegians in 1911 to earn a hard living as one of a fleet of similar whale-catchers in both Arctic and Antarctic oceans; transformed into a French gunboat off the Brittany coast in the Great War, and in peacetime sold again as lowly bunkering tender delivering steam coal for a British line in the port of Piraeus. Embirikos, surrealist poet, psychoanalyst and optimist, had bought her for a song in 1928 to be converted into his private yacht; thus was explained the vestigial heavy-duty gear on the foredeck. But would the master also admit that in their whaling days these ungainly vessels were known for their tendency to *founder* in steep seas?

None of this fazes Moholy. He's a survivor, and ... wasn't the Berlin gallery that first brought him success called *Der Sturm*? He seems to have kept his good-humoured composure throughout, continuing his report to Sibyl:

> *... i didn't want to tell you so many geographical, ethnographical details. the entire letter—i can confess now at this point, is intended to describe my heroic deed—that i didn't get seasick. in short, at santorini a rather strong*

storm blew up, that had our little boat dancing around so much that the entire party became seasick. i—thanks to your despised vasano—survived two bad days and was one of the few that didn't get seasick.

At some point early on Wednesday, 9 August, the *Afros* made it to less stormy waters closer to the mainland. Hubacher photographed the crew members on the bridge, FIG. 43 their stoical expressions betraying the merest flicker of relief, while Ghika, as if to celebrate their delivery from the bursting waves immortalises an intriguing vignette that survives in his archive as a single torn print. FIG. 44 If we include the photographer and two members of the *Afros* crew who gather up and furl the now-redundant canvas awning, there are six players. Anchoring the shot, back to the camera and hunched under his flat cap, is the ubiquitous Léger: we can almost hear his grumpy *Why did I ever leave Normandy?* Beyond him and to the right, we recognise Le Corbusier huddled in a waterproof, apparently absorbed in watching the seamen at work, while plumb centre in Ghika's composition is a young man whose wildly flying locks suggest a mildly mischievous Medusa. Not an entirely inappropriate analogy, since he is Gaston Bonheur, 20-year-old poet and songwriter and, around this time, founder of a provocative surrealist review—*Choc.* Native of Languedoc and fluent in the regional language, Occitan, we conjecture that he and Le Corbusier have found common ground in their heretical Cathar roots, their close proximity also implying that, by this stage of the voyage, Le Corbusier has overcome any aversion he may have had to surrealism. Bonheur and fellow surrealist poet Pierre Guéguen, also on board, constitute the entire editorial staff of *14 rue du Dragon* and since Le Corbusier would remain friends with both poets—it was Guéguen who would later introduce him to the wild rockscapes of his native Brittany—we conclude that if there

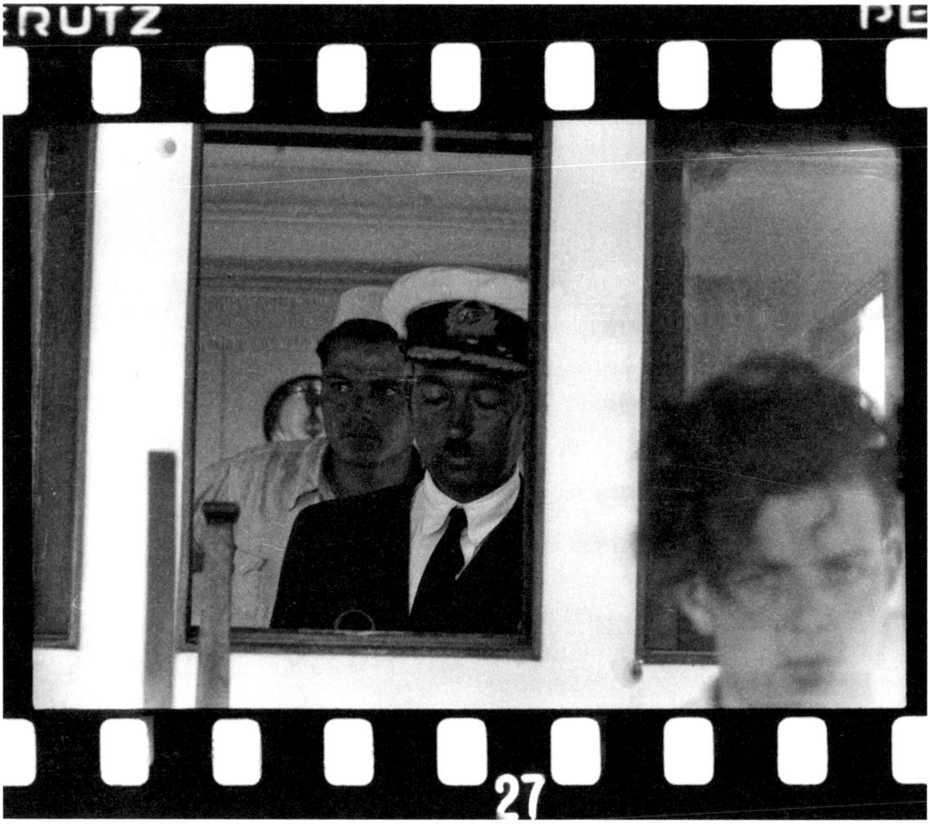

43 *Afros* captain and crew members on the bridge Photo by Carlo Hubacher

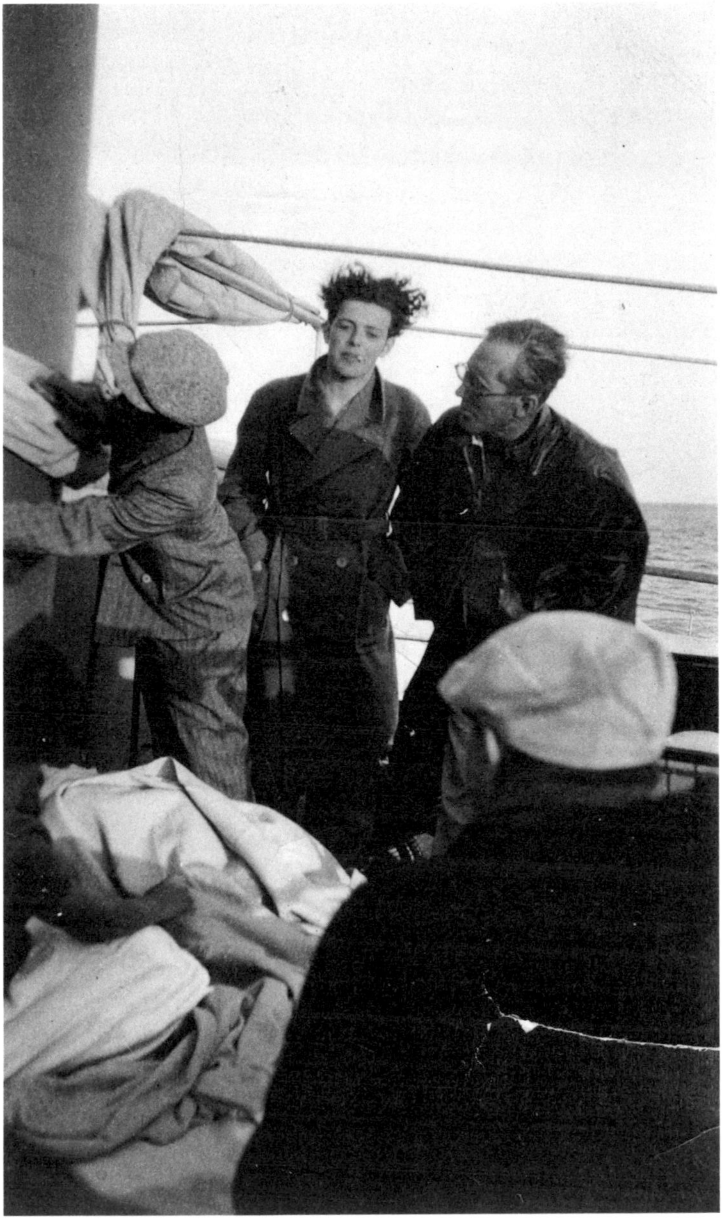

44 Léger (back to camera), Le Corbusier, Bonheur and crew members on the upper deck of *Afros* after the storm Photo by Ghika

really *was* a *brouille* with Zervos, it was limited to architectural matters.

Later that morning the party from *Afros* landed on the beach below the Temple of Poseidon at Cape Sounion; the significance would not have been lost on Le Corbusier, who would surely have imagined this spot as the Ithaca that had so nearly eluded them. Giedion later reflected, no doubt with a nod to the sea-god, 'Had the ship foundered during the night a good slice of art history might never have been written.'[112] The *gesellschaft* of Saturday afternoon, now a *gemeinschaft* of intrepid survivors—albeit flawed by the cracks of certain *brouilles*—dried off their equipment and possessions while recovering their equilibrium. Presumably they were then chauffeured back to Athens in the fleet of large American automobiles we have seen earlier in Moholy's film. There they would rejoin the congress for one more day of discussions before their departure from Piraeus on the Friday. FIG. 45

2 after the party: Moholy scrambles to complete his letter while the CIAM agenda begins to seem somewhat distant

Emerging from the 'film within', Moholy returns to the main documentary with the title *The Return Voyage*, panning over a large crowd gathered on the Piraeus dockside to wave off the visitors. It is an emotional parting; some among the crowd running along the quay after the *Patris II* as she picks up speed and heads towards the open sea. Anticipating an uncertain future,[113] the Greek representatives of CIAM are anxious to maintain contact with the departing visitors who already seem like charmed personages. Moholy is back in theatrical Eisenstein territory: he cuts unsentimentally to an intimate evening sequence in which a gramophone is set up on deck, wound up, and a pile of records played to the surrounding passengers. A small boy is enthralled as the machine emits sounds which we can only

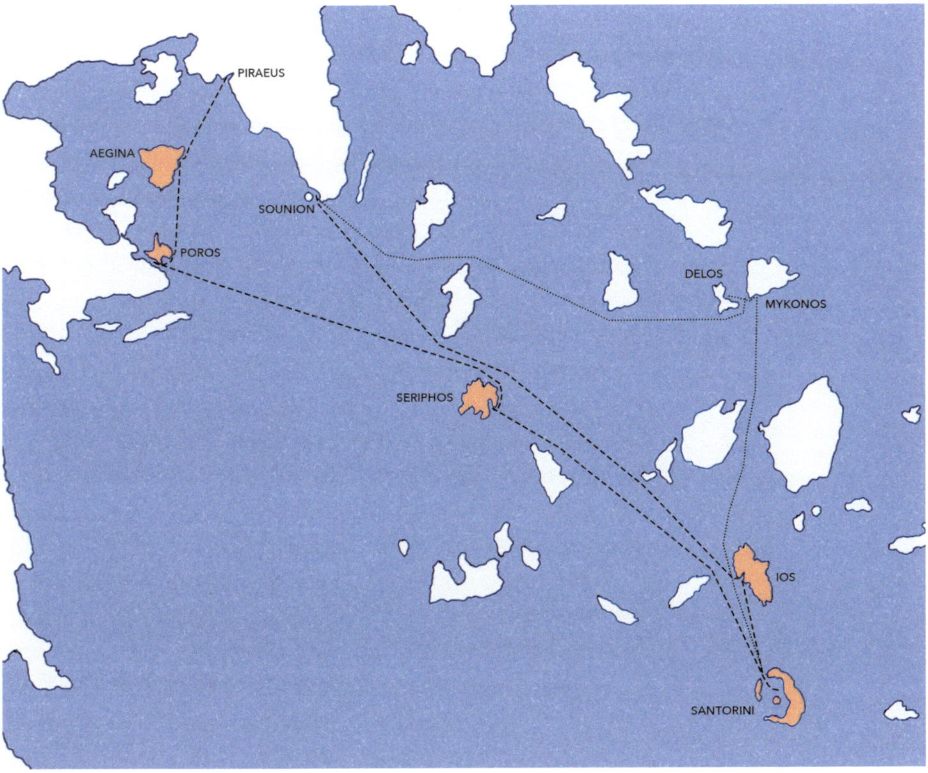

45 Course of the *Afros.* The cruise party sailed from Piraeus on the afternoon of Saturday, 5 August 1933, calling first at Aegina and Poros. They called at Serifos on Sunday, 6 August, and Santorini on Monday, 7 August. The intention was to then sail directly to Delos and Mykonos; however, this leg of the cruise had to be aborted due to the storm, and Tuesday was spent sheltering on Ios. The cruise party eventually landed on the beach below the temple of Poseidon at Cape Sounion on Wednesday morning, 9 August. Drawing by the authors

imagine. FIG. 46 Albert Jeanneret and his younger brother had a passion for what we would now call 'world music', and they had left Athens with an armful of records of Greek *rebetiko.* In launching these exotic *modes* into the night air they imagine themselves prolonging the spell of the islands.

During the two shipboard days that follow, Moholy films the congressists as they wake from painful nights curled up in deck chairs, while secretaries are seen urgently typing up the numerous minutes and resolutions. He snatches a few minutes to continue his report to Sibyl:

> *... i am all right, you must know letter writing on the boat demands a real decision, because in general one is extraordinarily focused animal-like on looking, loafing around and eating. but it is impossible that i do not answer your dear letters in detail, so love is the only force that drags me out of my passivity. the word 'passivity' doesn't apply to me at all, really. until now i've been working all day everyday. and yesterday it happened for the first time that i spent 3/4 hour in a deckchair without chasing after the various goings-on. / though actually this chase is worthwhile in itself; the day before yesterday i was able to show the—admittedly uncut—film in chronological sequence of shooting (apart from the island cruise, about which i want to tell you more later). people were delighted by the shots, understandably so, as the entire film is exclusively about 'family scenes', i.e., the congress at work, a bit on the passage through the isthmus canal and athens. / at the moment i'm taking a few metres of 'after' shots of heads that have not featured up till now etc; the island cruise—c. 130 m—hasn't been developed yet.**

And with his asterisk he explains,

> *the american speed of athenian development and copying was, of course, quite hard work but, in the end, people*

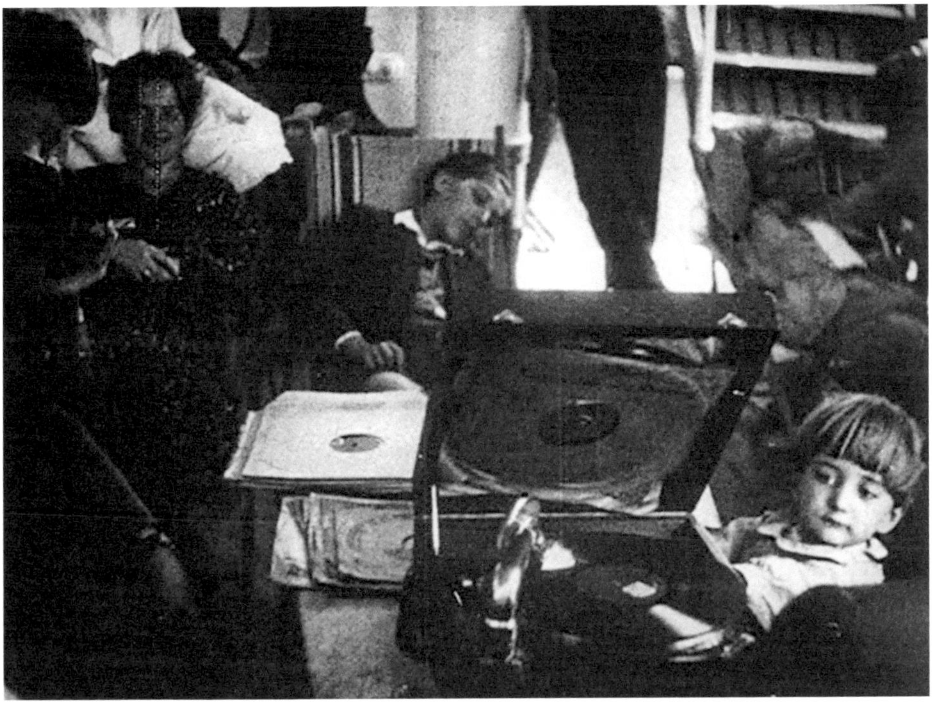

46 On the return voyage Moholy films some of the Greek passengers listening to records being played on a wind-up gramophone. Le Corbusier would later write, 'Albert Jeanneret, purest of musicians who, through the magic of twenty gramophone records, reassembles profoundly suffering souls on the bridge of the *Patris II* [...] releasing on the calm of the night the hollers and cries [...] of the peasants of Epirus or the Peloponnese.'

> *saw that i wasn't just running around mindlessly with my equipment*
>
> *early this morning on deck at half past six i filmed some of those in our group who [...] preferred to sleep in the open air. / Incidentally, i have done this quite often myself on our island cruise, and if i could give a real portrayal, i would be very happy, because it was an unusual experience.*

But to over divulge details at this stage, Moholy realises, would detract from his enthusiasm for the whole adventure; and as for the cruise footage—still 'in the can'—that will need inspired editing ...

Ultimately Moholy will edit his *'after' shots; heads etc.* into a few seconds of running time as the voyage of *Patris II* nears its end. He focuses on animated discussions between friends who seem anxious to make the most of these last few hours—it may be years before they meet again ... There's a close-up of Aalto's face betraying the exhaustion of last-minute deadlines followed by a frantic dash by plane and train from Helsinki, via Warsaw, Budapest and Thessaloniki[114]—just in time to spend one day in Athens before the departure from Piraeus. Moholy reveals a toothy Badovici darkly silhouetted against the horizon, followed by a close-up of a jovial Zervos deep in conversation. The final vignette has Pierre Jeanneret—Le Corbusier's cousin and technical partner—in earnest conversation with Badovici's gamine companion 'Mado' Goisot, while Léger turns his back to the camera. As Le Corbusier enters the frame, the mood palpably stiffens; we remember that while the others were cruising the islands, Pierre Jeanneret had hiked across the Peloponnese with Le Corbusier's indispensable collaborator Charlotte Perriand. There are accounts of strange and unusual experiences to be exchanged, of course—but perhaps Moholy is also subtly reminding us that there are aspects of life that even a famous architect cannot control. At this point the title *Marseille again* abruptly appears: soon we're passing factories and warehouses—and *Architects' Congress* concludes, as it began, with the daring *Pont Transbordeur* soaring high above the old port.

Filming complete, Moholy scrambles to finish his letter to Sibyl before disembarking:

> *my letter should have been more long-winded as it will be now, but i couldn't finish it on-board ship and we have just arrived in marseille. getting on and off the boat belong to my most terrible memories, and also the present getting off just now is so tiring, that i am happy to just say adieu to you. on the boat (just now) i received a letter from mme de mandrot, that i should go to la sarraz for at least a week, but i prefer to stay in the area, although i don't have a penny left*), because i would like to relax a bit.*

He is expecting a transfer and must go to the post office to check if it has arrived.

> *we will remain here today and possibly tomorrow, then we will tarry somewhere in the area with alvar aalto* [...] *and with s.g's.* [Sigfried and Carola Giedion].... *lucia—she wrote me to athens—would definitely like to speak with me before my return and suggested several different places for a rendezvous in different parts of the world (tyrol, ČSR, vienna; wherever i want).*

If his first wife, who lent him her camera, feels compelled to speak to him, it is probably to alert him to recent developments in Berlin and insist that now he really *must* make plans—but *i don't know at all if i should want this?* It appears that, in emphatically framing his penultimate sentence to Sibyl, his thoughts are still 'at sea': *till now, this journey—except for losing the suitcase—was wonderful, wonderful!!!* **FIG. 47**

Mme Hélène de Mandrot, owner of the Chateau of La Sarraz and sponsor of the first CIAM meetings, expects a report

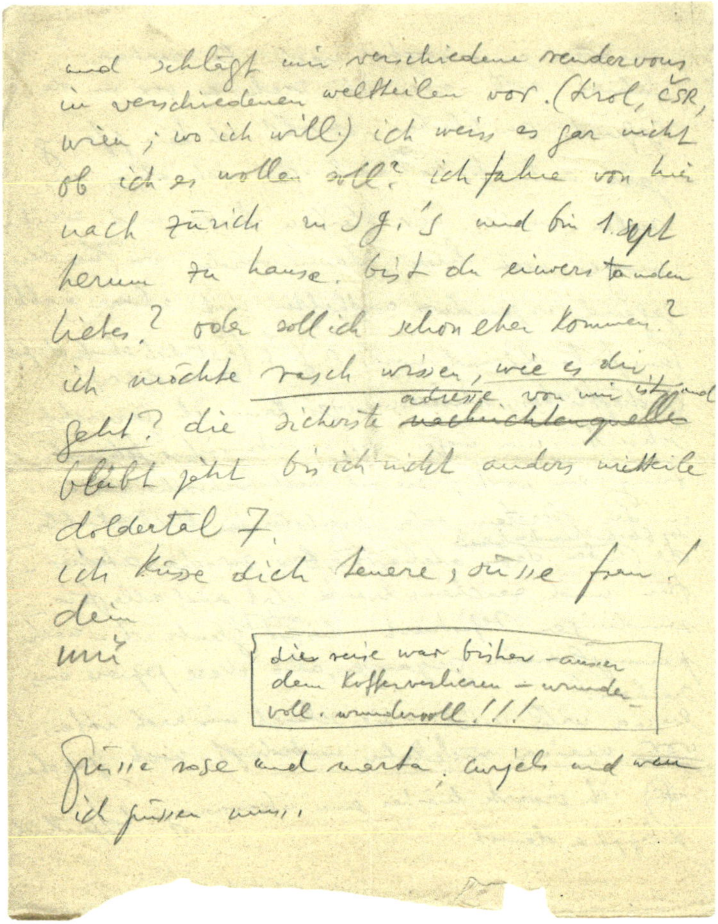
und schlägt mir verschiedene rendezvous
in verschiedenen weltteilen vor. (tirol, ČSR,
wien; wo ich will.) ich weiss es gar nicht
ob ich es wollen soll? ich fahre von hier
nach zürich zu g.'s und bin 1. sept
herum zu hause. bist du einverstanden
liebes? oder soll ich schon eher kommen?
ich möchte rasch wissen, wie es dir
geht? die sicherste ~~nachrichtenquelle~~ adresse von mir irgendwo
bleibt jetzt bis ich nicht anders mitteile
doldertal 7.
ich küsse dich teuere, süsse frau!
dein
mi

dies reise war bisher – ausser dem kofferverlieren – wundervoll. wundervoll!!!

grüsse rose und marta, angela und wen ich grüssen muss.

47 The last page of Moholy's six-page letter to Sibyl, which he scrambled to complete in the minutes before disembarking from the *Patris II* at Marseille.

on the congress; after their Greek epiphany, however, neither Giedion nor Moholy are inclined to comply. To keep a hold on the precious *mode* they must find a calm refuge, well away from meetings and manoeuvrings, where they can think things over. The agenda for CIAM 4 had been 'The Functional City', but that seems somewhat distant now; as Giedion would write,

> These problems of the subconscious became fully clear only after the conference was over. They were a development of the purely functional tendencies in architecture toward a greater inclusiveness of the elements, aesthetic, social, biologic. The full evaluation of this new, independent platform had been helped immeasurably through the contact with the past and our Hellenic heritage.[115]

3 *sachlich* deformation: impetuous kick scores unexpected revelation

It appears that Le Corbusier was confronting crises of a practical nature at this point in time;[116] perhaps his cousin had updated him on some of them during their meeting on the return voyage. Ultimately, he would leave it to Pierre Jeanneret, as technical partner, to resolve these tedious matters while he re-established that part of his personality which preferred to paint and have poetic thoughts. In September 1933 *L'Architecture d'aujourd'hui* publishes a special double issue comprehensively reviewing his *oeuvre* so far. With such ambitious projects as the League of Nations in Geneva, the Palace of the Soviets and the Centrosoyuz Headquarters in Moscow—in addition to a portfolio of exceptional and justly celebrated individual houses—he is, beyond doubt, the most important architect of his generation. Nevertheless, there are persuasive dissenting voices, and he feels sufficiently stung by one in particular to make a stand; thus, in the same issue he reprints a lengthy 'credo': 'In Defence of Architecture'. This had originally been written in 1929 for the

Czech journal *Stavba* with a dedication, significantly, 'to Alexander Vesnin, founder of "Constructivism"'.

Adopting a self-consciously discursive literary mode, Le Corbusier defends his project for the Mundaneum, the 'world city' project intended for Geneva which had been commissioned by the Belgian peace activists and pioneers of information science Paul Otlet and Henri La Fontaine. Anticipating the internet by half a century, the Mundaneum was conceived as a documentation centre for the world's ever-expanding knowledge, and Le Corbusier had seized on the 'Museum of Knowledge' element of the plan as a unique opportunity to develop his revolutionary *Musée à croissance illimitée* concept. To Le Corbusier it was self-evident that such a significant building type should be dramatised in 'constructivist' manner; thus, he expressed the Museum as a spiral pyramid raised on pilotis. The austere Karel Teige, however—arch-functionalist and ally of Hannes Meyer—insisted that such unrestrained architectural rhetoric was proof of Le Corbusier's bourgeois romanticism; his a priori 'harmonious' forms, leading inevitably to academicism, ipso facto could not be objectively functional—or *sachlich,* to use the more seductive German term.

It's a provocation familiar to 'poets of architecture' and levelled, in this case, by a vocal representative of those non-attendees of CIAM 4—German-speakers in the main—who viewed the voyage to Greece as an escape from reality. Le Corbusier accuses Teige of

> playing hide-and-seek with words. If one deprives words of their meaning, no further dialogue is possible, and confusion results. In your case, it is [the] dilettantism of a new romanticism, a romanticism of the machine. With the others (the practitioners), it is a police measure which is perhaps opportune (blinkers to keep people from losing their way, or better, blinkers with which to fix the eyes of the masses,

48 Le Corbusier's didactic sketch of the waste basket in his studio with '*sachlich* improvement' by Alfred Roth. From *L'Architecture d'aujourd'hui* (September 1933).

> so that they can be pushed like a flock of sheep into a new adventure with which they are not yet comfortable [...].[117]

To demonstrate the absurdity of Teige's 'hide-and-seek', Le Corbusier recounts how, when the Mundaneum drawings had been completed,

> there was a minor revolt in our studio. The younger members of the group criticised the pyramid.... On other drawing boards, the drawings of the Centrosoyuz for Moscow were being finished and had received everyone's approval. They were reassuring because that scheme was clearly a rational problem of an office building. Nevertheless, the Mundaneum and the Centrosoyuz both emerged from our heads during the same month of June. / All of a sudden the decisive argument popped out of someone's mouth: 'what is useful is beautiful!' At the same moment Alfred Roth (of such impetuous temperament) kicked in the side of a wire mesh wastebasket which couldn't hold the quantity of old drawings he was trying to stuff in. FIG. 48 Under Roth's energetic pressure, this wastebasket, which had a technically *sachlich* curvature (a direct expression of the wire netting), deformed and took on the appearance shown in the sketch. Everyone in the office roared. 'It's awful!' said Roth. 'Ah, but this basket now contains much more,' I replied; 'it is more useful, so we could say it is more beautiful! Be consistent with your principles!'

On his return to Paris from CIAM 4, Le Corbusier would surely have been intent on finally moving from his cramped apartment at 20 Rue Jacob on the Left Bank to the spacious new rooftop studio and apartment under construction at Porte Molitor,[118] which would, in his imagination, represent a fragment for demonstration purposes of his 'Ville Radieuse'—the final expression of the 'Contemporary City'. Yvonne Le Corbusier, however, was

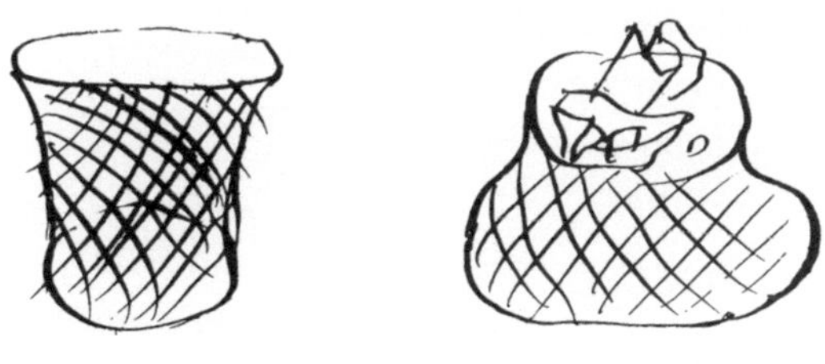

less enthusiastic and must have been delighted that progress at Porte Molitor was so slow. At this point in time, and with the economy deep in depression, several of the contractors involved were bankrupt; worse—from Le Corbusier's point of view—few of the apartments had sold, and he was compelled to enter into a risky deal to procure additional finance. When the move was at last made, late in 1934, Le Corbusier could instal himself in the famous vaulted studio with rough limestone masonry party wall. Ghika was perhaps wide of the mark in writing, 'It was charming, unexpected and quaint. It had been inspired by the houses on Santorini, of which I did not hesitate to remind him.'[119] The truth is that Le Corbusier had long been intrigued by the possibilities of vaults and had possibly seen photographs of Santorini architecture years earlier; however, section drawings of the Porte Molitor block demonstrate that the harmonious form was also an ingenious solution to the stringent Paris building regulations intended to preserve daylight at street level, thus perhaps qualifying—even in Teige's severe terms—as *sachlich.* The asymmetric vaults of the rooftop studio carry echoes of the deformed waste basket, and we can imagine Le Corbusier and Roth having a chuckle over this during their sojourn on Santorini.

4 Zervos's agenda absorbed and new interest in 'archaism'

Le Corbusier would return to the archaic mode that had been advocated by Zervos at the outset of the island cruise in a text titled 'Explications'.[120] This appears alongside *témoignages* by Pierre Guéguen, Fernand Léger, Gaston Bonheur, Amédée Ozenfant and the critic Maurice Raynal—all of whom had been members of the group on the *Afros* who 'liked to keep to themselves'—in *L'Art en Grèce.* The sumptuous large-format volume, published by Zervos on New Year's Day 1934, FIG. 49, 50 carries high-quality black-and-white photographs of pre-classical Greek art, Zervos insisting that only works which remained in Greece—and could therefore be seen in Greek light—should be shown. Thus, we see exquisite Bronze Age Cycladic marble figurines and the enigmatic ceramic vessels that are now misnamed 'frying pans', a number of *korai* and *kouroi* including the famous *Moschophoros* from the Acropolis Museum. In his introduction, Zervos presents a perceptive analysis of themes that had become fundamental to this group during their 'odyssey' in the Cyclades, focusing in particular on the plastic preoccupations of the generation of the 'modern spirit' vis-à-vis the arts described at that time as 'primitive'.

Since Zervos has dedicated *L'Art en Grèce* 'to the 4th Congress of Modern Architecture' whose theme was urbanism, he takes the opportunity to remind the Western architects of the

> profound lesson from Greek art which profits our generation, importuned on all sides by confused and contradictory ideas. / It is a question of confidence [...] in that collective consciousness which had produced miraculous results in Greece. From its formation Hellenism has, in fact, shown itself to be concerned to elaborate a collective conscience and take root solidly among the masses. More than any other part of the world, Greek cities, in particular those where the principles of necessity and liberty were harmoniously combined, had opened up very broad ways for development of the personality.... As long as Greece knew how to achieve victory over the isolated limitations of the individual, its personality retained its full value... Some Greek cities produced much more powerful and complete personalities than those of the big cities of the western Mediterranean where the individual was totally separated from the collective. [Conversely,] with the development of Renaissance spirit, the antagonism between the individual and the collective is accentuated. All the levers of command, on the

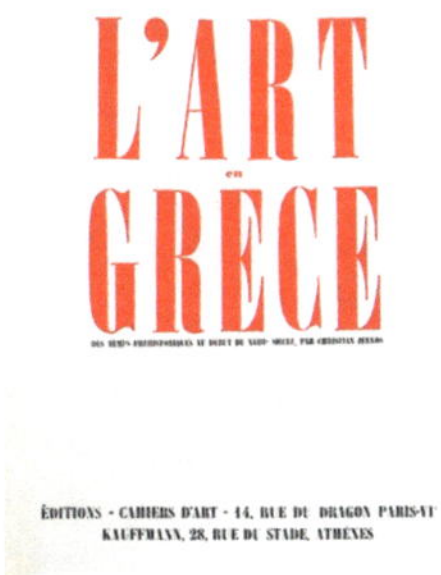

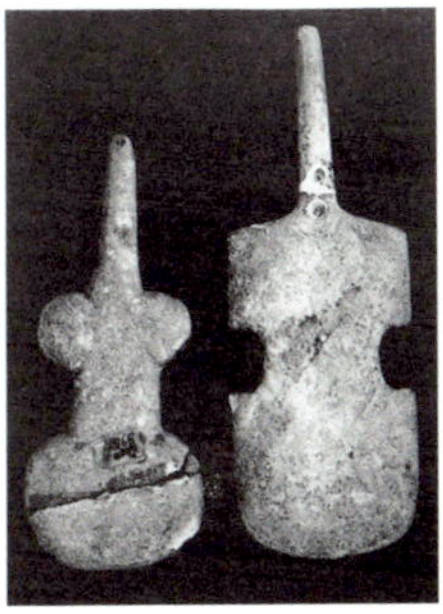

49 Title page of *L'Art en Grèce,* the luxurious *hommage* to CIAM 4 published by Christian Zervos on New Year's Day, 1934

50 Page from *L'Art en Grèce*, with image of Neolithic Cycladic 'violin form' figurines

> spiritual plane as much as the plane of action, are held by individuals filled with profound desires, insatiable appetites, violent passions—voluntarily detached from the masses, and consequently deprived of the freshness which could offer them yet unexploited strengths.

Finally, there was the contact and communion with a Greek art which issued directly from the landscape and the exceptional plastic atmosphere created in the plains, mountains, sea and islands under the 'inconceivable' Greek light. Greek works of art, integrating the felicitous geometry of nature and bathed in a pure light 'appearing not just as a miracle of the human spirit, but as a fragment of life linked to the ensemble of the universe'. Here Zervos is articulating similar thoughts to those of Pikionis in his August 1933 *Technica Chronica* article. He had returned to Athens early in September, staying on until November while working closely with Ghika on the images for *L'Art en Grèce.* Ghika and Pikionis were close friends, subsequently teaching together at the Polytechnic for many years; thus, a critical response, independent of both the rationalist findings of CIAM 4 and the authoritarian 'Greekness' advocated by Tombros, must have been discussed during those months. However, the regenerative influence on European architecture of these potent ideas would only become apparent after the turmoil of the 1930s and 1940s had subsided.

In the months following CIAM 4, Le Corbusier began to interpret 'archaic spirit' through an idiosyncratic mix of Homeric and Rabelaisian mythological images in which he imagined himself playing a central role:

> For 2,000 years Greece has been masked with a false sign: static, philosophising philosophy, Corinthian fluting, white eyes, limbs of ice, noble *peplum* and arm upraised under the peristyles, impassiveness or petrified drama: *white sign. /*

51 Double-page spread from Le Corbusier and Pierre Jeanneret *Oeuvre Complète, 1934–1938*, with photographs of the exhibition titled *Les Arts primitifs dans la maison d'aujourd'hui*, installed in Le Corbusier's recently-completed apartment and studio at Porte Molitor

> We of the 4th Congress of CIAM have marked Greece with a *red sign* and have breathed, nosed-out, strolled about, found intact again on the islands and evident in the ruins the pulse of life with its immanent drama: initiative, agility, speed, acuity. / Corneillian dilemma, white sign! Such is the mark of received lessons. Our notion: rather Rabelaisian—but yes—with Aeschylus at one of the extremities.... And yes! this land whose reality is a contour measured like the abscissa drawn on the sea's horizon, this land can only be that of *true measures.* Guéguen—poet, at Aegina or Marathon—hears the song of the pine needles and combines it with the Corneillian theme of the acanthus; that acanthus which we saw nowhere except on the capitals which it in no way puts in order. Albert Jeanneret, purest of musicians who, through the magic of twenty gramophone records, reassembles profoundly suffering souls on the bridge of the Patris II on the return voyage, releasing on the calm of the night the hollers and cries—or healthy and robust gaiety—of the peasants of Epirus or the Peloponnese.[121]

While, in 1923, the youthfully heroic author of *Vers une Architecture* had insisted that Greek art and architecture were a 'pure creation of the spirit', he now reveals in the didactic exhortations of 'Explications' the more nuanced viewpoint that he had acquired in the company of Zervos. Greece is still the land of 'precise proportions', but it is also a land of *archaics* having a sense of the cosmic and a measure of the abyss that separates human work from that of fate; 'Greece is a land which had heroes and created gods.'

Le Corbusier's rediscovered interest in 'archaism' and the small scale is demonstrated in his contribution to an exhibition titled *Les arts primitifs dans la maison d'aujourd'hui*, FIG. 51 which he organised with his new neighbour, the art dealer Louis Carré, and installed in the Porte Molitor penthouse in 1935.[122]

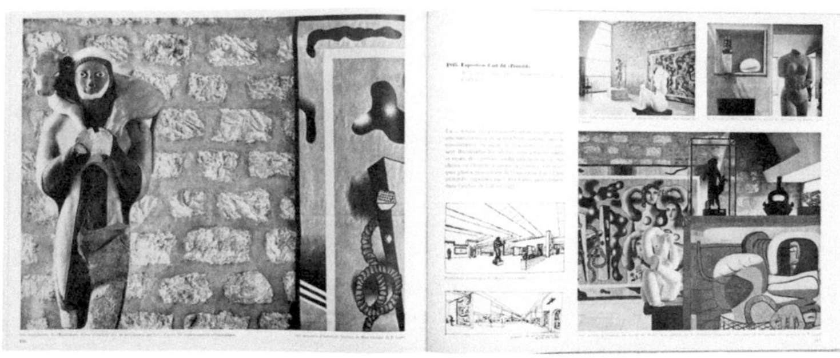

The published photographs of the exhibition are carefully composed to emphasise a felicitous concordance between the modernity of the architecture—which nevertheless also evokes the timeless vaults and masonry of the islands—and the primal energies of the art. Le Corbusier's main contribution, evoking his August morning eulogy to Greek colour on the Piraeus *paralía,* was a polychromed copy of *Moschophoros*—the celebrated early 6th century BCE sculpture of a *kouros* bearing a calf on his shoulders. In preparing this exhibit, he had consulted the curators at the Louvre for a guide to the intense colouration that the archaicera sculptor, like the sculptors of the Cycladic figurines before him, might have employed.

Greek light and 'archaic spirit' would begin to enter European cultural discourse later in the decade as an antidote to the malign atmosphere fomented by the relentless advance of 'dark powers'. Though the bulk of the 1934–38 volume of Le Corbusier's *Oeuvre Complète* is taken up with ambitious city plans relying on technology in the functionally zoned CIAM format, there are significant exceptions. A *primitiviste* vacation house in Brittany known as the 'Maison au Mathes', and an elemental 'Maison de Weekend' built in rustic masonry and with concrete vaults, stand out against the rationalist formulae. The latter small house, as Max Bill wrote in his editorial introduction,

> is as much part of the landscape as a hill or hollow: it has grass all round it and on the roof.... The result is the effect of naturalness without any suggestion of the romantic. The essentially human quality which comes out in these small creations is the best answer to the accusations of inhumanity and over-scaling which are levelled against his big projects.[123]

In the latter half of the 1930s, as war-clouds gathered, Le Corbusier—together with such modernists as Georges Bataille,

Jean Cocteau, Fernand Léger, Michel Leiris, Raymond Queneau, Roger Vitrac and Marguerite Yourcenar—contributed articles to the review *Le Voyage en Grèce* published from 1934 to 1939 by Ioannides's Neptos agency. Ioannides, the bohemian 'traveller without baggage' engaged his friend Tériade FIG. 52 as art editor, thus establishing a direct connection with the sumptuous surrealist magazine *Minotaure* founded by Tériade and Albert Skira in 1933. The primary purpose of *Le Voyage en Grèce* was, of course, to promote high-end tourism to Greece, and perhaps Le Corbusier's three contributions should be read in this light. Nevertheless, the Ioannides-Tériade duo also had a political agenda, combining surrealism with a commitment to the extreme left; thus the juxtaposition of Le Corbusier and Giorgio de Chirico on a two-page spread in the first—Spring / Summer 1934 issue FIG. 53, 54—generates a certain electrical charge.[124] The Greek-born de Chirico, who had known Pikionis since they had been students together at the Polytechnic in 1904, contributes the fantastical account of a night spent on the Acropolis, closing with an image of the sacred rock as a ship drifting away on a sea of mist that has obliterated the city of men. In *Point de Départ,* on the other hand, Le Corbusier is in didactic mode. Rather than 'drifting away', he urges his readers to promptly pack their bags: 'The insatiable machine dominates us; it is preparing to make a banal subspecies of us.... Life has been forgotten: intensity, fire, joy, violence and laughter.' Claiming that he desires 'to return there often', he insists

> that every man who is in love with life, tortured by the slow shipwreck of conscience in the tempest of early mechanisation, should embark at Marseilles and head for Greece.... It is there that is the point of departure for our Occident. It is, in an exceptional simplicity (still intact today), an integration of design with the landscape, quality of light, adequate vestiges of a human civilisation, earth, sun and ourselves.

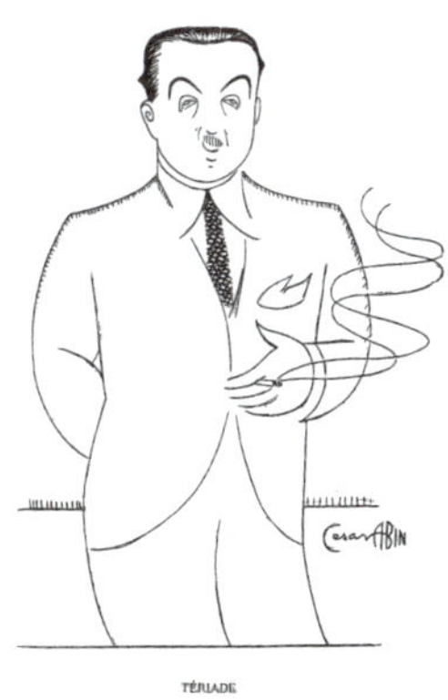

César Abin, 1932 caricature of Tériade (Stratis efteriades), fine-art publisher and art editor of oth *Minotaure* and *Voyage en Grèce*. From *Leurs gures*, with commentary by Maurice Raynal

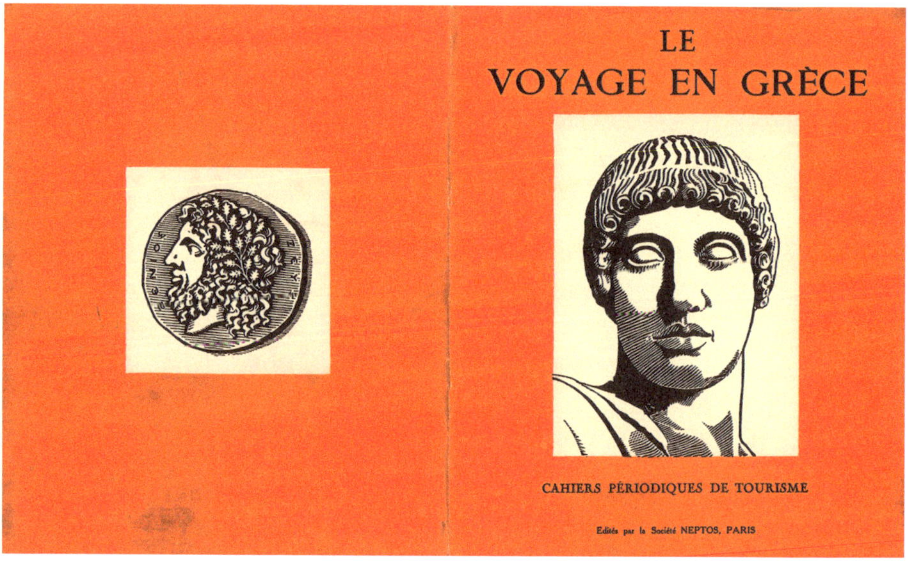

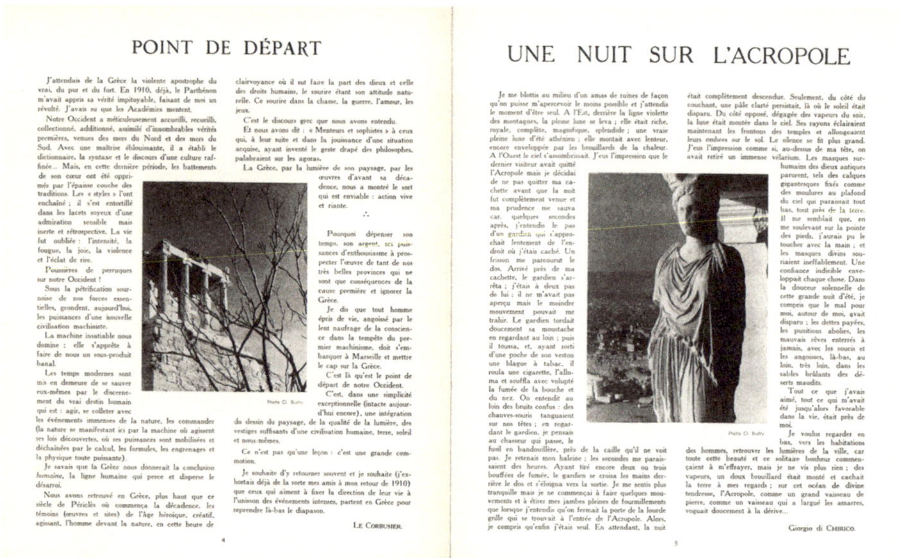

53 Cover of the first, Spring 1934, issue of *Le Voyage en Grèce.* Published by Neptos SA

54 Double-page spread from the same issue with contributions by Le Corbusier and Giorgio de Chirico

5 *La Sarraz*

We can imagine Le Corbusier formulating these thoughts on his way home to Paris from Marseille; the map of his future work—morning and afternoon—clear in his mind. Moholy, though, faced a dilemma: Berlin, the city he had called home for the past thirteen years, had become hostile. He appears to have finally accepted the inevitable some time after he, along with Alvar Aalto and the Giedions, had succumbed to Madame de Mandrot's persuasion and travelled to La Sarraz. Staying on at the chateau after his friends had left for Zurich on 17 August, Moholy tells Sibyl[125] that 'the CIAM trip had been very important for contacts' and he therefore has letters to write. The English architectural writer and *bon vivant* P Morton Shand is setting up a company to market Aalto's birch furniture; Sibyl should therefore leave Berlin for London, where Moholy will join her in November during the Aalto exhibition. In the meantime, he intends to stay on at La Sarraz for several days before going to Zurich to edit the CIAM film.

Mme Hélène de Mandrot (1867–1948), a wealthy widow and promoter of the modern movement, had created 'La Maison des Artistes' at the chateau of La Sarraz in 1922; subsequently hosting the first meeting of CIAM in 1928 and the first international congress of cinema in 1929. In Sibyl's account, Moholy 'was devoted to La Sarraz', spending part of each summer at the chateau, where 'Mme de Mandrot maintained [...] open house for a select circle of European artists. Women were not admitted to the circle.... This monastic arrangement was to provide an opportunity for concentrated creative work, and for exchange of ideas, undisturbed by sex competition.'[126] Freed also from the vexations of life in Berlin, Moholy had simultaneously found the space to resume painting and a new artistic direction; thus, one of his most memorable paintings, titled *La Sarraz*,[127] FIG. 55 had been created at the chateau in 1930. In this work Moholy has stepped outside the familiar orbit of Western European painting and seems to be exploring inexpressible intangibles of light, time and space. The picture appears to be constructed as a series of layers: celestial body like a full moon in zigzag motion, rusty grillage, striated light-blue and yellow angular planes—all floating freely against the profound darkness of a sidereal universe. The work will await critical scrutiny for twenty-five years, until Colin Rowe and Robert Slutzky attempt an interpretation in their celebrated 1955 essay 'Transparency: Literal and Phenomenal'. Here they write: 'Moholy seems to have flung open a window onto some private version of outer space [...] his superimpositions of form [...] overcome space and time fixations. They transpose insignificant singularities into meaningful complexities.'[128] A strategy that might also describe the construction of Moholy's 'film within'—and surely, also, a distinctive artistic space which he constantly strove to regain. The La Sarraz idyll had been short-lived; by the summer of 1932 'space and time fixations' had intruded and Moholy felt constrained by 'the significant psychological changes in the spiritual climate of the times',[129] to the extent that he and his fellow members of the 'select circle' had been unable to work. Now, in the dog days of 1933, he takes advantage of the monastic peace of La Sarraz to write letters, essentially exploring opportunities for employment.

Still, though, Moholy procrastinates about making the final break with Germany; as Sibyl wrote,'He felt a deep loyalty to the country that had given him creative maturity and artistic recognition.'[130] While his friends in France, Holland and England are urging him to leave, he finds the decision too difficult to make; however, November finds him in London prospecting at the invitation of Morton Shand and the poet and critic Herbert Read. On the 22nd he writes from the Regent Palace Hotel to Sibyl, now the mother of six-week-old Hattula, to let her know that he 'spent all day editing the CIAM film'.[131] We imagine him in a rented edit-

55 László Moholy-Nagy, *La Sarraz* oil on canvas 60.5 × 72 cm. In this work, created at the Chateau of La Sarraz in 1930, Moholy seems to be exploring inexpressible intangibles of light, time and space. Painting in private collection. Reproduced from Sibyl Moholy-Nagy, *Moholy-Nagy: Experiment in Totality* (MIT Press, 1969)

ing suite in Soho—once again, up against a deadline—reliving his Aegean adventure. Moholy had been commissioned by Giedion to make a documentary record of the 4th Congress; no doubt the overall running time of 29 minutes had been agreed between them in the knowledge that the film would be avidly scrutinised by cognoscenti of CIAM for generations to come. As an artist, this presents Moholy with a dilemma. The 'official' congress footage had been processed in Athens and rushes shown to the delighted congressists during the return voyage on the *Patris II*, as he describes in his shipboard letter, and he was confident that his finished film would gratify CIAM members as a record of their most successful congress. Moholy was also conscious that he had 'freelanced' extensively; shooting 130 metres of film on the island cruise,[132] simultaneously abandoning documentary conventions and experimenting as he had done in those now celebrated films of his early independent career: *Berliner Stilleben, Marseilles, Old Port* and *Urban Gypsies*. It had not been possible to process the island footage in Zurich as originally planned, and it seems likely that Morton Shand was the Maecenas who facilitated this in London.[133]

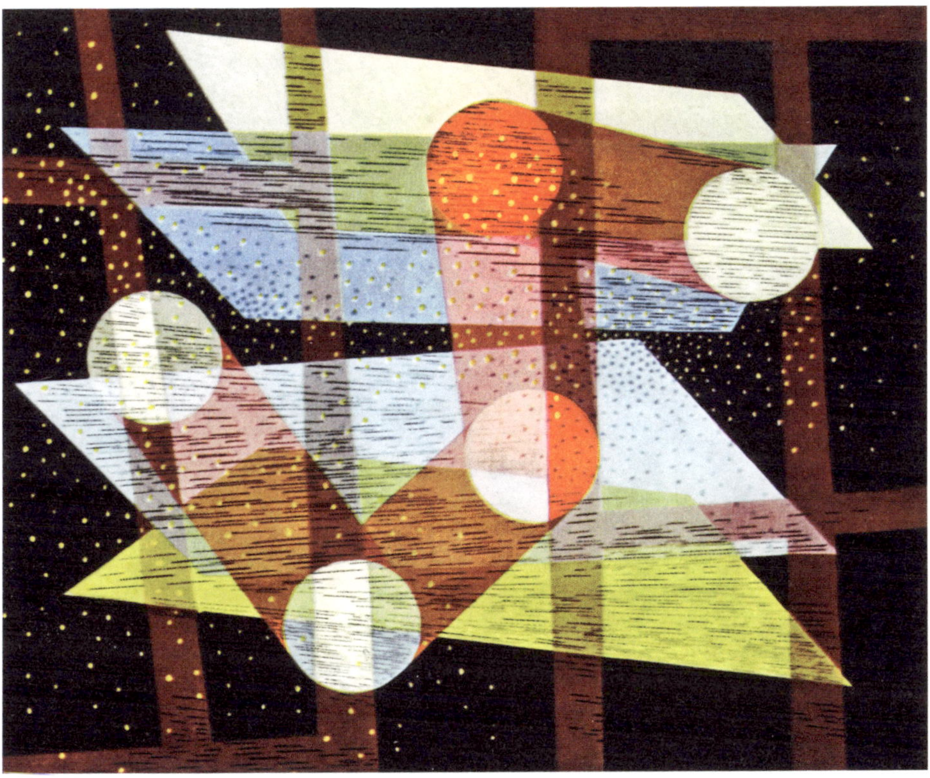

Uncut, the island footage would run for almost 11 minutes. Moholy's intuition tells him that it will almost certainly be perceived as too idiosyncratic—and thus 'peripheral'—to the authorised annals of CIAM. How much of that brilliantly illuminated and enlightening abstract 'other world' can he reasonably retain—and how to edit it? At this point he remembers Dziga Vertov's technique of rapid cutting: creating 'a sense of motion (that) is impressionistic rather than constructive'—and he finds that he can distil his 'film within' into a time frame that occupies less than 16 per cent of the overall. Consequently some 80 metres of 'pure Moholy' end up on the cutting-room floor.[134] After a low-key 'premiere' at the London Film Society later that winter, Moholy's edit of *Architects' Congress*—the CIAM film with a dual personality—sets out on an odyssey of its own.

IX 'experiences which we rarely expressed in words'

The 'heterogeneous group of younger cinéastes ... and the intelligentsia' who had started the London Film Society in 1925 may not have fully appreciated the significance of *Architects' Congress.*[135] Nevertheless, we can imagine that as the audience at the first screening followed the action on the flickering screen, its interest would have been divided between the two main protagonists: celebrity modernist architect on-screen, and avant-garde film-maker off-screen. The two men appear side by side in a photograph FIG. 56—taken at some stage during the filming process—which survives as a unique 8.5 × 6 cm print. A quick 'snap' taken impulsively into the sun, the negative was clearly battered; nevertheless, the image is doubly eloquent—both for its unconscious hierarchically layered diagonal composition and the inscription on the reverse side. Le Corbusier's gaze is fixed straight ahead—a *cigarillo* clamped firmly between his lips. Moholy, on the other hand, appears to be talking enthusiastically, perhaps commenting on the unfamiliar scene; the metal superstructure above their heads belongs to the *Patris II*—and shipping in the background suggests that they are in the port of Piraeus.

Turning the print over we read: *An die Meister mit Verehrung* (To the Masters with veneration) and the name of the photographer: *I.Saporta.* Thus, we conjecture that his photo commemorates their arrival at this point on the periphery of Europe, since Isaac Saporta—at twenty-three the youngest Greek participant in CIAM 4—was one of the welcoming delegation that Moholy had filmed coming out in a launch to meet the *Patris II* as she emerged from the Corinth canal. A Sephardic Jew from Volos, Saporta would join Le Corbusier's rue de Sèvres studio later in the 1930s. During the German occupation he fought with the partisans, as did many of the younger Greek architects, subsequently being obliged to flee the hostile post-war political climate to the US, where he established one of the first masters-level urban design courses.

The image records a momentary interlude of anticipation following the intense mental exertions of the voyage from Marseille, both men looking ahead to the island adventure which, if nothing else, they will always have in common. There is an eight-year age difference and already, at forty-six, the elder of the two is accustomed to being venerated as 'Master'. In attempting to understand his character, Ghika thought it necessary to define the 'Master's' origins: 'He was not French, but Swiss; he was not Roman Catholic, but Lutheran; he was not a scholar, but self-educated—and he was also a member of Swiss Rousse, so consequently an avid revolutionist [...] in his life and art a fighter and anthropic.'[136] And from that particular philosophical tendency, Ghika believed, came Le Corbusier's 'too visionary and [...] grandiose radical urban plan'. Since this 'grandiose' plan underlay all his interventions in the *Patris II* sessions, we can be fairly confident that it was uppermost in his mind as he stood on the ship's deck gazing into the distance. Ghika, as a Sorbonne-educated Greek renowned for his cultivated and 'correct' metropolitan tastes, understood only too well the limitations of self-taught anthropism.

The younger man, as his letter to Sibyl and film eloquently demonstrate, possessed a broader, more correlative view of existence. A phenomenologist if ever there was one, he is firmly in the 'here and now'—perhaps at that very instant reaching for his Kinamo to capture some context ... His origins—rural Hungary, Great War battlefields, revolutionary artist in Weimar-era Berlin—suggest an incompatibility: what could they have talked about? And in what language, since Le Corbusier's German was probably closer to *Schweizerdeutsch,* while Moholy's—learnt 'on the hoof'—was notoriously described as *moholisch.*[137] Some years earlier Le Corbusier had scornfully dismissed photography, while his companion on the deck of the *Patris II* considers himself photographic artist and film-maker first and foremost. He has dedicated the past two days to documenting activities on the ship—the 'Master's' above all—as he addressed the assembled congressists, 'buttonholed' various sub-groups and chatted to his cronies. Obsessively image-conscious, Le Corbusier must be wondering what kind of document is going to result from all this sleuthing around with the whirring Kinamo; after all, he knows this man primarily as one-time Bauhaus lecturer and Giedion's graphic designer/collaborator on his 1928 book *Bauen in Frankreich.* Perhaps, also, as the inventor-constructor of the *Light-Space Modulator,* but he's not sure what to make of that elaborate demonstration of mechanical wizardry.

For his part, Moholy clearly admired the older man, including a photo of the Maison la Roche in his revolutionary Bauhaus primer *Von Material zu Architektur* of 1929. To put it in context, though, it appears as a restrained interior view taken from a glass manufacturer's catalogue in more daring company: no less than ten works by Picasso and numerous Brancusis, Pevsners, Archipenkos and Gabos among others. As an indication of his true feelings about the 'Glass Architecture' to which he aspires, Moholy also includes—following the title *Raum* (space)—Stefan Sebok's drawing of his 'Kinetic Construction System', Gropius's Total Theatre for Piscator, striking abstract photos by Feininger and Itting of the Bauhaus building, an ephemeral diagrid planetarium structure and a dream-like positive-negative image of van der Vlugt's constructivist Van Nelle factory in Rotterdam. Now, in August 1933, everything has changed; quite apart from the muddled naïvety of *throwing knives*—allied with his overbearing 'positiveness, insistence, and rigid thoughts'[138] exhibited during the voyage from Marseille—the undogmatic Moholy would have found Le Corbusier's opinions on photography, painting, and art generally, reactionary.

Moholy was manifestly inspired throughout the island odyssey; *extraordinarily focused animal-like* on that unfamiliar world, while consciously advancing his visual explorations. His transcendent film and playfully ironic letter make light of egotism, in marked contrast to the 'Master' whose world view appears to have been ballasted with classical preconceptions; from that standpoint failing at first to 'see' the extraordinary *difference* of those unique places. Nevertheless, it had been an experience Le Corbusier could not ignore, necessitating months of earnest reflection on his part before eventually composing the literary narrative 'Explications', in which he redefines his mythical relationship to Greece.

Denied the luxury of reflection, Moholy was obliged to act: in early 1934—still hoping against hope that the dire situation in Germany would be of short duration and the 'Hitlerian' menace evaporate—he moved to Holland where a position as typographical consultant to a large printing firm offered him the opportunity to explore colour photography, then in its infancy. Moholy's convictions about the use of colour, however, soon led to tensions with his collaborators; as he wrote at the time,

> All these experts aim at the closest possible imitation of natural colour, and they always fall short of their goal. They're delighted if they can picture an apple looking red instead of brown and the surface of a lake blue instead of green. That's alright for scientific recording and reportage. But it has done great harm to photography as a creative process employing techniques unique to its concept. The language of gradation we've finally mastered in black and white is totally invalidated. We're back where realistic painters started in the Renaissance—the imitation of nature with inadequate means.[139]

Moholy stubbornly pursued his path as an artist; however, the Dutch printers—no doubt motivated by a commercial *Sachlichkeit* of their own—lost patience and refused him permission to use their colour laboratories. Once again without a firm footing, in the bitterly cold March of 1935 Moholy and Sibyl visited Paris,[140] there to renew friendships with a number of artists including Brancusi, Lipschitz, Arp, Delaunay, Mondrian and his *compagnon* from the *Afros,* Fernand Léger—though there is no record of a meeting with Le Corbusier. Rejecting the alternatives—Scandinavia, Switzerland, America—and persuaded by 'the British tradition of free thought', which, Sibyl reported, 'gave his first London years the exuberance of a confirmed faith', Moholy would briefly thrive in that unfamiliar setting.[141]

Nevertheless, his adventures in the Anglo-Saxon world take us far away from the *mode* of his 'film within' in which we glimpse—intensified and in sharp focus as though viewed through a pinhole camera—a network of meanings and possibilities in limitless space. The advent of colour photography and the simultaneous loss of the 'language of gradation' becomes a metaphor for the fragility of that vision; as inspired educator and innovator in several media, he finds the predominantly commercial commissions which come his way in London unfulfilling. An invitation from Gropius to revive the Bauhaus in Chicago brings him to America in July 1937; however, in an environment of rampant expansionism he is obliged to battle almost daily with arbitrary patrons and political intrigue. He feels compelled to write extended texts elucidating his life's work; thus, two years before his untimely death—in 'Abstract of an Artist'—he also 'nails his colours to the mast', as Le Corbusier had done in 'Explications'. However, the standpoint Moholy adopts is at the opposite end of the philosophical spectrum:

> The so-called 'unpolitical' approach to art is a fallacy. Politics is taken here, not in its party connotation, but as a way of realising ideas for the benefit of the community. Such a *Weltanschauung* is transformed, in the arts, into an organised, felt form by the concrete means of the different modes

> of expression. This content can be generally grasped directly through the senses, on a subliminal level, without a conscious thinking process.... As a young painter I often had the feeling, when pasting my collages and painting my 'abstract' pictures, that I was throwing a message, sealed in a bottle, into the sea. It might take decades for someone to find and read it.[142]

Inevitably, as he wrote these words, an image of *Afros* tossed by the storm floated up from his subconscious—as it must have done again in April 1944 when he was briefly reunited with Léger during the artist's wartime exile in New York. The two friends reminisced

> over a bottle of Rosé about that nightmarish dinner in the Arts Club [on the occasion of the Container Corporation Poster Exhibit]. Léger imitated the speaker who was a poll-taker for advertising agencies and who reported so proudly how the designs of Moore, Helion, Kepes, Bayer, Léger rank by plus and minus points against the output of the commercial studios. We both felt ashamed in a strange sort of way that none of us had protested, save under our breaths. I guess art directors buy artists to advertise advertising, and to camouflage the mediocre quality of the anonymous designs. The provocative statement of modern art is constantly annulled by chequebook and cocktail party.[143]

Somewhere around the time Moholy and Léger were exchanging farewells in New York, Le Corbusier—isolated in voluntary exile in the village of Ozon in the Pyrenees, having failed to make any headway with the Vichy regime—began to assemble thoughts which he would ultimately distil into a poetic text: 'L'Espace indicible' (Indescribable Space):

> The *fourth dimension* is, I believe, the moment of boundless freedom brought about by an exceptionally happy consonance of the plastic means employed in a work of art. / It is not the effect of the subject chosen by the artist, but a triumph of proportioning in all things [...] owing its being to intuition, that miraculous catalyst of knowledge; acquired, assimilated, perhaps even forgotten. For a finished and successful work holds within it a vast amount of intention, a veritable world, which reveals itself to those who have a right to it.[144]

Intuition was a loaded word and he had a good memory; van Eesteren, summing up on the *Patris II*,[145] had acknowledged that while architects often talked *intuitively* about urban planning they must, above all, have factual knowledge; *because it is only what gives certitude that should guide our actions.*

For four days and nights in August 1933 Le Corbusier had imagined himself liberated from any obligation—self-imposed, or otherwise—to functionalist certitude. For proof, if it was needed, there was the revelation brought about by Alfred Roth's impetuous kick. Now, as his mind ranged over those times, he recalled that Aphaia's repeated Doric order had unsettled him: *de rigueur* badge of dictatorial regimes, columns had acquired oppressive connotations—as his 'throwing knives' implied. Leaving the rigid trabeated system behind, the luminous 'plastic' vaults of Santorini had, in conspiring with the objections of his artist friends Léger and Ghika, shaken his faith in the 'new political order' that was a prerequisite for his rationally ordered *Ville Contemporaine,* in the process revealing a possible way forward. Later still, when the archaically sensual acropolis of Ronchamp had somehow emerged, surreal and *indicible,* from his subconscious he would emphatically conclude, *architecture is not an affair of columns, but an affair of plastic events. Plastic events are not ruled by scholarly and academic formulae, they are free and unquantifiable.*[146]

Dimitris Pikionis, whose profound reservations about a functionalist methodology established the grounded starting point for this odyssey, was Le Corbusier's exact contemporary. Both architects had been born in small countries considered at the time to be politically and culturally marginal. Largely self-taught, they had pursued unconventional peripatetic learning experiences; thus, it is not surprising that Pikionis should have been equally unimpressed by 'academic formulae'. Throughout the decades following the departure of the CIAM *personae* from Greece, when modern architecture was, as Candilis wrote, 'inscribed in red on the map of Power which [...] considered it subversive, communist and dangerous', Pikionis maintained a low profile as revered teacher, adapting his limited architectural production to Greek tradition. In the years of reconstruction following the Greek civil war, he was at work patiently restoring the sacred character of the Athenian Acropolis with a series of inspired landscape interventions. Finally completed in 1957, it is a work that today brings him universal acclaim; the confluence of marble pathways and viewing points are so authoritative and delightful that the multitudes who make the pilgrimage to the Acropolis and nearby Philopappos Hill spontaneously experience raised expectations as they approach their goal. It was the inspired idea of the poet-architect—known to his students for his passion for Japanese architecture—to devise a 'threshold' to the ancient site which would, in keeping with Soseki's insight, reveal the austere Periclean monument in an entirely new light. In hitting on the subtle irony of crafting the Acropolis pathways as a collage of marble fragments salvaged from the mindless destruction of 'neoclassical' Athens, Pikionis deflated in a stroke the pomposity of Le Corbusier's 'Decisive Manifestation' of 1933—a Dionysian gesture that would have met with Zervos's approval.

The means adopted by Pikionis and his collaborators in composing this sublime intervention *sur le vif* evokes the film-maker's technique of montage. It was also, like the architecture of the islanders, 'free and unquantifiable':

> The ancient Greeks were masters in this respect as in so many others. Up on the Acropolis, it never occurred to them to interfere with the terrain's rich repository of aesthetic feeling. The Parthenon rises out of the rock; the first step of its stylobate is hewn directly from the rock. This is how the *passage* from nature into art is effected. Breaking up lifeless rectilinearity with the *tension* of the curve, delicately and judiciously balanced, art carries over and embodies in its works the plasticity of nature.[147]

Ultimately, architectural thinking could not resist the forces of nature and, two years after the completion of the Acropolis pathways, an international gathering of younger-generation architects met at Otterlo in Holland and resolved to dissolve CIAM. Their manifesto,[148] in rejecting the functionalist certitudes which had dominated discussions at CIAM 4 and which were enshrined in the 'Athens Charter', advocated instead an approach to urbanism that learnt directly from the daily lives and 'free and unquantifiable' architecture of indigenous peoples. It is not surprising, therefore, that among the core group of prime movers who would become known as Team 10 was Pikionis's student, Georges Candilis, who had been inspired as a 20-year-old by Le Corbusier's address to CIAM 4. As soon as the Second World War was over, he had taken up a French government bursary and moved to Paris, eventually working closely with Le Corbusier for five years on the *Unité d'Habitation* at Marseille. Candilis's account of the difficult gestation of this controversial revolutionary structure, which would become one of the undisputed masterpieces of twentieth-century architecture, illustrates the paradoxical influence of the Cycladic experience on Le Corbusier.[149] Viewed from the perspective of the islands, it is an unequivocally plastic

Mediterranean building in which he so faithfully incorporated the 1933 critique of his friend Léger that it could be interpreted on one level as a monument to the artist. The *Unité* is arranged as a vertical 'village' in which each of the 337 cave-like apartments—conceived of by the architect as 'bottles in a bottle-rack'—is oriented to sun and sea, while evoking the timeless vaulted dwellings of Santorini.

To conclude this odyssey of a rediscovered sensibility with an obscure reference to 'a message, sealed in a bottle' begs the obvious question—an omission that Moholy, as inventive and generous teacher, ever sympathetic to his students' fallibilities, would have considered irresponsible. His vivid descriptions of the minutiae of Place, and the beings—human and animal—who *belong to it* demonstrate a unique grasp of language. In revealing the 'thingness of things', he is, inevitably, making a political statement—an awareness formed very early in his artistic life. Thus, as he and Léger lamented their failure to protest the baleful influence of 'chequebook and cocktail party', his thoughts may have returned for confirmation to those audacious first years in Berlin, when he had come under the influence of a young photographer and lecturer in art history, Lucia Schulz. In Sibyl's words, 'To the delirious sense-perception of his new vision she added her superior intelligence and the sober working discipline of a scholar. In collaboration with her, Moholy acquired the ability to think and express himself logically and intelligibly.' This was against the revolutionary background of Germany following the First World War, in which psychological reform was to be achieved by a strict personal regime including vegetarianism, outdoor living and long hikes. It was on these hikes that Lucia taught Moholy photographic skills and a reverence for landscape.[150]

Moholy's personal revolution in art had begun to crystallise in 1922 with the arrival in Berlin of El Lissitzky as emissary of the Russian avant-garde, in particular Rodchenko and the suprematists. Shortly afterwards Kazimir Malevich, the inventor of suprematism, exhibited in the city and established a close bond with Moholy which would ultimately result in their joint authorship of the 'abstract and metaphysical' Bauhaus book *Die gegenstandslose Welt* (The World as Objectlessness).[151] In 1923 Moholy was invited by Gropius to teach the foundation course at the Bauhaus, and in the summer of 1924 he and Lucia collaborated in the writing of *Malerei, Fotografie, Film.*[152] Radical in scope and direction, the book presented 'ideas still in ferment, or but partly clarified',[153] dealing with the relationship—and antagonism—between the traditional and new genres: pigment and light, easel painting, photography and film. Lacking the necessary technical and financial resources, Moholy was able to realise few of his 'artist-engineer's ideas': the *Light-Space Modulator,* for example, took eight years to achieve. Undeterred, Moholy addressed the problem in his writings—his chapters discussing the new technology remain prescient and exciting to this day.

A connection between these revolutionary artistic ideas and the revelations of August 1933 is anticipated in a discussion in *Malerei, Fotografie, Film.* This concerns the phenomenon Moholy and Lucia referred to as *Gesamtwerk.* In seeking its origin, they identified cubism and constructivism as the first attempts to 'purify the expressional elements and means themselves without intending to produce "art" in the process'. These pioneering movements, they believed, had been succeeded by attempts to combine hitherto isolated 'fields of creation' into singular entities—de Stijl being an example. However, the resulting *Gesamtkunstwerk*—total, or comprehensive, work of art—failed from their point of view because it was separated from life. In its place they advocated 'a synthesis of all the vital influences, spontaneously forming itself into the all-embracing *Gesamtwerk*': in other words, *life itself,* which abolishes isolation. Since these ideas would remain uppermost in Moholy's mind, it is highly likely that in his ecstatic experience of the distant islands—where the visitor finds reflection on the phenomenon of isolation unavoidable—he found evidence of a precious pre-existing *Gesamtwerk.*

Nine years after writing *Malerei, Fotografie, Film*, Moholy was presented by Giedion with an opportunity to test his ideas in that strangely surreal, peripheral environment. His letter to Sibyl suggests that in the unconscious modernism of the islanders' architecture he also found confirmation of his belief that 'modern art is a way of life'. Making use of the latest available technology, 'which reacts upon nature not only directly, physiologically, but in a wider sense as well', he demonstrated the unique quality of film and photography: that they are able to 'make us see the whole world with different eyes'. Having absorbed the teaching of the suprematists in rejecting traditional studio painting, Moholy identified Malevich's work as 'a remarkable example of the new cultural outlook'.

A clue to how this new outlook might influence architecture can be glimpsed in Alexander Korda's 1936 movie based on H G Wells's sci-fi novel *The Shape of Things to Come.* Wells had separately approached Léger, Le Corbusier and Moholy for set designs to represent the fabulous city of the future: 'Everytown'[154]. Though in-house designs would ultimately be used, ninety seconds of Moholy's visionary design were included, albeit uncredited, in the final cut; as Sibyl described it,

> The fantastic technology of the Utopian city of the future would, so Moholy dreamed, eliminate solid form. Houses were no longer obstacles to, but receptacles of, man's natural force, light. There were no walls, but skeletons of steel, screened with glass and plastic sheets. The accent was on perforation and contour, an indication of a new reality rather than reality itself.[155]

Sigfried Giedion, whom Moholy acknowledged both as authority on art history and valued collaborator, attempted to distil Moholy's interpretation of reality:

> All his life Moholy had concentrated in giving expression to the intangible quality of light in his paintings. Colour and pigment were secondary compared to the language of light which nowhere was more articulate than in Greece. Here the light had the power to clarify, modify and enhance. Whether it was the boat's screw in the water, accentuated into a luminous apparition, a precipice surmounted by the columns of the Parthenon, or olive trees against the white reflections of the houses, it was always the coincidence of light and structure that gave intensity to the world of vision. It is only what lies prepared within ourselves that is revealed to us in the nature of materials. For Moholy it was *light* that he absorbed in the phenomenon Greece. / These were experiences which we rarely expressed in words. They gave atmosphere to our community, and they reached a climax on a cruise to the Greek islands.[156]

Confident in his didactic role as exponent and custodian of a venerable and avowedly Western historical narrative that progresses logically towards an inevitable goal,[157] Giedion would nevertheless come to perceive, in Moholy's self-styled 'faulty' vision, its origins in the East, a vital dimension that twentieth-century architectural culture had hitherto lacked. There is surely a Moholian irony in the title he gave to his account of the 1933 Greek adventure: *CIAM at Sea:*

> It was not till later on that those 'problems now beginning to emerge' became clear to us and defined themselves as the extension of architectural expression over and beyond its purely functional aspect and the need to resume an independent contact with antiquity—more particularly the Hellenic heritage—from our newly acquired standpoint.

Thus, while future historians might consult the documentary *Architects' Congress* for clues to the once-current idea of the Functional City, Giedion saw to it that the 'experiences which we rarely expressed in words' would also be preserved for the benefit of those who knew how to 'see'. And in creating the distilled edit—a mere 4 minutes and 28 seconds—of his idiosyncratic 'film within', Moholy re-projected that phenomenal light, in the process conducting us to a yet more daring standpoint. One that is less anchored in certitude and more enlivened by the language of gradation.

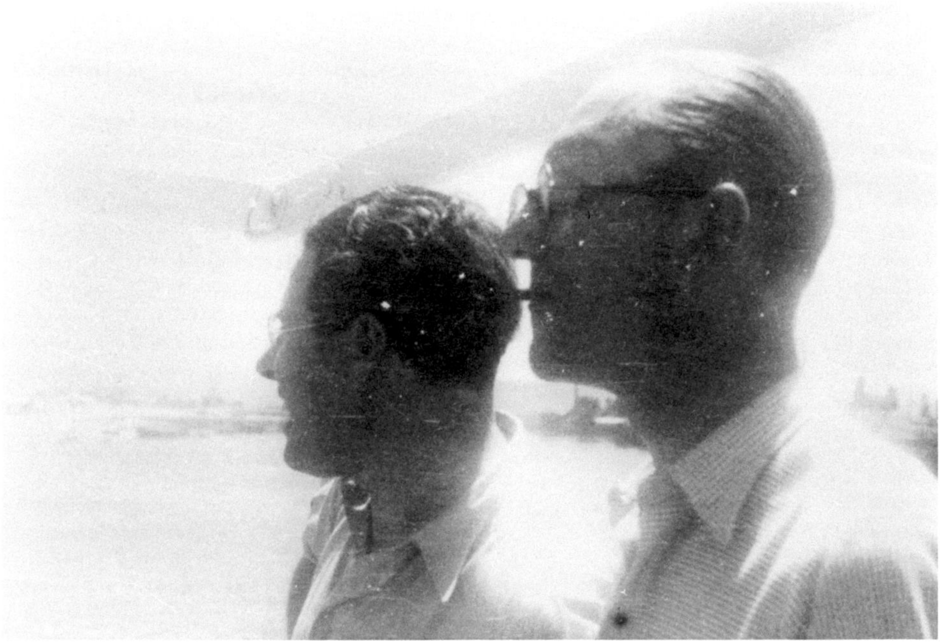

56 Moholy and Le Corbusier together on the deck of *Patris II* in the port of Piraeus: battered print of a 'spontaneous' shot taken into the sun by the youngest Greek CIAM member Isaac Saporta, soon after their arrival in Greece on 1 August 1933

1 Dimitris Pikionis, 'About a Conference' [Γύρω από ένα συνέδριο], *Technica Chronica* 4/39 (August 1933), pp. 775–76. The article was brought to our attention by Agni and Dora Pikioni (email, 17 March 2014) [translated by Kathryn Koutelieris / Agni and Dora Pikioni].
2 Georges Candilis, *Bâtir la vie* (Gollion: Infolio éditions, 2012), p. 75 [translated].
3 Jean-Pierre De Rycke, 'Greekness and Modernism (1933–1934)', in *Ghika and Avant-garde in Interwar Europe* (Athens: Ephesus Publishing, 2004), p. 103.
4 Ibid., p. 109.
5 Sigfried Giedion, 'CIAM at Sea: The Background to the Fourth (Athens) Congress', trans. P. Morton Shand, in *Architects' Year Book* (London: Paul Elek, 1949).
6 Nikos Hadjikyriakos-Ghika, 'Memoirs of Le Corbusier', *Zygos* 8 (1965), pp. 15–21 [translated by Kathryn Koutelieris].
7 Ibid.
8 Irène Soetaert-Ioannides, 'Héraclès Ioannides: Mon père' (international colloquium organised by the École française d'Athènes and Basil & Elise Goulandris Foundation, Andros, 2006) [translated by the authors].
9 Sigfried Giedion letter in gta archives dated 11 July 1933: 'On 25 July I'm driving to Marseille, a seat is reserved for you. You'll be making a film about the congress and about Greece. The film will be paid by us as raw material. It is most likely that any travel expenses you incur during the trip will be covered, just that at the moment I can't commit on this conclusively. Léger and Arp will also travel with us. Anyway I've added your name to the list. So make up your mind. Please let me know!'
10 Sibyl Moholy-Nagy, *Moholy-Nagy: Experiment in Totality* (Cambridge, MA: MIT Press, 1969), p. 78.
11 Göran Schildt, *Alvar Aalto: The Decisive Years* (New York: Rizzoli, 1986), p. 94. Quotes from an entertaining report on CIAM 4 by Nils-Gustav Hahl, a young art historian whom Aalto persuaded to attend the congress as his representative: 'A man who does not feature on the official programme but is nonetheless one of the central personalities of the congress is the Hungarian László Moholy-Nagy. . . . I shall merely point out that he has had a greater impact than anyone else on the break-through of the modern feeling for form, e.g. in film and typography, and that his contribution to modern photography cannot be overestimated. On the *Patris II* he and his perfect little film camera are ubiquitous, he finds subjects everywhere, whether group portraits or perspectives. At the break of dawn, sleeping in our folding chairs on top deck–few of us sleep in our cabins—we are sometimes awakened by a faint whirring: a few feet of film have turned in Moholy's camera. He gives a sly wink and tiptoes up to the next chair: the camera whirs and the facial movements of the sleeping Alvar Aalto are immortalised. One evening Moholy-Nagy's travel film is shown on the quarter deck: a realistic report which expands into a fantastic picture poem on life aboard ship. When it is completed it may attain the same quality as his famous film *Marseilles*.'
12 Joseph Rykwert, email to the authors, 29 Nov 2013. 'The only time I saw it was when Alfred Roth brought his copy to the Venice Biennale some years ago.'
13 Jos Bosman, 'Sur le *Patris II*, de Marseille à Athènes', in *Le Corbusier et la Méditerranée*, exh. cat. (Marseille: Editions Parenthèses, 1987), p. 75 [translated by the authors].
14 László Moholy-Nagy, letter to Sibyl, 13 August 1933 [translated by Hattula Moholy-Nagy].
15 Georgios Simeoforidis and Georgios Tzirtzilakis, 'Le Dernier Voyage en Grèce', in *Le Corbusier et la Méditerranée*, op. cit.: 'The other congressists visited Ossios Loucas, Delphes and the islands of the Argo-Saronic, scarcely comparable from the point of view of plastic qualities to those of the Aegean.' Nils Gustav Hahl, in *Alvar Aalto – The Decisive Years*, op. cit., also informs us that 'During the voyage a clique of twelve similarly-

minded people toured the Peloponnese by car' but omits to identify them.
16 Sibyl Moholy-Nagy, *Experiment in Totality,* op. cit. p. 8: 'Late in 1916, in a battle along the Isonzo River in Venezia Giulia, his whole battery was wiped out, he alone escaping, with a shattered thumb and a fast-spreading infection that kept him for months in military hospitals.'
17 Fernand Léger, 'De l'Acropole à la Tour Eiffel', *Le Voyage en Grèce* 1 (Spring 1934) [translated by the authors].
18 Bosman, 'Sur le *Patris II,* de Marseille à Athènes', op. cit.
19 Fernand Léger, 'Discours aux architectes', *Quadrante* 5 (September 1933) [translated by the authors].
20 Candilis, *Bâtir la vie,* op. cit. p. 85.
21 Panayotis Tournikiotis, *I Diagonios tou Le Corbusier* [The Diagonal of Le Corbusier] (Athens: Ekkremes, 2010), pp. 210–11 [translated by Kathryn Koutelieris].
22 Candilis, *Bâtir la vie,* op. cit. p. 85.
23 Bosman, 'Sur le *Patris II,* de Marseille à Athènes', op. cit.
24 Damarice Amao, '*Le Voyage aux Cyclades* film 1932', in *Zervos et Cahiers d'Art,* ed. Christian Derouet (Paris: Centre Pompidou, 2011) [translated by the authors].
25 Giedion, 'CIAM at Sea', op. cit.
26 Translated as 'Problems of the Modern Film', in Krisztina Passuth, *Moholy Nagy* (London: Thames and Hudson, 1985), p. 311.
27 Olivier Lugon, 'Neues Sehen, Neue Geschichte', in *Sigfried Giedion und die Fotografie,* ed. Werner Oechslin and Gregor Harbusch (Zurich: gta Verlag, 2010), p. 88–105 [translated by Christina Hoechst].
28 László Moholy-Nagy, letter to Sibyl, 13 August 1933.
29 Giedion, 'CIAM at Sea', op. cit.
30 Candilis, *Bâtir la vie,* op. cit. p. 87.
31 Tim Benton, *Le Corbusier: Secret Photographer* (Zurich: Lars Müller 2013), p. 23.
32 Le Corbusier, *Journey to the East,* ed. Ivan Žaknić (Cambridge, MA: MIT Press, 1987), pp. 218–19.
33 Vincent Scully, *The Earth, the Temple and the Gods* (New Haven, CT: Yale University Press, 1962), pp. 164–68.
34 Dimitris Pikionis, 'About a Conference', op. cit.
35 'Paul Vanderborght et le mouvement de "La Lanterne Sourde"', published online by Université Libre de Bruxelles – Bibliothèques, https://www.bib.ulb.ac.be/fileadmin/user_upload/Web_Bibliotheques/documents/lanterne_sourde.pdf.
36 Lawrence Durrell, *The Greek Islands* (New York: Faber and Faber, 2002), p. 211.
37 Le Corbusier et Pierre Jeanneret, *Oeuvre complète de 1929–1934* (Zurich: Les Éditions d'Architectures, 1935), pp. 53–57.
38 Catalogued in the archives of the Fondation Le Corbusier as FLC_C_recto-13.
39 Giedion, 'CIAM at Sea', op. cit.
40 The classic description of arrival at Poros by boat is to be found in Henry Miller *The Colossus of Maroussi* (London: Minerva 1991), p. 54.
41 Rebecca Goldstein, *Incompleteness: The Proof and Paradox of Kurt Gödel* (New York: W. W. Norton, 2006), p. 81.
42 László Moholy-Nagy, letter to Sibyl, 13 August 1933.
43 Giedion, 'CIAM at Sea', op. cit.
44 Sigfried Giedion quoted in Sibyl Moholy-Nagy, *Experiment in Totality,* op. cit. p. 91.
45 Kees Somer, *The Functional City: The CIAM and Cornelis van Eesteren, 1928–1960* (Rotterdam: NAi Publishers, 2007), p. 165.
46 Nader Vossoughian, 'Otto Neurath, the International Congress of Modern Architecture (CIAM), and the Politics of Information Design', *MIT Design Issues* 22, no. 3 (Summer 2006).
47 Giedion, 'CIAM at Sea', op. cit.
48 Evelien van Es et al. (eds.), *Atlas of the Functional City: CIAM 4 and Comparative Urban Analysis* (Bussum: THOTH, 2014).
49 Vossoughian, 'Otto Neurath', op. cit.

50 Passuth, *Moholy Nagy,* op. cit. p. 10.
51 Sibyl Moholy-Nagy, *Experiment in Totality,* op. cit. p. 13.
52 László Moholy-Nagy, 'New Film Experiments', in Passuth, *Moholy-Nagy,* op. cit. p. 320.
53 Ibid., p. 13.
54 Ibid., pp. 176–83.
55 Ibid., p. 318.
56 In this comment made to a student in 1950—quoted by Eric Mumford in *The CIAM Discourse on Urbanism, 1928–1960* (Cambridge, MA: MIT Press, 2000), p. 204—Gropius was being disingenuous. In 1930 he had attended CIAM 3 in Brussels, presenting high-rise housing projects in Berlin. According to correspondence between Giedion and Ioannides in the gta archives, Gropius was interested in attending CIAM 4, and Ioannides, at Giedion's urging, went to considerable lengths to obtain accommodation at special rates for him. Ultimately, Gropius cancelled his reservation in a letter to Neptos dated 17 July 1933, which Ioannides immediately forwarded to Giedion: 'M Gropius would have participated in this congress in the exceptional conditions which you have been granted, that is to say that you would have paid the 3rd class fare for him and we would have placed him in a 1st class cabin.' Soon after this date Gropius would be in England prospecting for work (email from Evelien van Es, 16 May 2014).
57 Somer, *The Functional City,* op. cit. p. 165.
58 Catalogued in the archives of the Fondation Le Corbusier as FLC_C_recto-16.
59 Simeoforidis and Tzirtzilakis, 'Le Dernier Voyage en Grèce', op. cit.
60 Somer, *The Functional City,* op. cit. p. 169.
61 Giedion, 'CIAM at Sea', op. cit.
62 Dimitri Analis, a Greek poet established in Paris, quoted in Josyane Savigneau, *Marguerite Yourcenar: Inventing a Life,* trans. Joan E Howard (Chicago, IL: University of Chicago Press, 1993), p. 100: 'Her writing, before meeting Embirikos, is beautiful, but it does not touch life.... has no feeling for the earth, or the sky. It is after their meeting, in all her writing, that her sensuality explodes. It was he who made it possible for her to link together the materiality and spirituality of life. He showed her, in Greece, the permanence of things.'
63 Tournikiotis, *I Diagonios tou Le Corbusier,* op. cit. p. 207.
64 Catalogued in the archives of the Fondation Le Corbusier as FLC_C_verso-14.
65 Catalogued in the archives of the Fondation Le Corbusier as FLC_C_recto-16.
66 Savas Condaratos, 'Dimitris Pikionis in Context', in *Dimitris Pikionis, Architect 1887–1968: A Sentimental Topography,* exh. cat. (London: Architectural Association, 1989), p. 27. See also Candilis, *Bâtir la vie,* op. cit. pp. 9–14.
67 Le Corbusier, sketch in 'Carnet no. 9, 1924', Fondation Le Corbusier (FLC).
68 Le Corbusier, letter to Sotiris Papastratos, 25 November 1933, FLC [translated by the authors].
69 Hadjikyriakos-Ghika, 'Memoirs of Le Corbusier', op. cit.
70 Christian Zervos, letter to Sigfried Giedion, 14 February 1931, gta archives [translated by the authors].
71 Hadjikyriakos-Ghika, 'Memoirs of Le Corbusier', op. cit.
72 De Rycke, 'Greekness and Modernism', op. cit. pp. 116–26.
73 Ozenfant & Jeanneret [Amedée Ozenfant and Le Corbusier], *La Peinture Moderne* (Paris: Les Éditions G. Crés, 1925), p. 152 [translated by the authors].
74 Reinhold Hohl, 'C. G. Jung on Picasso (and Joyce)', *Source: Notes in the History of Art* 3, no. 1 (Fall 1983), pp. 10–18.
75 De Rycke, *Ghika and Avant-garde in Interwar Europe,* op. cit. p. 112.
76 Carlo Belli, 'Le Corbusier, L'Italia e il Gruppo 7' and, in particular, 'Notes on Le Corbusier and Italy 1931–1941', *Domus* 687 (October 1987), p. 23.
77 Hohl, 'C. G. Jung on Picasso (and Joyce)', op. cit. p. 10.

78 Sigfried Giedion, letter to Christian Zervos, 2 November 1932, gta archives.
79 Jacques Sbriglio, *Apartment Block 24 N.C. and Le Corbusier's Home* (Basel: Birkhäuser Verlag, 1996), p. 73.
80 László Moholy-Nagy, *Vision in Motion* (Chicago, IL: Paul Theobald & Co., 1947), pp. 344–350.
81 http://www.moma.org/collection/works/79039
82 http://www.moma.org/collection/works/79762
83 http://www.moma.org/collection/works/79078
84 Carolyn Lanchner, *Fernand Léger* (New York: Museum of Modern Art, New York, 2010), p. 17.
85 Bosman, 'Sur le *Patris II,* de Marseille à Athènes', op. cit. p. 75.
86 László Moholy-Nagy, letter to Sibyl, 13 August 1933.
87 Christian Zervos, introduction to *L'Art en Grèce des temps préhistoriques au début du XVIIIe siècle* (Paris: Editions *Cahiers d'Art,* 1934) [translated by the authors].
88 Giedion, 'CIAM at Sea', op. cit.
89 The construction method is described in detail in Dimitri Philippides, *Santorini,* Greek Traditional Architecture series (Athens: Melissa, 1987). The traditional Santorini vaults appear to have been a direct influence on the housing project known as 'Roq et Rob' proposed by Le Corbusier for Roquebrune-Cap Martin in 1949. Paradoxically, it was to that project that the Greek government architects responsible for reconstruction work after the catastrophic Santorini earthquake of 1956 turned for inspiration. However, when the new vaults, constructed of reinforced concrete, cracked and failed after a few years as the reinforcement corroded, they became known to the islanders as *kaláthi* (baskets). The latter information was given to the authors in May 2014 by Triantaphyllos Pitsikalis, their host in Oia and descendant of many generations of vault-builders.
90 Kadio Kolymva, *Oia in Santorini: A Journey in Space and Time* (Athens: Armos, 2002).
91 Sibyl Moholy-Nagy, *Experiment in Totality,* op. cit. p. 53.
92 Sigfried Giedion, 'CIAM at Sea'. op. cit.
93 Robin Schuldenfrei, 'Images in Exile: Lucia Moholy-Nagy's Bauhaus Negatives and the Construction of the Bauhaus Legacy', *History of Photography* 37, no. 2 (2013), pp. 182–203.
94 Benton, *Le Corbusier Secret Photographer,* op. cit. p. 239.
95 László Moholy-Nagy, letter to Sibyl, 29 July 1932, quoted in Sibyl Moholy-Nagy, *Experiment in Totality,* op. cit. p. 77.
96 *Le Voyage en Grèce* (Spring-Summer 1934), op. cit. p. 13.
97 Filine Wagner, email to the authors, 16 April 2014, gta archives.
98 Bosman, 'Sur le *Patris II,* de Marseille à Athènes', op. cit. p. 76.
99 Panos Djelepy: 'Les Maisons de l'Archipel Grèque observées du point de vue de l'architecture moderne', *Cahiers d'Art* 1–4 (1934) [translated by the authors].
100 Benton, *Le Corbusier Secret Photographer,* op. cit. pp. 88–89.
101 Passuth, *Moholy Nagy,* op. cit. p. 16.
102 From Sibyl Moholy-Nagy, *Experiment in Totality,* op. cit. p. 57, we learn the sinister aspect of Hubacher's film cassette box: '[In 1931] I took over the scenario office of a large motion-picture company in Berlin. In a thickening atmosphere of nationalistic isolation, the level of the Tobis production was above that of the average commercial firm.... I hoped that the international character of Tobis would save it from a Fascist mentality. But in shrewd anticipation of future developments, the Dutch and Belgian stockholders suddenly sold out their interest to I. G. Farben, which acted as spearhead for Hermann Göring's planned consolidation of Germany's industry under Nazi rule. This transaction, involving millions of marks, emphasised a sense of impending disaster spreading slowly among German progressives.' The activities of I. G. Farben during the Second

World War are too well known to require repetition.
103 Vanessa Morisset, 'Christian Zervos: Un éditeur face à l'art de son temps', Dossiers pédagogiques, Centre Pompidou (May 2011), http://mediation.centrepompidou.fr/education/ressources/ENS-zervos/ENS-zervos.html#zervos2 [translated by the authors]. Correspondence in the FLC archives (Le Corbusier, letter of 26 February 1934) reveals that Le Corbusier accused Zervos of 'tricking him' into giving him a short-term loan of 5,000 francs, which he had failed to repay. Zervos, though, seems to have regarded the sum as a 'subvention'—perhaps towards the cost of publication of *L'Art en Grèce.*
104 Simone Brott, 'In the Shadow of the Enlightenment: Le Corbusier, Le Faisceau and Georges Valois', in *Proceedings of the Society of Architectural Historians, Australia and New Zealand: 30, Open,* ed. Alexandra Brown and Andrew Leach (Gold Coast, Qld: SAHANZ, 2013).
105 Le Corbusier, 'La Ville Radieuse' first published 1935, quoted by Jacques Sbriglio, 'Air, Mer, Soleil, Verdure', in *Le Corbusier et la Méditerranée,* op. cit. p. 101 [translated by the authors].
106 Sigfried Giedion, letter to Christian Zervos, 23 February 1932, gta archives [translated by the authors].
107 Le Corbusier, *The City of Tomorrow and Its Planning,* trans. from the 8th French edition of *Urbanisme* with an introduction by Frederick Etchells (Cambridge, MA: MIT Press, 1971). Best demonstrated by chapter 10 'Our Technical Equipment', pp. 139–56, here: p. 154.
108 Christian Zervos, 'La Sculpture: Domaine de prédilection', in *Zervos et Cahiers d'Art,* p. 132 [translated by the authors].
109 Giedion, 'CIAM at Sea', op. cit.
110 Le Corbusier, 'Explications', in *L'Art en Grèce,* op. cit.
111 See '1911 Horta', Lardex, http://www.lardex.net/TONSBERG/salvesen/skipstekst/1911horta.htm1.
112 Giedion, 'CIAM at Sea', op. cit.
113 Candilis, *Bâtir la vie,* op. cit. p. 17. Describing the official reaction that followed CIAM 4: 'But, paradoxically, since all of that is new, therefore disturbing, this movement of modern architecture is inscribed in red on the map of Power, which, in the end, considered it subversive, communist and dangerous. Under the same heading, moreover, as other groups of spiritual research which developed in parallel around us—for example, the movement towards simplification of the Greek language and research into populism in art, poetry and literature.'
114 Schildt, *Alvar Aalto,* op. cit.
115 Giedion, 'CIAM at Sea', op. cit.
116 See, for example, Deborah Gans, *The Le Corbusier Guide* (New York: Princeton Architectural Press, 1987), p. 36, for discussion of the 'severe overheating' caused by the sealed south-facing *pan de verre* of the 'Cité de Refuge', completed in 1933.
117 Giedion, 'CIAM at Sea', op. cit. 'Our adversaries taunted us, as the representatives of Contemporary Architecture, for going to Greece. They interpreted this as an escape, if not, indeed, as something worse. In my opening address to the Congress, I said, "The fact that we are now bound for Greece does not imply a retreat on our part. Our voyage simply affords us the opportunity for undisturbed work, together with the investigation of certain problems that are now beginning to emerge, and also something in the nature of an interval for reflection."'
118 Sbriglio, *Apartment Block 24 N.C.*
119 Hadjikyriakos-Ghika, *Memoirs of Le Corbusier,* op. cit.
120 Le Corbusier, 'Explications', *in L'Art en Grèce,* op. cit. The other témoignages were 'The Radiant Ruin' by Pierre Guéguen, 'Country of Light Where the Shadow Finds No Place' by Fernand Léger, 'Greek Baggage' by Gasto Bonheur, 'The Parthenon Pre-exists in Each of Us' by Amédée Ozenfant, and 'Triangulation of Greece' by Maurice Raynal.
121 Ibid.

122 Le Corbusier et Pierre Jeanneret, *Oeuvre complète, 1934–1938,* ed. Max Bill (Zurich: Les Éditions d'architectures, 1945), pp. 156–57.
123 Ibid., p. 12.
124 *Le Voyage en Grèce* (Spring-Summer 1934), op. cit. pp. 4–5.
125 László Moholy-Nagy, letters to Sibyl, 17 and 20 August 1933.
126 Sibyl Moholy-Nagy, *Experiment in Totality,* op. cit. pp. 75–76.
127 60.5 × 72 cm, oil on canvas. The painting was sold to a private collector by Sibyl Moholy-Nagy (Hattula Moholy-Nagy, email to the authors, 28 September 2016) and has, to our knowledge, only ever been published once in colour—in ibid., facing p. 75.
128 Colin Rowe with Robert Slutzky, 'Transparency: Literal and Phenomenal', first published in *Perspecta 8: The Yale Architectural Journal* (New Haven, CT: Yale University School of Art and Architecture, 1963), p. 48.
129 Sibyl Moholy-Nagy, *Experiment in Totality,* op. cit. p. 77.
130 Ibid., p. 85.
131 Hattula Moholy-Nagy, *Moholy-Nagy Chronology,* unpublished document dated December 2000. '1933 Nov 22 LMN to SMN on Regent Palace Hotel letterhead. He spent all day editing the CIAM film. Friday evening he'll go to Amsterdam to meet with Katz and then on Sunday to Basle.'
132 László Moholy-Nagy, letter to Sibyl, 13 August 1933 op. cit.
133 Correspondence between Giedion and Ioannides in the gta archives (letters dated 1 November 1933 and 7 November 1933, translated by the authors) reveals that Giedion asked Ioannides to send 15 metres of film showing *Patris II* 'en voyage'—'at the latest on 14 November'—for incorporation in Moholy's film, which 'will be presented for the first time in London on 19 November'. On 7 November Ioannides confirms that he has sent 18 metres of film to P Morton Shand's address: 73 Ladbroke Grove W11. In the event Moholy could not find space in his edit for Ioannides's footage, perhaps feeling that a sequence of the ship 'at sea' was too evocative of conventional travelogue material. *Architects' Congress* eventually premiered in the Film Society programme of 10 December 1933 (Hattula Moholy-Nagy, *Moholy-Nagy Chronology,* unpublished document dated December 2000: '1933 Dec 16, LMN letter to Franziska and J. G. Crowther').
134 That the unused 80 metres were binned seems likely because, as Hattula wrote regarding Moholy's attitude to his original work (email to the authors, 1 November 2013), 'Generally, Moholy seemed to be very casual about asking for the return of photographs that were eventually published. Many seem to have vanished and might have been discarded by the publishers.' This in contrast to Giedion, who was fastidious about keeping all forms of documentation.
135 Documentation of the Film Society (1925–1939) exists online: http://www.screenonline.org.uk/film/id/454755/index.html
136 Hadjikyriakos-Ghika, *Memoirs of Le Corbusier,* op. cit.
137 Louis Kaplan, *László Moholy-Nagy: Biographical Writings* (Durham, NC: Duke University Press, 1995), pp. 191–92: 'In a eulogistic letter, Xanti Schawinsky imparts a piece of information about his friend's monstrous relationship to the German language. "Some of his German writings are almost incomprehensible, their writing so complicated that '*moholisch*' has become a new term in the German vocabulary, just like *'faustisch'.*"'
138 Hadjikyriakos-Ghika, *Memoirs of Le Corbusier,* op. cit.
139 Sibyl Moholy-Nagy, *Experiment in Totality,* op. cit. pp. 104–5.
140 Ibid. p. 113.
141 Ibid. pp. 116–17.
142 László Moholy-Nagy, 'Abstract of an Artist', in Passuth, *Moholy Nagy,* op. cit. p. 364.

143 Sibyl Moholy-Nagy, *Experiment in Totality,* op. cit. pp. 215–16.
144 Le Corbusier, 'L'Espace Indicible', *L'Architecture d'aujourd'hui* (June/July 1961).
145 Somer, *The Functional City,* op. cit. p. 165.
146 Le Corbusier, *Textes et dessins pour Ronchamp* (Genève: Presses Coopi, 1981), unpaginated [translated by the authors].
147 *Dimitris Pikionis, Architect 1887–1968,* op. cit. p. 94.
148 Alison Smithson (ed.), *Team 10 Primer* (Cambridge, MA: MIT Press, 1962). First published as 'Team 10 Primer 1953–62', *Architectural Design* 12 (December 1962).
149 Candilis, *Bâtir la vie,* op. cit. pp. 137–82.
150 Sibyl Moholy-Nagy, *Experiment in Totality,* p. 21.
151 Passuth, *Moholy Nagy,* op. cit. pp. 42–44.
152 László Moholy-Nagy with Lucia Schulz, *Malerei, Fotografie, Film,* originally published in 1925 as vol. 8 in the Bauhausbücher series, subsequently in English as *Painting, Photography, Film* (London: Lund Humphries, 1969).
153 Passuth, *Moholy Nagy,* op. cit. p. 47.
154 Mark Duguid, 'Things to Come (1936)', BFI screenonline, http://www.screenonline.org.uk/film/id/438287/index.html.
155 Sibyl Moholy-Nagy, *Experiment in Totality,* op. cit. p. 129.
156 Sigfried Giedion, quoted in ibid., p. 94.
157 The classic exposition of Giedion's positivist narrative is *Space, Time and Architecture*—first edition published by Harvard University Press in 1941 based on lectures delivered at Harvard in 1938–39, which were in turn developed from his teaching at ETH Zurich earlier in the 1930s. In later editions Giedion reconsidered many of his opinions, reinstating as 'constituent facts' those which he had earlier dismissed as 'transitory': 'Expressionism' for example. A 1937 essay (in *Architecture, You and Me,* published by Harvard University Press in 1958) titled 'Art as the Key to Reality' begins: '*Why is our age so sick?* Every creative art has the task of creating its own approach to the world.... Its task lies within the realms of irrationality: to give expression to the emotional feeling of a period. When this is not done it is a sign that that period has lost contact with its own inner self.'

Appendix

The *Personae*

CIAM cruise of the Greek islands: 5–8 August 1933

László Moholy-Nagy: Artist, film-maker, writer
Le Corbusier: Joint founder CIAM
Cornelis van Eesteren: Chairman CIAM
Vrouw Frieda van Eesteren
Sigfried Giedion: Art historian, joint founder and secretary CIAM
Carola Giedion-Welcker: Art historian
Fernand Léger: Artist, writer
Christian Zervos: Writer, publisher *Cahiers d'Art* and *L'Art en Grèce*
Yvonne Zervos: Gallery owner
Ghika (Nikos Hadjikyriakos-Ghika): Artist
Antigone 'Tiggie' Kotzia: Artist, Ghika's wife
Andreas Embirikos: Poet, photographer, later psychoanalyst—owner of *'Afros'*
Marguerite Yourcenar (Crayencour): Writer
Heracles Ioannides: Editor *Le Voyage en Grèce*, director of Neptos travel agency
Tériade (Stratis Elefteriades): Writer, publisher
Amédée Ozenfant: Artist, writer
Albert Jeanneret: Composer, musician, older brother of Le Corbusier
Pierre Guéguen: Poet, critic, co-editor of *14 rue du Dragon*
Gaston Bonheur: Poet, songwriter, co-editor of *14 rue du Dragon*
Maurice Raynal: Critic
Jean Badovici: Architect, editor *L'Architecture Vivante*
Madeleine 'Mado' Goisot: Badovici's companion
Stamo Papadakis: US-based Greek architect, organiser of CIAM events in Athens
Michael Tombros: Sculptor, publisher and editor of *20th Century*
Kurt Seligmann: Artist
Otto Neurath: Philosopher of science, originator of 'Isotype' graphic language
Dr Pierre Winter: Medical reformer and urban theorist
C. Werner Moser: Architect
Rudolf Steiger: Architect
Alfred Roth: Architect
Carlo Hubacher: Architect/engineer
Frau Greta Hubacher: Film-maker

Total: 32

Sources

From Moholy's letter to Sibyl:
... it was an unusual experience. imagine a small nutshell on a rough sea, manned by a captain, helmsman and several sailors, and 25 chosen guests of the congress, mostly french, who like to keep to themselves, and several swiss, dutch and greeks + me.

From Sigfried Giedion, 'CIAM at Sea':
'Though these reflections were seldom, if ever, uttered, they were constantly in our thoughts—thoughts untroubled by cares of the day and the gathering oppression of that ominous period. Hence, it is only right that I should mention the cruise among the Aegean Islands to which some of us devoted a short respite from Congress labours at the beginning of August. The "yacht" we managed to hire was a converted English collier, and since the only cabin was reserved for the ladies of the party, its crew slept on deck. It was a mixed and merry company of some twenty painters, architects, poets, musicians, and writers who met at lunch in Piraeus and then embarked together. Among the party were Fernand Léger, Moholy-Nagy, the surrealist painter Kurt Seligman, Le Corbusier and his brother the musician Jeanneret, Christian Zervos, Jean Badovici, the Dutch town-planner van Eesteren, one or two French men of letters, a few of the best Swiss architects, and a well-known French physician.

From 'Le Dernier Voyage en Grèce' by Georgios Simeoforidis and Georgios Tzirtzilakis, in *Mediterranéitée et Modernité*, 1987:
'Le Corbusier and most of the French, accompanied by Giedion, Moholy-Nagy, by certain Greeks and also by intellectuals, artists and poets not participating in the Congress but present in Athens as friends of CIAM, such as Raynal, Guéguen, Bonheur, Ozenfant and Léger, cruised the Aegean on the small boat "Agros" [*sic*]. Some stages of this long and complicated voyage remain mysterious: Delos, Mykonos, Santorini, Serifos ... before or after Aegina. The other congressists visited Ossios Loucas, Delphes and the islands of the Argo-Saronic, scarcely comparable in terms of plastic qualities to those of the Aegean.' Evidently the authors did not have access to *Architects' Congress.*

Zervos published *témoignages* by Pierre Guéguen, Fernand Léger, Le Corbusier, Amédée Ozenfant and Maurice Raynal in *L'Art en Grèce*, 1934

Evelien van Es, historian, editor of *Atlas of the Functional City: CIAM 4 and Comparative Urban Analysis*, published in 2014, wrote to the authors (12 Feb 2014):

'I am on behalf of the EFL Stichting working on a huge project about CIAM 4. As far as the project team and I know, at least Giedion, Van Eesteren, Le Corbusier, Jeanneret, Léger, Moholy-Nagy, Zervos, Badovici, Winter and a few Swiss joined the trip to the Aegean. Giedion wrote about the trip; S. Giedion, 'CIAM at Sea', in *Architects' Year Book 3,* ed. J. B. Drew and T. Dannat (London: Paul Elek, 1949), pp. 36–39.'

Other, less reliable, accounts

From Ghika, 'Memoirs of Le Corbusier':
'Eventually we boarded the yacht owned by Embirikos, Giedion, the painter, Fernand Léger, the poet Guéguen, Christian Zervos with Yvonne who had produced *Cahiers d'Art*, Le Corbusier's brother (the musician), a cousin of Jeanneret who was the technical officer of the Rue de Sevres office. There was also a Romanian architect, Badovici with Mado, a Spanish architect, Sert, a Greek Papadakis who lived in America and others.'
We know that neither Pierre Jeanneret nor Sert were on the Aegean cruise.

From *Isaac Saporta: Professional Architect* (Athens: Untimely Books, 1996):
'The conference days in Athens were unforgettable. I recollect one evening; following a celebration in Kifissia, at "Cecil", I think, about fifty people continued on to Faliro, to go skinny dipping.... After that we were to head all together for the islands. I was to accompany the Spanish team—Sert and the others. I had my bag there, ready. I had to tell van Eesteren something. I boarded a beautiful yacht comprising the "leaders". I began to speak, then, after a moment, I saw the boat sailing away with my luggage along with my friends. I went to jump—however, I said to myself, leave it, you might get knotted up in the anchor. I held myself back. I found myself there on board with just a shirt and nothing else. Along with Mrs van Eesteren and Mrs Giedion, the first place we anchored, we bought some material similar to that which the shepherds use—in this manner they sat and sewed me a jacket. I still have it. And so it happened by chance that I was there with the group consisting of Moser, Steiger, Giedion, van Eesteren, who was an extraordinary man, Le Corbusier. I was there with the group of people who later on published the famous "Charter of Athens".'
Saporta was reminiscing towards the end of his life in America; if he was indeed on the cruise, it's curious that he has nothing to say about it.

Image Credits

Moholy's letter to his future wife, Sibyl, was scanned and printed thanks to the kind permission of Hattula Moholy-Nagy.

Scans of figures 13, 14, 16, 22, 24, 27, 29, 30 were provided by the Fondation Le Corbusier.

1, 2, 39, 40 gta Archives / ETH Zurich (Holding Sigfried Giedion)
3, 4, 18, 19, 26, 28, 33, 49, 50, 52, 53, 54 Personal collection of Dr Nikos Paissios
5, 6, 12, 17, 46 Stills from *Architects' Congress,* courtesy of the Moholy-Nagy Foundation
7 Philadelphia Museum of Art, A. E. Gallatin Collection, 1952-61-58, © 2018, ProLitteris, Zurich
8, 13, 14, 16, 22, 24, 29, 30, 48 © FLC / 2018, ProLitteris, Zurich
9, 11, 25, 32, 41, 42, 43 gta Archives / ETH Zurich (Holding Karl Hubacher)
10, 27, 44 Benaki Museum / Ghika Gallery, Photographic Archives, Athens
15, 33 © Fonds d'archives Eli Lotar; Cabinet de la photographie Musée nationale d'art moderne, Centre Pompidou, Paris
20, 56 gta Archives / ETH Zurich (CIAM Archive)
21 From *La Cité—Revue d'Architecture et d'Urbanisme* 8 / 1934, p. 125
23 From *Voyage en Grèce* 2, 1935, p. 37. Personal collection of Dr Nikos Paissios
34, 37, 40 © Stiftung Sigfried Giedion, Zurich
35 Still from 'Man with a Movie Camera' by Dziga Vertov, 1929
38 gta Archives / ETH Zurich (CIAM Archive)
45 © Chris Blencowe and Judith Levine
47, 55 Courtesy of Hattula Moholy-Nagy
51 © FLC / Fernand Léger / 2018, ProLitteris, Zurich

Although all reasonable efforts have been made to provide accurate copyrights for the images used in this book, it was not possible to identify all copyright holders and photographers. Should despite our intensive research any person entitled to rights have been overlooked, legitimate parties should contact Lars Müller Publishers.

Glossary

Borías	from an old wind rose; strong persistent north wind, also known as *vorías* or boreas.
ČSR	Czechoslovakia
kafeneíon	small café serving mainly coffee
Katastrofí	Catastrophe
korai, kouroi	statues of young women or young men from the pre-classical period
monopáti	ancient donkey/mule track
naós	the inner chamber of a Greek temple
orológio	clock tower
Sachlichkeit	objectivity, sobriety—tenets of Functionalism
Schweizerdeutsch	Swiss German
skála	flight of steps
paralía	harbour promenade
plateía	square in a town or village
pleonasmós	the use of more words than are necessary to convey meaning
vólta	a stroll—as, for example, 'evening *vólta* along the *paralía*'
xénoi	plural of *xénos*: stranger

Author biographies

Chris Blencowe was born in Hampshire and grew up in the north of Ireland. He worked in architects' offices in London for several years before entering the Architectural Association School, graduating in 1966 with the gold medal of La Societé des architectes diplomés par le gouvernement, Paris, for his thesis project: a layered restructuring proposal for Soho.

Judith Levine was born in Toronto and spent her early years in Canada and the USA. She graduated from Manchester University in 1961 and researched and designed a Museum of First Nations Art and Culture, Ottawa, which was exhibited at the UIA Congress London in 1961. She has also exhibited artworks and photographic projects, including at the Canadian Cultural Centre Paris, 1974–1975.

Inspired by the landmark 1959 exhibition of Le Corbusier's architecture, painting and sculpture at the Walker Art Gallery in Liverpool, which they experienced independently, they broadened their architectural practice to include art, photography and writing. Meeting in 1962, they collaborated on school competitions in Ticino, Switzerland, with Livio Vacchini and Luigi Snozzi, subsequently working together and teaching in Vancouver, Canada—where they lived for twelve years—Europe and the UK.

As regular visitors to Greece and the islands since the 1990s, it was an epiphany prompted by their first early-morning sight of the Santorini vaults and caldera—after arriving at night during a power cut—that would provide the stimulus for their research into the little-known CIAM visit to the Aegean Islands in August 1933.

Timeline

1910

Culture

- Creation of the Mundanaeum (a forerunner of the Internet) by Paul Otlet and Henri La Fontaine
- Umberto Boccioni paints *The City Rises* as part of the new movement Futurism.
- Loos: *Steiner House*, Vienna
- Poelzig: *Water Tower*, Posen

1911

Culture

- Picasso: *Portrait of D. H. Kahnweiler*
- Braque: *Le Portugais*
- Gropius & Meyer: *Fagus Factory*, Alfeld an der Leine
- Expressionist movement *Der Blaue Reiter* formed in Munich

1912

History

- After more than two thousand years of imperial rule the Republic of China is established.
- First Balkan War. European holdings of the Ottoman Empire achieve independence.

Culture

- Marcel Duchamp commences work on *The Bride Stripped Bare by Her Bachelors, Even* in Germany. It will take him 10 years to complete.
- Mies van der Rohe, project for the Kröller House, Wassenaar

1913

Culture

- Berg: *Jahrhunderthalle*
- Paris: Guillaume Apollinaire publishes *Les Peintres cubistes.*
- Marcel Duchamp: *Bicycle Wheel*– the first 'readymade'

1914

History

- → June 28 Franz Ferdinan
- → August 1 Germany decla

CIAM

Culture

- Taut: *Glass Pav*
- Sant'Elia: *Casa*

1930 | 1931 | 1932 | 1933 | 1934

)ekulakization' in the deportation, starvation ation lead to an estimated illion peasants.

'ash

→ February 27
Reichstag fire: Suspension of fundamental in Weimar

→ March 24
Hitler calls on Reichstag members to vote f Enabling Act. He is 'temporarily' granted pl powers by the passage of the Act. The law him the freedom to act without parliamentar consent or constitutional limitations

→ August 28
The Nazis publish lists of people, whose German citizenship, passports and other privileges are withdrawn.

Third congress of CIAM, held in Brussels on the initiative of Victor Bourgeois. The theme was 'Rational Methods of Site Planning'.

→ October 16
Germany announces its intention to leave the League of Nations.

'ess of CIAM in Frankfurt, at of Ernest May. Walter Gropius, d José Luis Sert made their ce.

n Stuttgart: Moholy-Nagy and orate on didactic 'Room 1'.

ohn: *Russland-Europa-Amerika*

ie neue Baukunst in Europa

Barcelona Pavilion by Mies van Villa Savoie by Le Corbusier: ements, of the 'heroic period' of ecture

-Nagy publishes *u architektur;* shoots : *Marseilles*

Walter Benjamin: *A Short History of Photography*

International competition for the Palace of the Soviets. Walter Gropius, Erich Mendelsohn, Auguste Perret invited, but all sidelined and severely attacked. Iofan's monumental reactionary scheme prevails topped by colossal statue of Lenin commissioned

→ November
L'Architecture de l'aujourd'hui publishes *The Problems of Building Socialist Cities in the USSR* and 'The Architecture of the Workers' Club'

→ April
Telegram from Moscow to CIAM 'postponin CIAM 4

→ July 29–August 13
Patris II departs Marseille: CIAM 4 Congress held on the ship and in Athens

→ August 5–8
Afros cruise: Piraeus–Aegina, Poros, Serifos, Santorini, Ios–Sounion

→ May 10
Joseph Goebbels encourages Nazi student to burn 25,000 'un-German' books.

→ November 22
Moholy-Nagy edits *Architects' Congress* in London.

→ December
Premier of *Architects' Congress* at London Film Society

Sigmund Freud: *Civilization and its Discontents*

El Lissitzky: *Russland: die Rekonstruktion der Architektur in der Sowjetunion* published in Vienna

László Moholy-Nagy: Film of *Light Prop: Light Play: Black and White and Grey*

→ May–July
Deutscher Werkbund Exhibition Paris: Interiors by Gropius, Breuer and Moholy-Nagy

Ernst May arrives in Moscow with 'a brigade of planners' to meet the demand for 100s of new towns. Establishes design standards that survive for decades

Albert Kahn (Detroit) establishes office in USSR that is ultimately responsible for nearly 600 factories.

→ November
Luis Buñuel: *L'Age d'or*

Bauhaus relocates to Berlin. Mies appointed director

→ March
Voyage aux Cyclades film by Brunius, Lotar and Vitrac premiered in Paris

→ Spring
USSR: All existing literary and artistic groups and organisations are disbanded and replaced with unified associations of creative professions, bringing the history of postrevolutionary art to a close.

Extremely aggressive attacks targeting 'Korbusianizm' and 'Leonidovizm' published in Soviet press

'Socialist Real becomes state when the First Congress of S Writers meets. Subsequently enforced ruthl in all spheres c endeavour. Art who stray from official line are punished.

1916 | 1917 | 1918 | 1919 | 1920

→ April 6
The United States enters the war.

→ October
Bolshevik Revolution and establishment of USSR

ıa Gandhi returns to India and joins an National Congress.

→ January
Berlin: Murder of Karl Liebknecht an Rosa Luxemburg

ajevo

→ February–December
Battle of Verdun

→ November 11
Armistice: End of First World War

Vladimir Tatlin: *Monument to the Third International*

El Lissitzky: *Proun* series—'a transiti from painting to architecture'

Fernand Léger: *The City*

Publication of polemical avant-garde (by Amédée Ozenfant, Charles Edou

Malewicz: *Black Square*

Bauhaus founded by Walter Gropius in Weimar

e Ozenfant, with Max Jacob and me Apollinaire, founds *L'Elan.*

Erich Mendelsohn: Sketches exhibite in Berlin Einstein Tower, Potsdam (completed 1921)

Duchamp emigrates to America.

van Doesburg and Huszar: *De Stijl*

→ February 5
Dada founded at Cabaret Voltaire, Zurich, by Hugo Ball, Marcel Janco, Richard Huelsenbeck, Tristan Tzara, Jean Arp and Sophie Taeuber-Arp

Carl Jung: *The Unconscious in Normal and Pathological Psychology*

Ozenfant meets C. E. Jeanneret and they jointly write *Après le cubisme* to coincide with first Purist exhibition, Paris.

Guillaume Apollinaire: *L'esprit nouveau et les poètes*

Oswald Spengler: *Decline of the West*

van Doesburg: *Black and white composition*

Sigmur *Pleasu*

Vkhute technic

1921 1922 1923 1924 1925

→ October 28
Mussolini appointed prime minister by King Victor Emmanuel III

→ June
Hyperinflation in Germany; continues until January 1924

→ November 8–9
Beer Hall Putsch, Nazis attempt coup in Munich. Hitler arrested and charged with treason. He writes *Mein Kampf* in prison.

d

nal stage

Le Corbusier: *Vers une architecture*

review: *L'Esprit nouveau.*
ard Jeanneret, Paul Dermée)

László Moholy-Nagy joins Bauhaus staff, taking over the metalworking shop and rewrites the *Vorkurs.*

Walter Gropius: Expressionist monument to the March dead

Jean Badovici starts *L'Architecture Vivante*—continues to 1932

d

Mies van der Rohe: Friedrichstrasse tower project in Berlin

Sigfried Giedion travels to Bauhaus; meets L. Moholy-Nagy and Gropius

d Freud: *Beyond the*
e Principle

nas, the Russian state art and
al school founded in Moscow

Klee, Kandinsky and van Doesburg join Bauhaus faculty

→ February
James Joyce: *Ulysses* published in Paris

Sigfried Giedion publishes his doctoral thesis in Munich: *Late Baroque and Romantic Classicism.*

Moholy-Nagy publishes *Buch neuer Künstler*, a pictorial survey of correlations in recent art, architecture, technology and music.

Ilya Ehrenburg in Berlin publishes *Veshch / Gegenstand / Object* with El Lissitzky.

Tatlin: *Monument to the Third International* reproduced by Bruno Taut in *Frühlicht* and by Le Corbusier in *L'Esprit Nouveau*

T. S. Eliot: *The Wasteland*

Léger and Ozenfant, teaching with Alexandra Ekster and Marie Laurencin, open painting school in Paris

André Breton: Surrealist Manifesto

1925 · 1926 · 1927 · 1928 · 1929

History

1929

- Stalin starts '[...]
  Ukraine. Mass[...]
  and collectivis[...]
  death of 11 m[...]
- → October
  Wall Street C[...]

CIAM

1928

- → June
  First meeting of CIAM at the Chateau de la Sarraz, organised by Le Corbusier, Cor van Eesteren and Sigfried Giedion as secretary general. Other members included Karl Moser, Hendrik Berlage, Pierre Chareau, Hugo Häring, Pierre Jeanneret, Ernst May, Hannes Meyer, Gerrit Rietveld and Mart Stam.

1929

- Second cong[...]
  the invitation [...]
  Alvar Aalto an[...]
  first appearan[...]

Culture

1925

- Bauhaus relocates to Dessau.
- Cor van Eesteren and Theo van Doesburg: Elementarist winning design for re-planning of Unter den Linden, Berlin
- Moholy-Nagy and Gropius co-editors of 14 Bauhaus Books on facets of modern art and design
- Moholy-Nagy writes *Malerei, Fotografie, Film* with Lucia Schulz and *Von Material zu Architektur.*
- El Lissitzky teaches at Vkhutemas-Vkhutein workshops (until 1930) combining suprematist experience with constructivism.
- *Architecture in the USSR* by El Lissitzky, a critique of Russia's 'mecanomania' published in *Kunstblatt*, Berlin
- *Exposition Internationale des Arts Décoratifs et Industriels Modernes* in Paris. Le Corbusier: 'Plan Voisin' for Paris. Konstantin Melnikov's USSR pavilion, first manifestation of the new Russian architecture in the West

1927

- Malewicz travels to Berlin, with a selection of his paintings and theoretical work, hoping to find employment at the Bauhaus.
- Malewicz exhibition in Berlin
- Moholy-Nagy collaborates with Malewicz on the Bauhaus book *The World as Objectlessness.*
- International competition for the League of Nations HQ. The project by Le Corbusier and Pierre Jeanneret awarded first prize —subsequently rejected by the jury on a technicality

1929

- → May
  FIFO exhibitio[...]
  Giedion colla[...]
- Erich Mendels[...]
- Bruno Taut: *D[...]*
  und Amerika
- Completion o[...]
  der Rohe, and[...]
  Definitive stat[...]
  modern archit[...]
- László Moholy[...]
  Von material z[...]
  10-minute film[...]

1926

- → March
  Werner Heisenberg: 'Uncertainty Principle'
- Completion of Bauhaus building in Dessau by Gropius and Adolf Meyer
- Mies van der Rohe: Monument to Karl Liebknecht and Rosa Luxemburg, Berlin
- Mart Stam: Prototype steel cantilever chair
- Louis Aragon: *Le Paysan de Paris*

1928

- Gropius and Moholy-Nagy resign from Bauhaus. Hannes Meyer appointed directo[...]
- Amédée Ozenfant: *Foundations of Modern Art*
- Sigfried Giedion publishes *Bauen in Frankreich* in Leipzig with typography by Moholy-Nagy.
- André Breton: *Nadja*
- Le Corbusier's first visit to USSR: writes several enthusiastic articles for French and Swiss newspapers
- Sergei Eisenstein: *The General Line*
- Le Corbusier wins commission to design *Centrosoyuz* in Moscow. Not completed until 1936

1936 | 1937 | 1938 | 1939 | 1940

1936 — Great Purge begins in the Soviet Union. Large scale repression, imprisonment and execution of Communist Party members, the Red Army staff, 'saboteurs', 'counter-revolutionaries', and peasants.

1938 — → November 9–10 *Kristallnacht*

1939 — → August 23 Molotov–Ribbentrop Pact

1939 — → September 1 Germany invades Poland.

1939 — → September 3 Britain and France declare war on Germany.

1937 — Fifth congress of CIAM, held in Paris, on the theme 'Housing and Recreation'

1939 — Sixth congress postponed ten years due to the war

… 10
…y-Nagy joins Gropius in London.
…nes a member of the avant-garde
…which also includes Barbara Hepworth,
…icholson, Henry Moore, John Piper,
…Grierson and Herbert Read. Also
…ments with 'space modulators' made
…sparent 'Rhodoid' plastic.

1938 — New Bauhaus forced to close due to lack of funds

1937 — → July *Degenerate Art* Exhibition organised by the Nazi party opens in Munich and is seen by over 2 million people. It includes 650 works by, among other artists, Paul Klee, Kurt Schwitters, Pablo Picasso, Piet Mondrian, Wassily Kandinsky and László Moholy-Nagy.

1937 — Moholy-Nagy appointed director of New Bauhaus in Chicago on Gropius's recommendation. The school opens on October 18.

1939 — → May 4 James Joyce: The complete *Finnegans Wake* published simultaneously in London and New York

Acknowledgements

In researching the event of August 1933, the breakthrough occurred in October 2013 when Hattula Moholy-Nagy emailed us with the news that she had 'just discovered a marvellous 6-page letter in which Moholy describes the yacht trip ... The not so good news is that it is handwritten in German in pencil on yellowed paper, which has faded and very difficult to scan.' Throughout our researches and writing Hattula has been more than generous in giving us access to her personal archive and patiently answering our endless questions.

Special thanks to Ioanna Moraiti, archive manager of the Ghika Gallery of the Benaki Museum, for making available previously unpublished texts and photographs by the painter Nikos Hadjikyriakos-Ghika, and for introducing us to the physician and art historian Dr Nikos P Paissios. Dr Paissios' unique archive of 1930s publications has proved an essential source of information on the Greek background to CIAM 4; a background which would be incomplete without Dimitris Pikionis' prescient August 1933 *Technika Chronika* article. We are grateful to Agni Pikioni for bringing her father's text to our attention, and to Kathryn Koutelieris for translating his formal *katharévousa* into demotic English.

Many thanks to Kathy Paraschi, architect-engineer and director of the Acropolis Museum, for discussing with us the refinements of pre-classical and classical architecture which so impressed the Western visitors in 1933; and to Christy Constantakopoulou of Birkbeck College and author of 'The Dance of the Islands' for her insights into the little-known world of political exiles on the Greek islands in the 1930s.

To our friends Katerina Samara and the late Iannis Diakakis in the village of Oia, Santorini, we owe an enthusiasm for the lighter side of island life—not to mention the colourful world of Greek music. In the same village, Triantaphyllos Pitsikalis—viticulturist and descendant of many generations of vault-builders—gave us a memorable lesson in construction.

For a clearer understanding of the Western background to the 1933 event we are indebted to Filine Wagner of the gta archives in Zurich; as the Greek island cruise had previously received scant academic attention, it was thanks to Filine's scholarly intuition that we were able to retrieve numerous unexpected documents and images. At the Fondation Le Corbusier in Paris the archivist Isabelle Godineau has been an invaluable source of documentation and high-quality imagery. The historian Evelien van Es in Rotterdam generously made many documents available to us from the van Eesteren archive.

For their perceptive and subtle translations from German we are indebted to Christina Hoechst on the island of Naxos, and to Kevin Galvin in London.

An earlier text on the 1933 event was published, much-edited by Tom Weaver, in 'AA Files 71'. That the complete text is now appearing in book form is thanks to the keen eye of Lars Müller, book *maestro extraordinaire,* and to his dedicated crew—editors and designers Maya Rüegg, Martina Mullis, Esther Butterworth, Chris Reding, Sabrina Hagel and Manuel Müller. Thanks to their enthusiasm, good humour and unequalled professionalism, this has been a shared voyage that we as authors were in no hurry to conclude.

This book could not have appeared in print without the generous support of the Riva Lindsay memorial fund.

moholy's edit

the avant-garde at sea
august 1933

Authors: Chris Blencowe, Judith Levine
Editorial team: Sabrina Hagel, Manuel Müller, Maya Rüegg
Copyediting: Simon Cowper
Proofreading: Stephanie Shellabear
Design: Integral Lars Müller / Lars Müller and Esther Butterworth
Production: Martina Mullis
Lithography: prints professional, Berlin, Germany
Printing and binding: DZA Druckerei zu Altenburg, Germany
Paper: Munken Lynx, 130 gsm

Lars Müller Publishers is supported by the Swiss Federal Office of Culture with a structural contribution for the years 2016–2020.

Lars Müller Publishers
Zurich, Switzerland
www.lars-mueller-publishers.com

ISBN 978-3-03778-566-9

Distributed in North America by ARTBOOK | D.A.P.
www.artbook.com

Printed in Germany

The film *Architect's Congress* is available in full length online:
www.vimeo.com/larsmuellerpublishers/ciam1933